WALTER P. REUTHER

SELECTED
PAPERS

THE MACMILLAN COMPANY
NEW YORK · CHICAGO
DALLAS · ATLANTA · SAN FRANCISCO
LONDON · MANILA

IN CANADA
BRETT-MACMILLAN LTD.
GALT, ONTARIO

WALTER P. REUTHER

WALTER P. REUTHER

SELECTED
PAPERS

*Edited and with an Introduction
by Henry M. Christman*

NEW YORK
THE MACMILLAN COMPANY
1961

First Printing

The Macmillan Company, New York
Brett-Macmillan Ltd., Galt, Ontario

Printed in the United States of America

Library of Congress catalog card number:
61–13339

Introduction

Few Americans can match Walter Reuther's consistent record of expressing new ideas and devising new programs that drive to the heart of contemporary economic, social, and political issues. He is one of the most provocative thinkers in the United States today.

From the perspective of American labor history, Mr. Reuther marks a sharp break with the approach of traditional old-line labor leadership whose concern was limited to winning a few cents more per hour for their separate union constituencies. Mr. Reuther challenges labor—and the United States as a whole—to seek new and broader horizons.

In order that the reader may proceed as rapidly as possible to examine Mr. Reuther's thinking firsthand, I shall restrict myself to the basic biographical facts and a few brief comments concerning some of his most noted ideas and programs.

Walter Philip Reuther was born in Wheeling, West Virginia, on September 1, 1907. He served an apprenticeship as a tool and die maker, and studied at Wayne University in Detroit for three years. He spent the late 1920's and early 1930's working in Detroit factories including the General Motors and Ford plants, and he became a foreman at the latter. He then devoted the next three years to travel in Europe and the Orient, working in factories and studying labor conditions.

In 1935, Mr. Reuther returned to the United States to serve as one of the original organizers of the United Automobile, Aircraft, and Agricultural Implement Workers of America. His first UAW office was as President of Local 174; by 1939, he was Director of the General Motors Division of the International Union. In 1946 he became President of the UAW, and in 1952, President of the CIO as well.

Since the merger of the AFL and CIO in 1955, Mr. Reuther has been Vice President of the new organization and President of its Industrial Union Department, meanwhile continuing to serve as President of the UAW. He is also Vice President of the International Confederation of Free Trade Unions, the coordinating body for democratic labor movements throughout the non-Communist world. In addition, Mr. Reuther has long been active beyond the labor movement, and is an official of the National Association for the Advancement of Colored People and of Americans for Democratic Action.

Mr. Reuther's concept of labor's role and responsibilities in a free society has attracted widespread attention. Condensed into a few words, his view is simply this: Labor can make economic progress only as the whole community makes economic progress. Although capital, labor, and the general public often have conflicting short-term economic interests, their long-term interests are inextricably interwoven. If a single group benefits at the expense of the other two, the result is an imbalance in the economy from which all three groups will eventually suffer. In collective bargaining, management and labor each have their respective responsibilities, but together they have an overriding responsibility to the whole of society.

The various economic proposals which Mr. Reuther has advanced over the years include not only new concepts of labor's interest in the total economy—such as the profit-sharing plan and the guaranteed annual wage—but also proposals to protect the consumer. For instance, Mr. Reuther has repeatedly pledged his union to cooperate with management to halt rising prices, and even to forego wage increases and other new benefits if management could demonstrate that the cost of such benefits could not be absorbed by industry but must mean higher prices for the consumer.

He has denounced the growth of monopoly in American industry, pointing to the effect upon the welfare of the American consumer. He has documented the practice of "administered prices," the practice of deliberately restricting the manufacture of needed products in order to arbitrarily maintain unnecessarily high prices and maximum corporate profits.

Mr. Reuther has supported automation, industrial use of

atomic energy, and other technological changes. He welcomes such innovations as opportunities to raise living standards for all Americans, and he has presented his own programs for implementing these changes in the most just and efficient manner.

Other matters that have claimed Mr. Reuther's attention— health and medical care, housing, federal and state pensions, and federal aid to education—are issues vitally affecting the public at large. Still other questions on which he has been particularly active—such as civil rights, political action, and the intellectual quality of education—range far beyond economics.

On the international scene, Mr. Reuther has been a dynamic link between the United States and the free labor movement abroad. He has been especially concerned with the problems confronting the nations of Asia, Africa, and Latin America as they seek industrialization and economic progress. As a labor leader, he has striven unceasingly to persuade labor everywhere that it has nothing to gain from Communism.

History already has proved Mr. Reuther prophetically right in a number of his programs. For instance, the proposal, "500 Planes a Day," Mr. Reuther's program to convert idle automobile factories to the production of military airplanes, was ridiculed by management when it was first advanced. However, when civilian automobile production was halted by the federal government following American entry into World War II, the automobile industry was converted to war production just as Mr. Reuther predicted it could be.

Another example of Mr. Reuther's foresight was his early and consistent opposition to Communism, and his leadership in driving Communists from the UAW and CIO. Only now is the general public becoming aware of his prophetic warnings concerning the nature of Communism and its callous but effective exploitation of poverty and social injustice.

The Peace Corps is yet another of Mr. Reuther's proposals now realized a number of years after it was first advanced. And, in regard to over-all foreign policy, Mr. Reuther has long advocated a new approach based upon mutual economic benefit rather than upon outmoded military alliances. He recommends a thorough reexamination of foreign aid, with the immediate elimination of those programs which have armed and enriched dictators and assisted them in repressing and exploiting their own peoples. He urges a foreign policy which recognizes that the major threat posed by Communism is not military, but economic and ideological.

All these subjects—both domestic and international—discussed in this introduction, and others as well, are analyzed at length by Mr. Reuther himself in the pages which follow.

In editing this selection of Walter Reuther's writings and speeches, it has been my desire throughout not only to present an accurate and balanced over-all view of his outlook, but also to give some indication of the dynamic character of the man himself.

As editor, I, of course, bear sole responsibility for the book, for the selections herein, and for the initiation of this publishing endeavor.

Henry M. Christman

Contents

CONTENTS

WALTER P. REUTHER
SELECTED
PAPERS

500 Planes a Day—A Program for the Utilization of the Automobile Industry for Mass Production of Defense Planes

A special study originated by Mr. Reuther while Director of the General Motors Division of the United Auto Workers, which was presented to President Roosevelt by Philip Murray, President of the Congress of Industrial Organizations, as a joint proposal of the UAW and CIO.

December 23, 1940

England's battles, it used to be said, were won on the playing fields of Eton. This plan is put forward in the belief that America's can be won on the assembly lines of Detroit.

In an age of mechanized warfare, victory has become a production problem. The automotive workers for whom I speak think our industrial system a productive giant capable of any task, provided it is not forced into battle with one hand tied behind its back. They also believe that we need send no men to a future conflict with the Axis powers if we can supply enough machines now to our first line of defense in Britain. The machines we and the British need most are planes, and the survival of democracy depends on our ability to turn them out quickly.

The workers in the automotive industry believe that the way to produce planes quickly is to manufacture them in automobile plants. The automotive industry today is operating at only half its potential capacity. This plan proposes that the unused potential of the industry in machines and men be utilized in the mass production of aircraft engines and planes. It is our considered opinion that it would be possible, after six months of preparation, to turn

1

out five hundred of the most modern fighting planes a day, if the idle machines and the idle men of the automotive industry were fully mobilized and private interests temporarily subordinated to the needs of this emergency.

Time, every moment of it precious, its tragic periods ticked off by bombs falling upon London and the Midlands, will not permit us to wait until new mass production factories for aircraft and aircraft engines finally swing into action late in 1942. Emergency requires short-cut solutions. This plan is labor's answer to a crisis.

Mr. William F. Knudsen says that airplane production is 30 per cent behind schedule. It will continue to be behind schedule so long as we continue to rely on the expansion of existing aircraft plants, and on the construction of new plants. Expansion of existing aircraft plants means the expansion of plants utilizing the slow and costly methods of an industry geared to hand-tooled, custom-made production.

New plants cannot be built and put into operation in less than eighteen months. In eighteen months Britain's battle, for all her people's bravery, may be lost, and our own country left to face a totalitarian Europe alone.

Packard and other companies are still digging the ditches and pouring the concrete for their new airplane engine factories. The Axis powers will not wait politely until these factories are finished.

New plants, when finally erected, must be filled with new machinery and this new equipment largely duplicates machinery already available in our automobile plants. The machine industry is overtaxed. The emergency of war cannot be met in the normal time necessary to construct new plants and equip them with the required production machinery.

We propose, instead of building entirely new machines, to make the tools required to adapt existing automotive machinery to aircraft manufacture.

We propose to transform the entire unused capacity of the automotive industry into one huge plane production unit. Production under this plan would not replace the output of the aircraft industry proper, which would continue to construct the large bombers and planes of special design.

No industry in the world has the tremendous unused potential productive capacity of the American automotive industry, and no industry is as easily adaptable to the mass production of planes. A careful survey will show that the automobile industry as a whole is not using more than 50 per cent of its maximum potential capacity if that capacity were properly coordinated and operated to the fullest degree.

The automotive industry could produce eight million cars a year. It is producing approximately four million. These unused plant reserves, as shown by the figures given in the Federal Trade Commission's report on the motor vehicle industry, are greater than the total motor plant capacity of England, Germany, France, Italy, Russia, and Japan combined. Adapted to plane production, this unused potential capacity would give us world plane supremacy within a short time.

At present the automotive industry never operates at more than 80 to 90 per cent of its maximum potential capacity, and then only for a few months each year. The rest of the year it operates on reduced schedules, and many plants shut down completely. If automobile production were spread evenly over a twelve-month period, it would be possible, without reducing the total output of automobiles, to convert a large portion of this machinery to the manufacture of planes.

During the automotive year ending August, 1940, Nash used only 17 per cent of its productive capacity; Dodge used 36½ per cent. Nash, working at maximum capacity, could have manufactured its total output for the twelve months in 49½ working days; Dodge, in 111 working days. Chevrolet, the largest single producer of motor cars, turned out over a million cars during the last model year, and yet used less than 50 per cent of its potential productive capacity. The main Chevrolet Motor plant at Flint, Michigan, produced 380 completed motors per hour at the peak of the 1937 production season, utilizing all four of its complete motor machining and assembly lines. At the present time, at the peak of the 1940 production season, the Chevrolet Flint plant is producing 282 motors per hour, with one motor line standing completely idle, while the three remaining lines are operating on a two-shift basis. Since 1937, Chevrolet has built a new motor plant in Tonawanda, New York, which at the present time is producing 65 complete motors per hour, with a plant capacity of 90 motors per hour. This would indicate that at the peak of the production season Chevrolet is building only 347 motors per hour, with an actual capacity of 470 motors per hour. With an unused capacity of 123 motors per hour at the peak of the production season, it is obvious that Chevrolet has an unused reserve which becomes tremendous during the month of reduced operating schedules.

The availability of automotive production facilities for plane production in Chevrolet is again shown in the case of the Chevrolet drop forge plant in Detroit, the largest drop forge shop of its kind in the world. If this shop were operated at full capacity, it could produce all the drop forgings required for the production of five hundred airplane motors per day, and still supply the Chevrolet company with sufficient drop forgings for one million Chevrolet cars a year. Skilled labor to operate this shop at full capacity is available. Other forge shops, including the Buick and the Dodge forge shops, are also working at far less than capacity.

Are the facilities used in manufacturing automobile motors adaptable to the manufacture of airplane motors? The answer is that they are.

Both the automobile and airplane motors are combustion engines, essentially the same mechanism for generating power by exploding gas. Both motors contain cylinders, carburetors, pistons, crankshafts, camshafts, valves, spark plugs, ignition systems, etc.

The same basic machinery is utilized in the manufacture of these basic parts common to both motors. True, there are differences between the automobile and the airplane engine, as there are differences of a lesser degree between the engine of the Chevrolet and the engine of the Cadillac. These differences between different engines are produced by adding certain tools, dies, jigs, or fixtures to the basic machine in order to make a difference in the product. The same "tooling" process adapts the same basic machinery to the production of the airplane engine. Graphic proof of this statement is even now being supplied by General

Motors. Many of the most difficult and precise parts of the Allison aviation engine are being manufactured in the Cadillac plant in Detroit, much of it with retooled Cadillac machinery. The new Allison plant in Indianapolis, still in process of expansion, is being used largely for assembly.

The experience of General Motors in making Allison parts with retooled Cadillac machinery should also dispose of the bugaboo of "tolerances." "Tolerances" are the allowable fractional variations in size of engine parts, and they must be far finer in the plane engine than in the automobile engine. But these more precise dimensions can be obtained by more precise tooling.

When the contemplated airplane motor plants are completed, it will be necessary to equip them with the same kind of basic production machinery already standing idle half of the time in the nation's automotive factories. This basic machinery will be duplicated, and after it is duplicated it will still be necessary to construct the special tools, dies, jigs, and fixtures required to adapt this machinery to the manufacture of plane engines.

In the process of duplicating basic machinery lies the most serious delay. This lag, which from all indications may continue, may well defeat our national defense program. An additional burden is placed on the already overloaded machine tool industry. We propose to short-cut the process by building only the tools, dies, jigs, and fixtures necessary to convert idle automotive machinery into plane engine machinery. A few special machines will be necessary, but these will be but a small part of the total equipment. In this way a job that will otherwise take at least eighteen months can be done in six months.

Certain basic machines are necessary to build both automobile and aircraft types of engines. These include gear cutters, gear shapers, screw machines, bullards, drill presses, punch presses, broaching machines, turret lathes, various types of milling machines, various types of lathes and Fay machines, lapping machines, various types of grinding machines, die casting machines, forge presses, header machines, foundry equipment, welding and riveting equipment.

The plane has three main parts: engine, wings, and fuselage.

Just as there is unused capacity for the production of motors, so there is unused capacity for the production of the wings and fuselage. The large body plants and the parts plants have metal stamping equipment now used for stamping out parts for the body of the automobile which can be adapted to stamping out the parts which make up the wings and fuselage of the plane. Proof of this is provided by the tentative plans being made by the automotive industry at the suggestion of Mr. Knudsen to manufacture parts of the wings and fuselages for large bombers.

A survey of the large body plants will show that their equipment for pressing and stamping metal parts is also not being used to full capacity. Murray Body, Briggs, and the Fisher Body plants show a 50 per cent over-all unused capacity in their pressrooms. Striking is the example of the Fisher Body plant in Cleveland, which contains one of the largest pressrooms in the industry. At present it is operating at but 40 per cent of capacity, although automobile body production is now at its peak. In 1936–1937 this plant made all the stampings for Chevrolet bodies, employing 9200 employees. Today it employs but 3500, for Fisher has built a new plant at Grand Rapids, Michigan, further adding to body capacity.

Technical problems are involved, of course, in constructing new dies to stamp the lighter aluminum alloys used in plane production. That these problems are not insuperable is shown by the fact that Murray and Briggs are already stamping wing parts for Douglas bombers.

Skilled labor is necessary to turn out the tools and dies required to adapt these various types of automotive machinery to plane production. The auto industry has the largest reservoir of skilled labor in the world. More than twenty-five thousand tool and die workers, jig and fixture men, patternmakers, draftsmen and designers, and allied craftsmen are employed in the auto industry at the peak of its tooling program.

Tooling is even more seasonal than production. Each year thousands of the industry's most skilled craftsmen work at top speed for a few months to complete the necessary tooling work to adapt the old machinery to the new models. When the tooling

program is completed, only a skeleton crew of these skilled craftsmen is retained for maintenance and duplicate tooling. Three or
four thousand skilled craftsmen are shifted to ordinary production jobs while more than ten thousand are laid off entirely until
their labor is needed for the next tooling season. During the past
five years more than half of the tool- and die-makers in the industry, or more than ten thousand, averaged less than six months'
work per year. At the present time there are approximately three
thousand tool- and die-makers unemployed in the auto industry;
some twenty-five hundred have been transferred to ordinary
machine-tending production jobs. Many of the remainder are
on a short work week.

In addition to the men who are unemployed, those working
on production and those employed only part time, there are at
least two thousand tool and die men who have permanently gone
into production jobs because of the short work year in the tool
and die industry. These mechanics could be combed out of production departments and made available again for tool and die
work.

Thus in manpower, as in machines, we have unused capacity;
the highly specialized and valuable skills of seventy-five hundred
tool and die workers are available to do the necessary tooling
for the plane production program here outlined.

Fisher Body Corporation, a division of General Motors, is now
working on wood models for a new body design. Chrysler also
is working on new models, for which some diework is likewise
under way. If the automobile industry goes ahead with plans for
new models, it will absorb unemployed tool- and die-workers.
However, if the introduction of new models in the auto industry
could be delayed for six months, from twelve to fifteen thousand
skilled mechanics could be made available to build the necessary
tools, dies, jigs, and fixtures for the production of an all-metal
pursuit ship on a mass production basis.

The tool and die shops of the automotive industry, like the tool-
and die-workers themselves, are partially idle. The ninety tool
and die jobbing shops in the Detroit area affiliated with the Automotive Tool and Die Manufacturers Association employ seven

thousand tool and die workers when operated at full capacity. In addition to these shops in the Association, there are some seventy-five additional tool and die shops which employ fifteen hundred tool- and die-workers at capacity production. And, in addition to these independent enterprises, there are large tool and die departments within the auto body and parts plants proper. These are known as "captive" tool and die shops. These great "captive" tool and die shops have a capacity beyond the available manpower if all the skilled men in the entire industry were employed on a full-time basis.

A typical example of the tremendous unused capacity of these captive shops is that of Fisher Body No. 23 at Detroit. This is the largest tool and die shop in the world. It builds the sheet metal dies, welding bucks and fixtures, and special machinery for all Fisher Body plants in the General Motors Corporation. In 1931 Fisher Body Plant No. 23 employed forty-eight hundred tool- and die-makers at the peak of the tooling program. In 1940 Fisher Body Plant No. 23 employed fourteen hundred tool- and die-makers at the peak of the tooling season. In December, 1940, this plant employed only 175 tool- and die-makers and even these few were on a reduced work week.

As important as the tool and die worker is the engineer who designs the tools and dies. Here, too, the same situation repeats itself. There are in the Detroit and metropolitan areas about twenty-one hundred designing engineers. Their drawings would be needed for the new tools and dies required to adapt automotive machinery to plane production. Designing engineers, like tool and die workers, are largely unemployed between tooling seasons. Here, too, a six-months' delay in new automobile models would make available an ample supply of the necessary skilled men.

Just as there is no shortage of skilled labor in the automobile industry, so there is no shortage of unskilled labor. Despite the defense program, there is a minimum of one hundred thousand former automobile workers unemployed or on WPA, not to speak of the thousands of young people in automobile production areas who would welcome an opportunity to work in plane production.

We propose that the President of the United States appoint an aviation production board of nine members, three representing the government, three representing management, and three representing labor. We propose that this board be given full authority to organize and supervise the mass production of airplanes in the automobile and automotive parts industry.

The first task of the board would be to organize a staff of production and tooling engineers and assign them to make a plant-by-plant survey of the industry to determine the capacity of each plant and the extent to which it is being utilized. The next task of the board would be to break down a blueprint of the type of plane chosen for mass production into its constituent parts and allocate the various parts of the engine, wings, and fuselage among the different automotive plants in accordance with their unused capacity and the kind of work to which that unused capacity is being adapted. Work is to be parceled out with an eye to spreading it as widely as possible, for much quicker results will be obtained if each plant has to cope with but one or two problems of design and tooling. As contrasted with the present method, which dumps half a hundred technical problems into the lap of one manufacturer who must build an entire engine or plane, this method has all the advantages of division of labor.

The production board should have power to allocate the tooling and designing necessary among the various tool and die shops in accordance with their capacity and their specialized qualifications.

Power to appoint inspectors for each plant in accordance with its part in the general plan should be given the production board and there should be close inspection of each part manufactured before its release.

We propose the establishment of a central motor assembly plant to which all complete parts shall be shipped after they pass inspection.

The automotive industry has unused floor space as it has unused men and machines. We suggest that the Hupmobile plant in Detroit (a plant which produced only 371 cars in 1939, and which at the present time is completely idle) be leased by the government for a central motor assembly plant. The plant is large enough for five assembly lines with a daily total production capacity of five hundred complete aircraft engines a day. The plant could be operated on a three 7½-hour shift basis and the unused machinery now in the building could be placed in other plants in accordance with the general production plan.

Similar methods can be applied to the manufacture and assembly of the wings and fuselage, and here, too, there is ample unused floor space for new assembly lines. Six complete floors of a building one block long and a half block wide are available at Fisher Body Plant No. 21, Detroit, which formerly made bodies for Buick. (This work has now been transferred to Fisher Body Plant No. 1 at Flint, Michigan.) Several floors are also available at the Fisher Body Plant No. 23 in Detroit, and there is also floor space available at the Briggs Highland Park plant and at the old Ford Highland Park plant.

An outstanding example of idle floor space is the Murray Body Corporation in Detroit, the third largest bodymaking corporation in America. Since its loss of the Ford body contract, Murray is not producing a *single* automobile body. There are 234,375 square feet of floor space in Building 107 in Murray Plant No. 1, 300,000 square feet in Building No. 121, and 20,000 square feet available in Building No. 129. This available space will probably be needed for the contract Murray has obtained to stamp the metal parts and assemble the wing sections for Douglas bombers, but there is still 200,000 feet more of modern floor space in the Murray plant which is now being used for storage. This could be turned to the uses of this production program.

Similar is the situation at the Fisher Body plant in Cleveland. The third, fourth, and fifth floors of this building are now being used for storage, and could easily be made available for assembly lines. This plant at one time made all metal stampings for Chevrolet bodies. Additional floor space is also available in the Cleveland area.

A final assembly plant would also be needed for the job of assembling the engine, wings, and fuselage into the completed plane. For this purpose we suggest the construction of cheap flat hangars in the open space around the Wayne County airport. Completed engines, wings, and fuselage would be trucked from the subassembly plants to these hangars and the completed planes could be flown from the airport. Similar flat hangars could be erected for final assemblies at the Cleveland airport.

We suggest that the subassemblies and the final assemblies be placed under the control of men carefully selected upon the basis of skill and experience from the various assembly staffs in our motorcar and body plants, and that these picked men be used as the core of the assembly staffs to be developed under this plan. Provisions for protecting the seniority of these men must be guaranteed.

The first few thousand planes produced will not meet 100 per cent performance requirements, for in mass production of planes as in mass production of automobiles a few thousand jobs must always be run before the "bugs" (technical problems of machining and assembly) are worked out. This is not serious since the first few thousand planes will more than meet the requirements as training ships.

The automotive industry workers believe that this plan is the only one which offers hope of quick production of planes. It seeks solution of our problem not in the costly and lengthy work of erecting entire new plants, but in the efficient organization of existing idle manpower, machines, skill, and floor space.

By dividing the parts among many manufacturers, the greatest possible number of minds is brought to bear on the production problems involved.

Though we propose payment of a fair profit to each manufacturer in accordance with his share in the work, we can foresee the fears this plan may arouse on the part of some managements. They may prefer a method whereby the government finances entire new engines and aircraft plants. Aviation companies may look with misgiving on a production program that would inevitably cut the cost of planes by putting their production on a mass production basis. But we believe the average management executive would not put forward these selfish considerations at a time of crisis.

Labor offers its wholehearted cooperation. All that labor asks is intelligent planning, a voice in matters of policy and administration, recognition of its rights, and maintenance of its established standards.

The merit of our plan is that it saves time, and time is our problem. Normal methods can build all the planes we need—if we wait until 1942 and 1943 to get them. This plan is put forward in the belief that the need for planes is immediate, and terrifying. Precious moments pass away as we delay. We dare not invite the disaster that may come with further delay.

Our Fear of Abundance

The New York Times Magazine
September 16, 1945

There is a widespread failure in Congress and with the public to appreciate the domestic implications of Japanese surrender. There is a general reluctance to confront the problems of transition from war to peace. If we do not face them soberly and soon we run the risk of creating a situation potentially as explosive and damaging as the atomic bomb.

Uncritical use of the term "reconversion" is itself a clue to the "normalcy" temper of our thinking in and out of Washington. We regard the next few crucial months almost exclusively as a period of relaxation or abolition of controls, of an automatic kicking over of wartime traces and return to some *status quo ante*.

Congress apparently intends to ignore the sound recommendations for action contained in President Truman's recent message. There is every indication that whatever slapdash emergency measures the Congress may contrive, we intend to rely almost solely on what J. A. Krug of the War Production Board has called "the natural resilience of the economy" to lift us out of the doldrums of contract terminations and mass layoffs. We are gambling on the effect of a combination of pent-up demand for civilian goods and a backlog of savings to prevent a tailspin into deflation.

This "coming in on a wing and a prayer" economics rests upon too many unwarranted assumptions. The first is that there is somewhere and something to go back to. Yet there can be no return to the balmy Palm Beach climate of the nineteen twenties —unless we are willing to take with it the inevitable aftermath of depression. And, if I am correct in my appraisal of the average American's present mood, there will be no easy road back to the serfdom which made outcasts of millions of unemployed in the thirties.

13

As for the "resilience" of our economy, it proved insufficient to stabilize boom conditions or to turn the corner of the slump. It could not convert from peace to war production without government prodding. And there is good reason to assert that, left to its own devices, it will be unequal to the task of converting another boom, if one arises, into continuing prosperity.

The third assumption, existence of a vast reservoir of savings which will immediately spring into action as purchasing power, is equally untenable. Most of the billions of dollars in War Bonds are held either by corporations and financial institutions or by individuals and families in the upper-income brackets who habitually save a great proportion of their income. These billions, therefore, will not prove a source of demand for consumer goods. Where will that demand come from? The rest of wartime savings, held by lower-income families, must serve to absorb the shock of reduced hours, downgrading, lower-paying civilian jobs, and unemployment. It will be used cautiously, dribbled out for necessities, not expended confidently and lavishly to confirm optimistic predictions of another lush era.

Thus our dilemma is a real one. It cannot be solved by hymns to free enterprise or by efforts to turn back the clock to the halcyon days of Harding. The road leads not backward but forward, to full production, full employment, and full distribution in a society which has achieved economic democracy within the framework of political democracy. We shall not attain these positive goals by a single-minded concern for the contract-termination pains of business or by grudging, belated, and negative action calculated to take care of the "human side of reconversion." Necessary as are such measures as adequate unemployment insurance, they remain poultices applied to an inflamed surface; our real ills lie deeper, temporarily forgotten during an ersatz wartime prosperity, but arising now to plague us again.

We suffer, to put it briefly, from what Thorstein Veblen called the "inordinate productivity" of the machine. We have mastered technology and possess a complex, high-octane B-29 production machine. But our productive genius has always been stalemated by our failure at the distributive end. We have found it impossible to sustain a mass purchasing power capable of providing a stable market for the products of a twentieth century technology. This disparity between our B-29 technology and our huffing and puffing Model T distributive system led to the crash of 1929 and ushered in a period of unprecedented waste of human and material resources—a waste estimated at 200 billion dollars in potential goods and services.

In the light of this diagnosis we see how precarious must be any postwar boom. We see, moreover, that the chief intent of national policies during the transition must be not merely to cushion the changeover to supposed normal ways of doing business, but rather to remedy the central flaw of our economy, wiping out the fitful succession of boom and bust, feast and famine, and providing stable mass distribution of the goods and services made available by mass production.

Any program designed to accomplish this end will require action along two lines: full use of our industrial plant and, secondly, a wage-price policy capable of creating and maintaining an effective demand for the products of that plant at capacity output.

On behalf of the United Automobile Workers thrown on the scrapheap by the closing of the Willow Run bomber plant, I recently proposed a plan providing for continued operation of the plant and of the thousands of other government-built war facilities which can be turned to the use of peace.

This plan, published by Willow Run Local 50, UAW-CIO, and now under consideration by government officials, recommends conversion of publicly owned war plants to the mass production of modern railroad equipment and low-cost housing.

Government authorities similar to the Tennessee Valley Authority would be set up in housing and transportation, and under their jurisdiction a survey would be made of the 20 billion dollars in war facilities, the vast bulk of which is public property, financed by the war bond investments of millions of Americans. Most of these plants have a high peacetime utility. They are ultramodern and contain the most efficient machine tools and equipment.

It is important to emphasize that most of these plants can readily be converted to production of civilian goods, just as plants were retooled for production of war matériel under the defense and war programs. Certain private management spokesmen will protest that this is not so; the same cry was raised in the fall of 1940 when I presented, on behalf of the technicians and production workers of the automobile industry, a plan to utilize its plant and equipment for the mass production of warplanes. Yet three years later, in testimony before the Truman Committee of the United States Senate, K. T. Keller, President of the Chrysler Corporation, admitted that 89 per cent of Chrysler's machines had been converted to war production—and could be converted back to civilian production.

What was true of Chrysler was true also of General Motors, Ford, and minor producers. The will to change corporate habits and to renounce a profitable civilian business simply wasn't there. After Pearl Harbor the government had to move in and force conversion.

After determination of the facilities adaptable to the program, these housing and railroad equipment authorities would place them in production either through direct operation, through lease to private manufacturers, or through lease to workers' producer cooperatives. In each case the plant would be operated as part of the total program, and its management would conform to three standards: an equitable wage pattern, a good low-cost product, and protection of the government's investment.

This program holds the promise of stimulating our whole economy through the progressive introduction of the most modern rolling stock and the proportionate retirement of obsolete equipment. Use of roller and ball bearings, of aluminum, magnesium, and Diesel power will increase the payload (just as important in freight car as in air transport) and will permit the radical scaling down of rail rates. As for housing, the same mass production miracles which have made us a nation on wheels can place a modern, durable, healthy house within the economic reach of the common man. Airplane, aircraft engine, magnesium, aluminum, electrical equipment, forge, foundry, and other government-owned war plants can be utilized in the mass production of complete homes, including all fixtures, complete bathroom, kitchen, garbage disposal, and air-conditioning units, electric dishwashers, and other appliances—all designed and constructed as integral parts of the house according to the latest standards of convenience and efficiency.

By giving the construction industry a public utility status, by fostering cooperative and federal housing projects, by working through a technical commission under the Housing Authority to revise and implement building codes and eliminate slum housing, the entire vicious circle of primitive methods and restrictive practices in the building industry can be broken.

Anyone familiar with technological advances made in the automotive industry cannot regard such a promise of low-cost prefabricated housing as visionary. These advances have been accelerated throughout industry in the last four years as a result of the pervasive demands of war. We have but to mobilize for peace the resourcefulness and technical know-how which put the B-29 in the skies over Tokyo and sent the atomic bomb crashing into Hiroshima—and we can wipe out the slums and substandard housing, both rural and urban, which sap the health and dignity of millions of American families. We have spent billions to destroy cities. Let us be lavish in the equally challenging and more creative assignment of building homes and rebuilding cities here in the United States, a victorious but poorly housed democracy.

The railroads and building industries are two vital areas of our economy which have not kept pace with technological advance in the past decades and whose practices are geared to scarcity rather than to that abundance which is now both physically possible and socially imperative.

In the building industry, outmoded construction techniques, inflated land values (often based on illegal but highly profitable use of slum property in violation of unenforced health and building codes), a multiplicity of small dealers and middlemen, and high interest rates on capital have combined to create high unit costs and general instability, and have made home ownership either impossible or impractical for a majority of American families.

In both industries only aggressive government action can cut through the tangle of inertia and vested interest and initiate sorely needed reforms. Housing and railroad equipment authorities would provide the administrative machinery to effect these changes.

The war has demonstrated to the American people that full employment is possible. They will not readily be convinced by conservative economic theorists that a return to peace must mean a return to a "normal float of unemployed" and "No Help Wanted" signs. Existence of a vast industrial empire of government-owned war plants, most of them adaptable to peacetime production, serves to dramatize, to focus more sharply than ever, the dilemma of American capitalism.

The proposals I have advanced deal chiefly with housing and transportation, but throughout industry the issue is the same: back to monopoly, to operation at a fraction of capacity, to cherished and (to a few) profitable habits in a scarcity economy— or forward to full use of resources, full employment, and an equitable distribution of the products of our labor. We cannot dodge the issue. If the right answer is too long delayed, Willow Run and the other giant plants of World War II will stand idle as rotting monuments to our fear of abundance—but our free way of life may well lie in ruins around them.

Physical plant and technical skill will avail us little if the complex process of production and distribution is impeded by an inequitable and unrealistic policy regarding prices and wages. The chief objective of that policy must be a general rise in the wage level without a concomitant rise in the price level.

The issue, viewed here from another perspective, is the same: will industry, in its search for profits, find them by exacting a high price per unit of a limited output, maintaining an artificial scarcity, pocketing the returns on advancing technology, and shutting millions out from employment and a stake in the preservation of the system? Or will industry, following the most respectable economic theory, pass on to labor its just share of the benefits of technical progress in the form of higher wages and seek its profits in capacity production for an expanded market?

Fantastic war profits, before and after taxes, and favorable government tax policy place most American corporations in an unusually strong position for adopting the high-wage, high-volume approach now, setting the pattern which will shape our peacetime economy. But there are ominous signs emanating from the oracles of government stabilization policy which suggest that the emerging pattern is just the opposite.

Sixty-five industries reporting to the War Production Board have revealed the volume of production at which they feel confident of breaking even in peacetime operations. Of the sixty-five, fifty-one stated that they could operate without loss at less than 70 per cent of capacity output. The break-even rate for the automotive industry is 55 per cent. Add to these figures the fact that the NWLB has held labor in the vise of the Little Steel Formula despite rocketing living costs, while the OPA has shown a disposition to grant price rises on flimsy evidence or none, and we have the elements of the postwar wage-price structure: low wages, high prices, high profit per unit, few units. The picture can be developed further: deficient purchasing power, shrinking markets, rising unemployment, a growing conviction on the part of those whom industry has thrust aside that the game of free enterprise, played at their expense, isn't worth the candle. It is to be hoped that we do not drift this far toward disaster.

There is, as we have said, an alternative: reduction of unit cost by high-volume production and constant technological innovation, enabling the masses of workers to get their bigger cut out of a larger pie and providing industry with an expanding market.

There are two other main items in a desirable wage policy for peace: industry-wide wage agreements based on the principle of equal pay for equal work, regardless of geographical area, and the introduction of guaranteed annual wage systems through collective bargaining between labor and management. The first will protect labor from exploitation as a pawn in the competitive struggle; the second will place responsibility for continuity of employment where it belongs—with employers—and will minimize the need for government intervention.

The logic of these two demands is simple. Competition, to be socially acceptable in a society which pretends to be at one remove from the jungle, must be founded upon the relative efficiency of management techniques, productive skills, technological improvements, and the resulting superiority of product. As for area differentials, the solution lies in raising low living standards, not in maintaining depressed conditions. General Motors does not charge less for a Chevrolet in Birmingham, Alabama, in deference to the lower standards of the South. Senator Bilbo receives as much for his services to democracy as do Senators Wagner and Vandenberg. UAW members in the South will not accept less for their sweat and skills than the auto workers of Michigan.

The guaranteed annual wage proposal represents a challenge to management to sponsor the greatest "back to work" movement in the history of labor relations. To businessmen, who have been known upon occasion to boast of their ability to meet payrolls and who in times of strikes and picket lines are extremely vocal about the "right to work," the annual wage proposal says, in effect: "You can't have your cake and eat it, too; if private enterprise wants to stay private, it has to stay enterprising. If you won't accept a continuing commitment to employ, the government will have to move in."

But the annual wage offers a positive alternative to government intervention. Besides being a powerful incentive to maintain capacity operations and a spur to labor morale and productivity through removal of layoff fears, it offers the expectation of a continually growing market by placing pay checks regularly in the hands of the millions of American workers, who are the great consumers of the products of this country's assembly lines.

These are the bare bones of a minimal program for making America as prosperous in peace as she has been formidable in war. The flesh and blood must come from our unswerving will to plan and work together for peace and abundance, just as we joined forces for death and violence. To assert that planning to fulfill the promise of American life in an economic as well as a political sense must degenerate into tyranny is to utter a counsel of despair and to resign ourselves to drift and ultimate disaster.

If we fail, our epitaph will be simply stated: we had the ingenuity to unlock the secrets of the universe for the purposes of destruction, but we lacked the courage and imagination to work together in the creative pursuits of peace.

How to Beat the Communists

Collier's
February 28, 1948

In 1939, in the course of our United Automobile Workers' negotiations with General Motors, William F. Knudsen, then president of the corporation, pointed a big forefinger at me and said, "Now see here, Reuther, we don't want any commissars in America!"

The answer I gave then is the answer I should give today to the question, "How can we stop Communism?" It is an answer bolstered by eleven years' experience in the day-to-day struggle for CIO survival and growth in America's pace-setting auto industry.

"Mr. Knudsen," I said, "we Auto Workers don't want commissars any more than you do. But what you and other powerful leaders of American industry do about helping to make democracy work in bread-and-butter terms for the average man and his family will determine—much more than anything we Auto Workers do—whether we get commissars or not."

I fear that such an answer will not comfort or please those who have been stampeded by the present anti-Red hysteria into the belief that there is some easy formula for beating the Communists. But we have beaten the Communists in the United Automobile Workers and we can speak with authority. There is no formula. There is only the never-ending task of making democracy work, keeping it alive and fighting against injustice; expanding and enriching it by tangible achievement. Stopping Communism is only a negative aspect of that positive, infinitely more important work.

There are quack cures for Communism. Hitler cured it by killing the limited democracy of the Weimar Republic. Mussolini stopped it by throttling Italian freedom. We in the United States still have time to avoid these fatal extremes and to prove that democracy is a militant, up-to-date creed—with the moral strength and the practical political and economic know-how to meet the challenge of totalitarianism.

The press, reporting the results of the latest UAW-CIO convention, stated that Reuther had scored a decisive victory over Communist forces. But to call this Communist defeat a personal victory for me is to obscure the most significant development in the Auto Workers. Hundreds of thousands of UAW members, not only in Detroit and the other large industrial centers, but in Kokomo, Oshawa, Kalamazoo; in Canada, New England, and the deep South—these are the men and women who stopped Communism in the Auto Workers by standing up, having their say, and being counted.

Communists cannot seize power in a nation or a union if the people are on their toes, if they know the issues, and are offered democratic leadership built around a positive program of action. The inertia and indifference of the average citizen or union member are the most valuable assets the Communists have. Working as a well disciplined minority, they cultivate this passivity and thereby seek to immobilize the democratic majority—especially those individuals and groups capable of providing leadership and direction in the fight against both Red and black totalitarianism.

The momentum of a positive democratic program is the only final answer to both the commissar and the storm trooper.

From our experience in the UAW-CIO, we have learned that there are two major obstacles to be overcome before decent unionists and honest liberals are ready to fight the Communists. The first obstacle might be called the united-front psychology; the second, fear of the Communists' highly developed technique of name-calling and character assassination.

We have just emerged from a period in which many non-Communist progressives made common cause with the Stalinists in the misguided belief that contemporary Communism operates from ethical and moral perceptions of a certain validity. The delusion still persists in many quarters; Henry Wallace's third-party movement was fathered by it. The liberal who succumbs to the united-front lure believes that Communists are simply democrats-in-a-hurry. He points to their concern over civil liberties (when it suits the party line), their loud support for price and rent controls, their advocacy of full employment, health, Social Security, and minimum-wage legislation. And he asks, "Since the Communists are going my way, why shouldn't I travel with them?"

The answer, of course, is that Communist concern for progressive reform under parliamentary democracy is little more than a temporary expedient, designed to enlist as many allies as possible against the day when the class struggle attains its climax in revolution and the "dictatorship of the proletariat." The Communist parties of the world are the self-appointed midwives of this violent historical birth. Moreover, in the course of the last generation, Communists have come to identify the interests of the world's peoples with the needs of the Soviet Union. Their subservience to the Kremlin and their shifts on trade union issues as Moscow winds veer can become the Achilles' heel of the domestic Stalinists if honest progressives in the labor movement carry the fight to them.

An amusing consequence of Communist acrobatics cropped up in the Wayne County CIO Council. Shortly before the invasion of Russia, the Communist clique in a UAW local union had slipped a resolution condemning the "imperialist war" past a sparsely attended local membership meeting and had forwarded it to the council for endorsement, after releasing it to the press. The Nazi attack followed. The Communists maneuvered a special meeting at the same local and quickly passed another resolution reflecting the new, superpatriotic line. The imperialist blood bath had now become a holy crusade.

This resolution was also given to the press as the official position of the local and sent to the council for action. When the council met, the two conflicting resolutions from the same local were read—and a motion was made to refer both of them back to their source, with the recommendation that the local union make up its mind.

Progressives must expose Stalinist duplicity without qualms.

To outlaw their party and drive them underground is not the answer. Such action would enable them to drape themselves in the cloak of martyrdom and would make more difficult the task of detecting their activities.

Exposure, not repression, must be our goal. We must get the Communists out of the political back alleys and walk them up Main Street in the full light of informed opinion. No sober public examination of their unadorned doctrine and purposes can fail to reveal them as frauds.

While the American Stalinists may quote democratic scripture for their purposes, they are neither good democrats nor good Americans.

Yet many genuine liberals who understand that the Communists have only a provisional interest in the democratic process are immobilized by fear of Communist character assassination and abuse—and they are disgusted by the stupid and indiscriminate Dies-Rankin-Thomas brand of Red-baiting. Such indiscriminate lumping of the Communists and the non-Communists gives to the Stalinists the protective coloration which is their most effec- tive means of defense. The hysteria engendered by the new "Republican Dies Committee" is creating the same confusion, hitting the very witch-hunt pitch required by Communist strate- gists. The Communists know how to exploit this confusion, how to intensify it. Witch hunts rather than legitimate and sober ex- posure, moreover, lend an aura of righteousness to the Stalinists' own technique of abuse and slander.

We in the UAW took the Communists on without illusions. We were determined not to be diverted from our program by any amount of Communist invective or distortion.

We understood that the alternative to a finish fight was Com- munist control of our union. Such an understanding comes pain- fully; nobody enjoys the daily diet of vulgar insult in the Com- munist press which is the lot of those who challenge the party. Morris Muster, former president of the CIO Furniture Workers' Union, for example, resigned under the incessant hammering of the Communists, after releasing a bitter statement exposing the extent of their infiltration in his union. But he should have considered the fact that when decent unionists lose stomach for the struggle, they surrender the field to the Communists.

Honest progressives in the UAW had ample cause for disgust as the Communist Party machine slipped into high gear in the preconvention struggle. The Stalinist bloc in the Auto Workers was responsible for publishing and distributing to the membership more than two million pieces of literature.

In addition to a weekly propaganda paper, they prepared and circulated nationally a 35-page magazine called *The Bosses' Boy*, replete with distortion, fabrication, and forgery, which sought to prove that I was a clever servant of General Motors and the National Association of Manufacturers. Responding to a full report which I had issued to the membership, which had minced no words in describing the conflict within our ranks, the left-wing majority on the International Executive Board adopted a resolution reflecting the Communist view that I was a traitor and an agent of Wall Street.

"Fulfillment of Reuther's program," the resolution charged, "would put him in such distinguished company that the Labor Management Relations Act of 1947 might well be called the 'Taft-Hartley-Reuther' Act."

This association of my name with Taft was a prelude to the more ambitious maneuver executed shortly thereafter by a press agent hired by the opposition. It soon developed that I was being boomed for Vice President as a running mate with none other than Senator Taft. This big-lie technique was perhaps brilliant as a public relations maneuver, but we exposed it as a repeat performance of a campaign by the Communists during the war, when they advocated a return to piecework and speed-up in the auto plants.

To those who are just beginning to face the unpleasant necessity of combating Communists in their local unions, veteran groups, and other organizations, we can offer only the simple recommendation: Names can't hurt you. We must have the courage to speak up.

Once committed to the struggle against Communists, honest

liberals must guard against the temptation to join forces with or accept help from those whose only badge of fraternity is their anti-Communism. It is fatal to resist Communism by courting reaction. The chief weakness of American foreign policy is the predilection of our State Department for dealing with anybody who will promise to hate Communism. And the most dangerous error into which any domestic offensive against Stalinism can fall is that of assuming that *every foe of Communism is a friend of democracy.*

We did not make that mistake in the UAW. At the height of our campaign against CP infiltration in our union, Michigan's Governor Sigler descended upon Washington as an expert witness in the Red probe. Mr. Sigler's authority on the subject of Communism derived from a few easy victories won on Michigan campuses over the American Youth for Democracy, latter-day name for the Young Communist League.

The governor, however, identified as subversive several groups which were nonexistent or highly respectable, and one organization whose members included Detroit's chief of police and a score more of that city's more prominent residents. Mr. Sigler's stock as an expert on Communist-front organizations fell suddenly, but not until he had made highly damaging allusions to Communism in the Auto Workers. The anti-Communist forces in the UAW, however, did not make the fatal mistake of regarding Sigler as a potential ally in our fight.

Anti-Communism is not sufficient. Hitler, Mussolini, Franco, Perón, Rankin, Bilbo, and Gerald L. K. Smith—all could pass that test. The fight against Communism can be transformed from a self-defeating clash by night into an honest engagement in which decent people can participate without embarrassment only by a passionate belief in democratic values and the will to give those values practical currency in the lives of the people.

The next step in any democratic move to combat Communism must be an awareness of how the Stalinist parties and their adherents function. Communist tactics in relation to the labor movement have shifted many times since 1917, but the central design has never altered. In 1921, the Third World Congress of the

Communist International, legislating on the "duties of Communist activity," laid down the following imperatives:

"Communist nuclei must be formed for the daily work in the different branches of the party activities. . . .

"These Communist units are the nuclei for the daily Communist work in military units, trade unions, etc. . . . If there are a greater number of party members in the same factory or in the same union, etc., then the nucleus is enlarged into a faction, and its work is directed by the nucleus."

The same Comintern directive contained clear instructions for Communist action in the unions: "In those capitalist countries where a large majority of the proletariat has not yet reached revolutionary consciousness, the Communist agitators must be constantly on the lookout for new forms of propaganda.

"The factions must carefully prepare the participation of the Communists in conferences and meetings of the trade-union organizations. For instance, they must elaborate proposals, select lectures and counsel and put up as candidates for election capable, experienced and energetic comrades."

The Daily Worker stated on July 16, 1928: "Communism is a revolutionary tendency in the labor movement and the only representative of revolutionary Marxism-Leninism; as such it is opposed to all other tendencies within the labor movement."

This fanatical preoccupation with conquest of organized labor, this elaborate apparatus of propaganda and disruption, the Stalinists, over the past several years, have brought to bear on the United Automobile Workers, which they regard as the strategic union of the CIO.

We have beaten them. The story of how we did it reads almost like the report of an experiment in creative democracy, and provides a demonstration of techniques which can be applied in the larger struggle to save democracy in the world.

Communists have never had much success in converting workers in any industry to their dogmas. But where the Stalinists had not been able to convert, they succeeded in exerting an influence far out of proportion to their numerical strength by exploiting the innocence and ambition of men and women in positions of leadership.

The Communists have a complete political valet service which they offer to those in public life and in the unions who, for whatever reason, accept their current policies and fail to challenge their motives. Henry Wallace is the most familiar contemporary example of a man who has accepted this service. This CP service provides its customers with ready-made thoughts on all subjects, ghost-writes speeches, arranges meetings, engineers applause, and inflates egos as required.

Recipients of the service ultimately discover, however, that they have become boxed-in, thoroughly dependent, and pliable instruments of the party linemen.

During the twelve years the UAW-CIO has existed as an international union, the Communists have placed only one party member in the top leadership and only two of the faithful on our International Executive Board. Yet they have prospered in our midst until recently, because they so skillfully cultivated persons who could be made, in some degree, to serve their purposes. It was through clever manipulation of such people that the Stalinists acquired an influence in the UAW vastly disproportionate to the numbers of their convinced adherents.

Working through such strategically placed victims, the Communists captured the leadership of a number of local unions and could count on assistance from certain members on the regional and international union staffs. Machine-made resolutions promoting the Communist line would pop up at union meetings, and Communist adeptness at parliamentary maneuver would get them by an unalerted membership.

The Communists are highly skillful in using the forms of democracy to subvert democracy. But in local after local union, non-Communist members, gradually and after many painful experiences, awoke to the party's contempt for the rank and file, to its methods of discouraging attendance at meetings, to its whole strategy of spreading conflict and sowing confusion.

The Stalinists suffered their first crucial preconvention defeat when their proposal to merge the Communist-dominated Farm Equipment Workers with the UAW was rejected by UAW local unions.

In the summer of 1947, a committee of UAW opposition board members had been meeting secretly with officials of the FE [Farm Equipment]-CIO. Without prior notice, they presented to a UAW Executive Board meeting a plan for merging the two organizations, both of which have jurisdiction in the agricultural implement industry. What followed might be regarded as a controlled experiment in the technique of fighting Communists without succumbing to the Communists' own vicious habit of generalized abuse.

The FE merger proposal was a complete fraud. Its sponsors had only one objective: to bring five hundred additional left-wing votes to bear in the UAW convention, then less than five months away. It did not provide for a true merger at all, but rather for the temporary establishment of a union within a union. Grant Oakes, FE president, admitted to a *Daily Worker* correspondent that the plan, if carried out, would set up a "powerful and autonomous FE Division of the UAW-CIO, throughout the U.S. and Canada."

The FE was to enter the UAW with its staff intact; FE members, together with UAW members in the farm implement industry, were to be given special membership cards in an "FE Division" of the UAW; the whole plan was in violation of the UAW constitution and organizationally unsound. It would have meant a retreat from industrial unionism to craftlike autonomy at a time when the industrial form of organization was under attack from Congress. But the Communists didn't care. They were making a bid for control of the nation's biggest union. This was the showdown.

The plan was approved by the left-wing majority of the UAW Executive Board. UAW locals were given less than a month to debate the issues and set up a poll in which no alternative set of proposals would be available. Those of us in the leadership and ranks who favored real merger but opposed the provisions of the left-wing plan were placed in the uncomfortable position of blocking "unity."

We went into the local unions with copies of the merger plan. Every time advocates of the measure waxed eloquent and general, we dragged them down out of the stratosphere by talking about the plan itself.

They railed at the Taft-Hartley Act. We insisted that all generalities be brought down to earth and measured against the specific provisions of the merger proposal. We were not against merger. We favored merger. But we objected to merger on the basis proposed. We knew that the FE merger maneuver was Communist-inspired. But to base our opposition to it on that ground would have confused the membership by involving them in a vague debate on the merits of Communism.

The Communists would have cried, "Red-baiting," and they would have succeeded in pushing the plan through on the basis of their general appeal to unity. When left-wing rhetoric had subsided and we had placed the facts before the membership, the proposal was rejected by a vote of better than 2 to 1.

A spokesman for the left-wing group, interviewed by a reporter for the *Detroit Free Press* (July 20, 1947) after the vote, had this to say: "We give Reuther credit. His workers covered the country from coast to coast and down to the Gulf."

His credit should have gone to the workers he mentioned rather than to me, but the point is clear. We had beaten the Stalinists on the merits of the issue—but the issues were rescued from the fog of double-talk and presented to the membership by hard work. That is the way to beat the Communists.

Since the UAW convention, we have offered the FE a sound unity proposal which their leadership has rejected. They have lost their zeal for unity.

An equally significant Communist defeat occurred at the last CIO convention. Here again, during debate on the foreign policy resolution, the progressive forces won an important victory for democratic unionism which has implications wider than the CIO—and we won it by hitting hard at the issue.

The resolution on foreign policy was among the most important adopted by the CIO convention, for it contained a clearly implied endorsement of the Marshall Plan. To the Communists, it was all-important, since they are always most sensitive in those areas where the interests of the Soviet Union are directly affected.

They recognized that the resolution itself was not so important as the interpretation it would be given by delegates and by the press. We, too, were fully aware of the importance of the setting. Secretary of State Marshall had been invited to address the convention.

What Marshall said before the CIO national convention was important, but more significant was the fact that he had been invited to address the CIO. For in its work of dispensing confusion to the hungry and troubled peoples of Europe, the Cominform would find it difficult to explain how the chief "agent of American imperialism and Wall Street capitalism" could be invited to address the delegates of millions of industrial workers.

The Stalinists attempted to maneuver convention action on the foreign policy resolution in advance of Secretary Marshall's speech. We blocked such a move. Marshall spoke first and debate followed. The democratic bloc was ready. Van Bittner of the Steel Workers took the floor. Anticipating the tenor of left-wing remarks, he gave the lie to Communist charges that Marshall was a "warmonger." Other similar speeches followed, attacking Communist hypocrisy.

Kehoe of the American Communications Association was the first speaker to echo the CP line. He had just finished attacking American policy in Korea and was in the middle of a free-speech peroration when Philip Murray interrupted him to inquire, "I assume that you also believe the heroes of Stalingrad are entitled to take the rostrum and the public platform in Russia to expound their views?" Kehoe replied lamely that he believed in free speech everywhere, even in Russia. The Communists were in full retreat.

The "secret battalion" had been licked before an international audience. Hundreds of thousands of decent unionists, watching from local union offices throughout the land, had won new heart. They knew now that it could be done; they had just seen it done.

And democratic trade unionists throughout Europe, who suffered the horrors of Nazi concentration camps, knew they had friends and allies in the ranks of American labor in their struggle against the new totalitarianism of the left.

As delegate elections preceding our 1947 convention were held and the campaign got under way, the results soon proved the effectiveness and soundness of our policy of fighting the Communists on the basis of principles and program. We entered the delegate elections with a militant union program. It was printed on every piece of our campaign literature.

We made specific recommendations for strengthening the internal structure of our union. We emphasized a broad program for union members acting not as producers alone but as consumers and politically conscious citizens. We developed a concept of unionism as an integral part of the community's life and sensitive to the relationship of its own function and the general good. We pulled no punches on the issues of Communism and Fascism, for we had no ulterior motives to hide. Whenever we could, we talked program, not personalities, in contrast to a left-wing campaign limited to personal slander and abuse.

It was our concern with program that provided our margin of victory in the UAW. Around our program we mobilized the energies of our people, the democratic unionist bloc. In every area where we clashed, militant democracy won out over Stalinist maneuvers.

In the Motor Building of the vast Ford Rouge plant, the leadership of the unit opposed our program. They fixed delegate elections for Sunday between 11:00 A.M. and 1:00 P.M., thinking that the inconvenient hour would discourage rank-and-file attendance and enable a disciplined minority to capture the delegates. It was a technique which had succeeded many times; this time it failed. We worked harder than the opposition.

We filled the hall and we elected nine out of ten delegates. The election was thrown out on a technicality by the leadership, and another election was scheduled. We went to work again. The results this time were perfect; we mobilized an even heavier vote and we carried ten out of ten delegates by better than three to one. Hard hitting on the issues; hard work on the double. There is no easier or surer way for democracy to win.

The Communists made a particularly ambitious play for the allegiance of our Negro members. They had in the past had undeniable success in exploiting the legitimate grievances of Negroes, both as citizens and as unionists. But here, as in other areas, the Communists have been more interested in playing upon misery and exploiting legitimate grievances for their own purposes than in making a principled and consistent attack on the evils of prejudice and discrimination. The cleverness of the Stalinist appeal to race emotions cost the UAW democratic bloc the Buffalo convention in 1943.

We persisted, however, in efforts to obtain equality of treatment and opportunity for Negro members. Our stand was not so spectacular as the Communist approach. We appealed to Negroes, not as racial nationalists but as unionists and fellow Americans. We could, moreover, afford to be steadfast in our actions. Throughout the war period, for example, we continued to press for fair play in the plants and local unions, at a time when the CP members preferred to look the other way, regarding a prosecution of Negro grievances (or any legitimate unionist grievance) as an offense against their newly acquired superpatriotic line.

At the latest convention of the UAW, the vast majority of Negro delegates joined the democratic bloc. Not only had we been more consistent—we had not waited for Communist-front organizations to champion the cause of civil rights.

The lesson is clear; it can be applied elsewhere. An honest but inactive liberal is no match for a devious but aggresive totalitarian in any engagement where democratic values are at stake. Democracy needs more get-up-and-go.

The lessons we learned in the UAW can fortify free men everywhere who stand at the crossroads today. We mobilized a third force, resisting the interference and blandishments of democracy's enemies on the right and the left. We talked program, and acted to implement program. The challenge to make democracy work is particuarly acute in America, where our great productive potential gives us the prime responsibility to provide leadership and sustenance to a world in crisis.

Communism is in perpetual war with what democracy preaches, for it cannot abide the sanctity of the individual or the interplay of honest differences. But Communism breeds on what democracy too often practices; it exploits the lapses of the democratic conscience and thrives on the shortcomings of democratic action. It is the task of democrats to bridge the gap between preachment and practice; we must wipe out the double standard in America, and in the world, which divides the masses of people from the minority that controls the preponderance of economic power. It is this double standard which embitters our society.

Democracy's heart is in the right place. It is grounded on the firm base of confidence in the intrinsic soundness and rightness of the ordinary person. Democracy affirms that the individual is more than a hired hand, more than a clock-card number, more than a servant of the authoritarian state. It rejects the Fascist and Stalinist notion that men must be herded and bullied through history's dialectic by vanguards and élites.

But you can't beat Communism by throwing embarrassing questions at witnesses in a Congressional hearing. You can't slug it to death with a club or a slogan. You can't burn it at the stake. You have to show it up in the market place of ideas, expose it by honest dealing. Communism breeds on hunger, poverty, human insecurity. The Catholic peasants of Italy have never read Marx or Lenin. But in desperation they will vote Communist for land and bread if Italian democrats fail them. Desperation knows and needs no ideology.

Whether in some small local union in some small American town or in the vast power vacuums of Europe and Asia, democracy needs program and the will to get up early and stay late in the running fight with totalitarianism of every stamp. Democracy needs less noise from the Thomas Committee and more quiet labor in the vineyeards Franklin Roosevelt had only begun to cultivate when he died.

Too Old to Work; Too Young to Die

Section of the opening address of the twelfth constitutional convention of the United Automobile, Aircraft and Agricultural Implement Workers of America

Milwaukee, Wisconsin
July 10, 1949

One of labor's long-range objectives is to achieve in every basic industry a guaranteed annual wage so that the consumers of this country can have a sustained income month in and month out, because only on that basis can we sustain an economy of full employment and full production and full distribution.

When we drafted the economic demands of our union in January of this year, we said that the workers in our industry needed a pension plan, that every day they were getting older and every day insecurity was clouding their future. We said that when a worker had worked twenty-five years and reached the age of sixty he was entitled to a minimum of one hundred dollars on top of the federal Social Security payments in order to be able to retire with a semblance of security and human dignity in his old age. We said that industry had to pay the bill because the workers have created the wealth that makes possible these great industries. We said that we wanted a hospital medical program financed on the basis of 5 per cent of payroll to give our workers and their families complete hospital and medical care. We said we wanted a wage increase to reestablish our real wage position back to where it was in June of 1946 when OPA was destroyed.

When we drafted these demands, we drafted them because they reflected the basic needs of our workers and they also reflected the basic needs of our nation's economy. Since we drafted these

36

demands the economic picture in America has worsened. There are soft spots developing. Unemployment is developing in serious proportions in many communities, like Muskegon, for example, and because of these worsening economic factors, these negative factors, the high priests in Wall Street say to us, "This is no time to rock the boat. Labor ought to demonstrate real statesmanship. Withdraw your demands and let's kind of weather the storm together."

And we in the UAW say to these people in industry, to the coupon clippers in Wall Street, every reason that necessitated our drafting our demands in January has been reemphasized and reinforced by the fact that we are getting into economic difficulty with growing unemployment. This is not the time for people in the leadership of American labor to be men of little faith or little courage. This is the time for labor to stand up and say we are getting in trouble in America because the little guy hasn't got enough, and therefore, he has to fight harder now to get what he is entitled to in order to avoid going into a depression. We have to say that loud and clear.

Industry tells us, when we are in a period of inflation, that we should not demand wage increases when prices are going up because they will create more inflation. Then when the inflation is leveling off and we are getting into trouble because people are being laid off, they say, "You should not do it now."

It is a good system: they get you coming and get you going.

We say the needs of our workers are simple and compelling, and we are not going to permit those demands to be ignored or postponed. We are going after them in 1949.

Big business again has welded a united front. The steel industry told Philip Murray and the Steelworkers the other day the answer was "no" on their wage and economic demands. The Ford Motor Company has told the Ford Motor workers "no." The Chrysler people have indicated their answer will be "no." And across America in industry you have this united front in the making.

We are going into these negotiations on the basis that we would like to see a situation in America where we can raise collective bargaining above the status of a struggle between competing economic pressure groups. We would like to resolve our economic demands on the basis of the economic facts and not upon economic power; but whether it is done one way or another is a decision and responsibility which industry must make.

We talk a great deal in our union about economic facts, and every time I get a chance to talk to you fellows I talk economic facts, because the kind of complex problems we have to solve cannot be solved just by table pounding or by picket line marching, no matter how militant you may be. Table pounding and picket line marching are part of the problem, but you have to base your demands and struggle on sound economic facts. We keep saying to our workers they have to understand these facts because these facts are the arithmetic of our future. What are the facts of the current economic situation as they relate to our demands? American industry has made profits higher than at any time in the history of America. Thirty-two billion dollars before taxes in 1948 and twenty billion after taxes, more than five times the profit rate of American industry before the war.

Profits have gone up three times as fast as wages and salaries. In the auto industry, eight companies, excluding the Ford Motor Company, in 1948 made profits 51 per cent higher than they did in 1947. In the first quarter of 1949, they made profits 35 per cent higher than in 1948, and these eight companies together made a return on their investment after taxes of 28 per cent. And that includes the little companies, Studebaker, Hudson, Packard, Willys-Overland, Kaiser-Frazer, in addition to General Motors and Chrysler. And despite these profits they are back at their old game of trying to cut corners and cut costs by sweating more work out of the workers. And I say to you the record of this union in its historic struggle in resisting speed-up with every weapon we have is clear. We have authorized 409 strikes since the last convention, the largest number in the history of this union, and almost 50 per cent of them involved the question of speed-up. We take the position we will mobilize our union to fight against speed-up wherever it raises its ugly head, whether it be in the small plant or Ford Motor Company or General

Motors or Chrysler, or any other company. The boys who are now making propaganda about the speed-up unfortunately are the same boys who tried to sell us piecework and were ready to lay their all on the altar for Joe Stalin at the Buffalo convention. They are not fooling anybody.

We say our economic demands are sound economically, and they are right morally. We have talked for a long time about destroying the double standards, and now we are finally in a position where we are going to do something about it. The trouble is that industry operates on the basis of these double economic and moral standards. They say to the worker when he is too old to work and too young to die, "You cannot have security in your old age: that is reserved to only the blue bloods, only the ones who were smart enough to pick the right grandfather before they were born. They can have security, but if you live on the wrong side of the railroad tracks you are not entitled to it."

And we say they are economically and morally and stupidly wrong.

Let me give you some of the figures. C. E. Wilson in 1948 got $516,000 in salary and bonus. He made, on the basis of a 40-hour week and 50 weeks a year, $258 an hour. Yet the Board of Directors of General Motors when they met in Wilmington said, "Poor old C. E., he is having a rough time of it, he can't get along on $516,000 a year; General Motors will give him $25,000 a year when he is too old to work but too young to die."

If you make $258 an hour they give it to you; if you make $1.65 an hour they say, "You don't need it, you are not entitled to it, and we are not going to give it to you."

We are going to change that in America, and we are going to start in the next couple of weeks.

Now don't get the idea C. E. Wilson is lonely. He has a lot of company in General Motors in this highly paid group. If you take the salary and bonuses of the top seven executives in General Motors, they averaged $426,799 last year. They averaged $213 per hour on a 40-hour work week, 50-week basis.

General Motors has made so much profit they declared a

$48,000,000 bonus. Eight million was laid aside for a rainy day, and forty million divided up. They had so much money they ran out of executives. They never run out of workers—just executives. And then they gave bonuses to people not on the pay roll of the General Motors Corporation, and they wrote a letter to the Chairman of the Securities and Exchange Commission to keep this information a secret. They didn't want anybody to know who got these bonuses, and why they got them and how much they were.

We have written the Securities and Exchange Commission, and we want this convention to pass a resolution, demanding they publish the information as to who is being bribed by the General Motors Corporation of America.

I don't want the Chrysler boys to feel badly, because I know they all love K. T. Keller. The four top officials in the Chrysler Corporation made last year an average of $225,000, or $113 per hour. And that does not include bonuses.

Let me tell you what happened on that. You fellows are all stockholders in the Chrysler Corporation. All of us together own one share. We bought one share of stock in every company under contract with our union, so that our Research Department could sit in on every Board of Directors' meeting, and see if we could not peep behind the Iron Curtain.

A brother from the Research Department went to the Chrysler stockholders' meeting, and after they went through all the rigamarole that they have at such meetings, the Chairman of the Board of Directors of the Chrysler Corporation stood before the meeting with a big brown envelope sealed tight. He said, "The Board of Directors has voted bonuses to some of the executives, and we want you to approve these bonuses. They are in the sealed envelope. We won't tell you who is getting how much. It is all in the envelope." And the fellow representing your one share of stock got up and said, "Mr. Chairman, I make a motion that we open up the envelope, so we can see who is getting how much of this bonus melon." He did not have enough shares—one share did not carry—and they voted him down. Imagine this! They voted themselves bonuses that are secret in a stockholders' meeting. I would just like to say to Brother Mazey and the other officers and Board Members, if we came before this convention, which is the stockholders' meeting of our union, and we had in a sealed envelope some bonuses for the top officers, and we said, you vote for them and approve them, without telling you who is getting what, I would want a jet plane out here to jump into and take off, because I would need it pretty quickly.

Now look at the Nash-Kelvinator Corporation. This is one of the little independents that is having a hard time getting along in the world. Mr. G. W. Mason of Nash-Kelvinator Company last year, got $300,925—$150 per hour, yet he got a pension plan.

International Harvester—so that the International Harvester boys do not feel slighted—Fowler McCormick made $161,000 last year, and when he is too old to work and too young to die he gets $40,000 a year pension from International Harvester.

And so the aircraft boys don't think that their industry is excluded, Mr. Leonard Hobbs of United Aircraft Company—he is just a measly vice-president—made $95,000 last year, and when he gets too old to work and he is too young to die, he will get a $12,337 per year pension. I just say to you people and we say to America—we say to American industry, if you can afford to pay pension plans to people who don't need them, then by the eternal gods you are going to have to pay them to people who do need them, the guys in the shop.

We want a hospital and medical plan. We want to remove the economic barriers which block good health to the average family in America. I don't speak with simply academic knowledge on this problem. I lay in four different hospitals over a period of months, and I tell you, you have to be a millionaire to afford medical care in America.

Let me just tell you the sort of things I have seen. I went into a hospital one morning to be treated and I met a young fellow twenty-eight years of age, a clean-cut looking boy with a smile in his eye, lying there on a hospital bed. The nurse asked me to go over and say hello to him and cheer him up, and I did. This boy has been paralyzed for nine years, and he lay at home. He could not afford hospital and medical treatment. I talked to him every morning, and after he had laid in the hospital about a month, after being paralyzed for nine years, I came in one morning and he was just overcome with joy. He said to me, "I have been reborn this morning." I said, "What do you mean?" And he said to the nurse, "Pull this sheet back so I can show Mr. Reuther." And the nurse pulled the sheet back and he could wiggle his big toe. It was the first time in nine years that he could wiggle his toe, and he was just like a kid on Christmas morning. I watched him every morning making progress, getting a new grip on life, with a whole new world opening up before him. Sometime later I came in to see him and he was crying like a kid. He was brokenhearted, and I said to the nurse, "What's the matter, hasn't he been doing so well?" And she said, "He hasn't got any more money; he goes home tomorrow."

I say there is something wrong in America when, if you happen to be born on the wrong side of the railroad tracks as these kids were, and you are paralyzed and you lie on your back for nine years because you can't afford the treatment that medical science can give you, I say that is morally wrong. No nation that has an ounce of self-respect or human decency, no nation that can spend $400,000,000,000 for war, can stand idly by and tolerate a continuation of that kind of double standard in America. And I say this convention has got to stand up and fight for these kids and give our people the kind of care to which they are entitled.

What made this thing so ironic—and you begin to see what is wrong in America—the same week this happened the *Free Press* came out with a story about C. E. Wilson's bull. C. E. Wilson had a bull and the bull had a bad back. We are sorry about that. But what happened to C. E. Wilson's bull compared to this boy who was paralyzed for nine years? In the case of C. E. Wilson's bull, the General Electric Company sent a special 140,000-volt X-ray machine into Detroit on a special chartered airplane. It was picked up by a General Motors truck and taken out to C. E. Wilson's farm. The bull didn't even have to leave home to get medical care. Then when they got the 140,000-volt machine there they couldn't operate it because they didn't have enough power, so the Detroit Edison Company ran a special power line out to C. E. Wilson's farm.

Then medical specialists flew in from all over the country and they gave this bull the best medical care that modern medicine and science knows how to deliver. Now why? Why? I ask that simple, honest question. Why did C. E. Wilson's bull get the best of medical care while millions of these kids all over America are not getting that kind of care? It is because C. E. Wilson's bull cost $16,000, and you get boys and workers for free. It is the age-old struggle between human rights and property rights, between people and profits, and this is just a dramatic illustration of how completely wrong some of our moral values are in America.

In the coal mines—and there are a lot of former coal diggers in this convention—they used to lay the coal miners off and they went hungry, but they always fed the mine mules because they owned the mine mules. They had to buy them but they didn't have to buy the coal miners. They got them for free.

That is the trouble in America, and we have got to change these things. We have to renew our faith in basic human values. We have to reassert the sovereignty of people above profits in America, and this convention has to do that. We want the pension plans and the medical plans and the wage increase. We need them. We are willing to sit down and do everything we can to resolve these problems intelligently and constructively, based upon the economic facts of life. But management must accept their responsibility in these coming negotiations, because if they try to continue the double standards we say to them here and now we are prepared to use all the weapons possessed by free labor in America in these negotiations. We know that we can't solve all of our problems through collective bargaining over the conference table.

We Shall March Together

Address accepting the Presidency of the Congress
of Industrial Organizations

Atlantic City, New Jersey
December 4, 1952

I stand before you humble in the face of the tremendous responsibilities which you have placed in my care. I thank you for the honor, and I pray that I shall have the strength, the courage, the wisdom, the understanding and vision to be worthy of your confidence. I am fully conscious, as would be anyone else standing in my place, that in assuming the presidency of the CIO and the responsibilities that go with that office, I am not in the remotest sense taking Phil Murray's place, because no man can take Phil Murray's place.

Phil Murray's death left our movement with an irreplaceable loss. His death robbed our nation of a truly great citizen. It robbed the labor movement of a courageous leader. It robbed each and every one of us who knew him of a good and kind friend. Bishop Haas said during the services in the Cathedral in Pittsburgh that Philip Murray was a great good man. He was right, but Philip Murray was more than just a great good man. He had many other qualities, and no one in our movement can take his place. Those of us who were called upon in the councils of the CIO to express ourselves on the loss of Phil Murray all felt wholly inadequate, because no one can put into words what you feel in your heart when you lose your best friend.

I remember the afternoon when the sun was bright and the day was clear and we all stood on the top of a hill outside Pittsburgh. All of us with heavy hearts and heavy hands laid Phil Murray down to rest eternally. I looked about me, and I saw my colleagues in the CIO and my friends with whom I walked on picket lines. I saw Cabinet members, I saw Senators, and I saw many dignitaries. I looked around and I saw old steelworkers who had retired on steelworkers' pensions, standing there on the top of the hillside with their heads bowed in sorrow, and with heavy hearts. And I thought to myself, "Those are the men that Phil Murray would want to come here and pay him homage." These horny-handed steelworkers whose lives are lighter and happier, into whose lives Phil Murray brought sunshine, and into their old age a sense of security and dignity.

Phil Murray would have been glad that they were there on the hilltop.

And then, I looked around and I saw hundreds of wonderful school children who had come there from the little parish school across the hill, who had come there to say their Rosaries and to pay their respects to that great good man, Philip Murray. And I said to myself, "These are the children that Philip Murray would have had come if he had drawn up the list," because Phil Murray's life and the CIO and the free labor movement of the world is all about people, about old people who have made their contribution to society, who have carried their portion of the common burden, and who in their last years have a right to look forward, not to fear and insecurity, but to enjoy the autumn of their lives in dignity with heads up, walking as children of God. And of children coming into the world, not handicapped by all of the economic and social disadvantages of an irresponsible and callous society, but children born into the world with the right to grow up strong in minds and body, limited only in their individual capacities, with the right to grow physically, intellectually, spiritually, and culturally into better citizens in a free world.

That is what Phil Murray gave his life for; that is what the CIO is all about. That is what you and I and the millions of people whom we have the honor, and the privilege, and the responsibility of representing stand for. All over the world there are other people who stand with us in the struggle for economic and social justice. We draw inspiration from them and their struggle, and we in turn give them strength, hope, and inspiration through our struggles.

This is what the free labor movement is all about.

Yesterday, we gathered in solemn ceremony to pay tribute, as an organization, to the memory of that great, good man, Philip Murray. There were many noble words said yesterday, said with the eloquence and the sensitivity of Adlai Stevenson. Those were wonderful, noble tributes to Phil Murray, but I say to you that the memory of Phil Murray, sleeping peacefully on that Pennsylvania hilltop tonight, is a challenge, a challenge that we cannot fulfill by noble words, no matter how noble they may come from your mind and your lips, and no matter how full your heart may be when you commend them to expression.

Ours is a more practical challenge. The CIO is the monument which Philip Murray left. He left it to you and me. He left it to the people whom we represent in the mills, in the factories, on the ships, on the high seas, in the textile plants, in the garment factories; and whether or not Philip Murray left an enduring monument is not for him to decide but rather for you and me to decide. What we do with our joint responsibilities in the challenging days that lie ahead, how individually and collectively we measure up to these great responsibilities which we share, will determine whether this CIO monument that Philip Murray gave his life to building is an enduring, living monument.

We need to draw inspiration from the life that he led and the examples that he set for men to follow. And then we need to rededicate ourselves to the cause of advancing the basic human principles, the idealism, to those basic human and social values which Phil Murray understood so well and for which he devoted his life so unselfishly.

We have had a convention, and if Phil Murray and our friends, Van Bittner and Sidney Hillman could have all been here, there would have been times when they might have prayed together, because there might have been times when they thought that the fabric of the CIO, which they wove together, was being torn asunder. But I say that they needn't worry because where individual delegates or unions stood on the candidates is of no importance. What is important is that we are all going to stand together inside the CIO and carry on.

Our enemies have been watching the proceedings of this convention from the cocktail bars of the Union League clubs and the millionaires' clubs all over America. Reading the stories in the press of the division in the CIO has filled their hearts with hope, filled their minds with designs to take us on if we are divided, drive us back and rob us of our hard-won social and economic gains. I say to the men who sit on the plush cushions in the Union League clubs of America, I say this for you who are delegates, and I say it for the millions of CIO members back home, that the fat men on the plush cushions are wrong. We are not going to go out of here divided; we are going to go out of here united to carry on this struggle for social justice until we win.

In the halls of government we shall speak with one voice. We shall stand together at the collective bargaining tables, doing the practical work on the bread-and-butter front. If and when reactionary managements are unwilling to give the workers of America the things to which they are entitled, we shall exhaust every means of resolving these issues across the bargaining table through the use of logic and reason, but, failing to get economic justice through that process, we shall march together on the picket lines of America to win what is rightfully ours.

There has been some talk that we have division in the CIO between the big unions and small unions. Nothing could be further from the truth. I think the majority of little unions maybe felt that this was their first opportunity to stand up and have their say—and, God bless them—they have that right. But what we need to do is to weld together the kind of practical, effective, working teamwork between all the unions, large and small and those in between. No one, not the biggest union down to the smallest union, can get along without being a part of the family of CIO. We want to help build the little unions. We want to help them do the practical job of organizing the unorganized in their fields so that they, too, can spread the good work that they are doing for their membership on the countless thousands of workers yet unorganized in their respective jurisdictions. We want the big unions to stand together, and I say this not only as a general statement, I say it as it relates specifically to two of the very biggest unions, the Steelworkers and the Auto Workers. We have the challenge in terms of practical collective bargaining of taking on America's giant industrial corporations.

We need each other. The Auto Workers need the Steelworkers. The Steelworkers need the Auto Workers. I say nothing, nothing, no matter where it comes from, and no one is going to divide either the leadership or the rank and file of the Steelworkers and the Auto Workers. We are going to work at this job together, because we need to. We have a slogan in the UAW—"Teamwork in the leadership and solidarity in the ranks." That is precisely what we are going to do inside the CIO.

There are many practical jobs ahead, jobs that will test the best that is in all of us. There is the job of organizing the unorganized. No union, no movement that rests upon past achievements will have the drive and the energy and the power without which we cannot succeed. We must recapture the crusading spirit we had in the early days, and we need to take on some of the areas of the unorganized and begin to do the kind of job that I know we are capable of doing if we pull together in the days ahead. But, our job is more than just organizing the unorganized. I think if we are going to be realistic, we must recognize the fact that when you sign up a worker in a union and he pays his dues, his obligation and his responsibilities do not end there. They just begin. All of our unions have too many people who are just card-carrying members. They pay their dues. They come to a meeting occasionally. Yes, they walk the picket lines when they are called upon. We have the job, not only to organize the unorganized, but we have the job of educating and unionizing the organized. We need to give our members a sense of participating in a great human crusade. We need to make them conscious of the fact that the free labor movement for the first time in the history of human civilization is trying consciously to give direction in the shaping of history. We are trying to participate in the great social changes that are taking place in the world in which we live.

When you belong to a union, when you understand where we are going and how we hope to get there, what tools free people have to use in the building of that better world that we dream about, then you have the satisfaction of knowing that as a free human being you have something to say about the kind of to-morrow that your children will grow up in. Until we do a better job of educating and unionizing the people whom we have or-ganized, we will not have mobilized the real potential power and the spiritual strength of our great, free labor movement.

We face some practical problems on the home front in terms of antilabor legislation, and I would like to say—not for the benefit of the people in this audience but to the people who will assume political responsibility in Washington come January— let them ponder a few simple understandable facts. What we do in America with the thing that we call freedom will determine the fate of freedom all over the world. We must get more people to understand that all of the truly basic human values, to which the free world dedicates its resources and its will to defend and extend, are invisible and inseparable. The questions of peace and freedom are indivisible.

The First World War taught us that you could not have peace in one part of the world with the rest of the world at war. At great cost we learned that peace is indivisible.

The Second World War taught us that freedom is indivisible, and when Hitler challenged the freedom of any country in the world he also was putting our freedom in jeopardy. But there is still one lesson we need to learn, and if we learn that lesson, the prospects of building peace on a lasting basis are greatly im-proved; and if we fail in learning that lesson then the future may be tragic. That lesson simply is that just as peace and free-dom are indivisible values so is the fact that in the world we live in, the questions of economic security and material well-being are likewise indivisible. You cannot make peace and free-dom secure in the world as long as hundreds of millions of people are denied the necessities of life, so long as millions and millions of people are committed to belong to the have-not nations, and they and their children are denied the right to achieve economic and social justice. Communism will continue to forge that poverty and that hunger and that human desperation into the weapons of political and military aggression. And what is true in the world in a larger sense is equally true in America.

In a police state, under Hitler, Stalin, or Franco, under any other kind of dictatorship, it is possible to achieve industrial peace in the absence of justice, but in a free society the only basis on which you can achieve peace is if that industrial peace is based upon a foundation of economic and social justice. We say to the men who will assume political power in Washington, "If you want to help build industrial peace and economic stability we will help you. We will work hard at that task at the bargaining tables of America, but remember, if you want to facilitate the achievement of economic and industrial stability, then pass legislation which will make it easier for people in America to realize their hopes and aspirations. If you try to build roadblocks like Taft-Hartley, or try to put other obstacles in the way of the right of American labor to move ahead to conquer broader social horizons, then you are not facilitating the achievement of industrial peace but you are sowing the seeds out of which will grow greater industrial conflict."

Representatives of industry and the men who will assume political responsibility in January have in their hands the power to make that decision. They have the initiative, and with that initiative goes the responsibility for what must follow.

We pray that reason will prevail, that they will understand something about the rights and the aspirations of free labor, because the better they understand those basic values the more rationally and intelligently will they discharge their legislative and administrative responsibilities.

Now, there has been some talk about restricting industry-wide bargaining. Let me say that here again reason must prevail, because there are no legislative magic formulas. Yes, some will point to the steel industry, and they will say that industry-wide bargaining is the problem. But they are wrong. The problem is that the industry people bring the wrong attitude to the bargain-ing table.

The Amalgamated Clothing Workers, over a long period of years, have developed a constructive and practical approach to their collective bargaining problems. They have industry-wide bargaining; and yet, in their industry, using that approach to its collective bargaining problems, they have established one of the most stable and constructive records in the history of labor-management relations.

What is the essential difference between the industry-wide ap-proach which the Clothing Workers have made and the way that idea is applied in other basic industries? The difference is not in form. The difference is in attitude. Free management must realize that in a free society there is no substitute for the voluntary dis-charge of social responsibility. All the laws that can be written cannot change this basic truth. You cannot go to the Supreme Court and change the basic fact of life—that free men, denied justice, will struggle to win that justice.

During the recent steel strike, the Supreme Court handed down a decision. I said to the boys in the Auto Workers union whom I talked to the day the decision came down, that the Court had made a decision but it had not solved the problem. All the learned men with all their wisdom, with all of the legal niceties they can put together on the finest of parchments cannot produce one ton of steel.

Steel will be produced, automobiles will be produced, the looms will weave textiles, and we will make all of the other things that we need, but free American labor will insist that while doing these things labor is entitled to a full measure of social justice.

There is no other way. This is not a matter of oratory, it is not a matter of eloquence; it is a matter of hard, cold, practical facts drawn from life. We hope that industry and the men who will assume political and social responsibilities will recognize these facts and will discharge their responsibilities accordingly.

We have the question of labor unity. I accept and I share the

spirit of the resolution adopted by this convention and the remarks made in support of that resolution. All of us, deep in our
hearts, recognize the fact that standing together in a united labor
movement we could be stronger than if we are divided, but this
must be qualified, for unity in itself will perform no miracles.

We must stand together in a united labor movement without
compromising the basic principles upon which the CIO is built.
We can never get ourselves in a position where we sacrifice
principle for expediency. No union, whether large or small, must
be sacrificed in working out these problems.

On taking this responsibility you have given me, I want to
make it abundantly clear that as far as I am concerned, as an
individual and as an official of this organization, I want to assure
you fully and completely that at no time will a question of vested
right in an office be the smallest obstacle in the way of achieving
a united labor movement.

I say that the real measurement by which we must judge
what is an honorable basis for working out labor unity is not
what happens to the status of those in positions of leadership.
There is only one measurement and that is the measurement
of what is good for the rank and file back home. We do not
count. You and I are not important, excepting as we are the
symbols, and as we are the collective instrumentality through
which the rank and file carries on its work. What is good for the
rank and file must be the only measurement of our judgment.

I want to assure you that within the CIO we are going to
go about the task ahead of us in a sensible, practical, and constructive way. This convention adopted several constitutional
changes. I am 100 per cent for all those changes. They make
sense. As long as we had our good friend Phil with us, his great
capabilities, his understanding, and his unlimited patience were
substitutes for many things that we now need. That is why we
need a team. I can say to you that had you asked me to run
the CIO alone I would have declined, because I am not capable
of that responsibility. But if you say to me, "Are you willing to
be a part of a team with Allan Haywood, Jim Carey, Jake
Potofsky, Emil Rieve, Joe Beirne, Buckmaster, Joe Curran, Jack

Knight, and all of these other fellows?" my answer is in the affirmative. I want to be a part of that kind of team leading the CIO.

We have worked out provisions for the officers to act as an Executive Committee. That is proper. That makes sense. We have worked out provisions for an Executive Vice President having a constitutional status. Such status is necessary in order to do his job properly. We have worked out provisions to call Executive Board meetings every three months. We intend to make these Executive Board meetings into working sessions, where you come with your problems and help work out programs and policies to meet such problems.

We have a big job to do in terms of political action. This is no time to hang crepe in terms of the political outlook. We lost the election. It was disappointing but it was not disastrous. Look at the centers in which we had large CIO membership and you will find that in those centers our people came through with flying colors. I say that the great challenge ahead is to lift the level of political morality on the part of the politicians in Washington, but you cannot raise the level of political morality in Washington until you first raise the level of political conscience on the part of the people back home. That is the job we must take on.

We need to build. We need to organize. We need to educate on the political front, because the kind of labor movement that we are building cannot find the answers to the many complex social and economic problems solely at the bargaining table. Therefore let us determine not to do less but to do more on the political front.

I take no credit in a personal sense for the fact that I am a trade unionist. I was raised in a trade union family. My father was an international representative of the Brewery Workers Union. He was President of the Central Trades and Labor Assembly in our home town when he was twenty-three years old. Along with my brothers at my father's knee, we learned the philosophy of trade unionism, we got the struggles, the hopes, and aspirations of working people every day. I was raised in the kind of trade union atmosphere that said to me when I was a boy that a trade union movement based upon the principles of pure and simple trade unionism could not adequately deal with the complex problems of the working people in the world in which we live. Our labor movement is a labor movement which integrates our efforts with the efforts of the whole people to move ahead in finding a practical and democratic solution to the complex problems that beset us. In a free and interdependent society, labor can make progress only to the extent that it helps to provide leadership in solving the problems of all the people. We have a job as free labor, of doing much more than just bargaining for our membership. We have to assume ever-increasing social responsibilities. We have a practical job of completing the task of organizing the unorganized, of unionizing the organized through educational work, and we must apply ourselves to the difficult, long-range program of finding a way ultimately, in a free society, to raise collective bargaining above the level of a continuing struggle between competing economic pressure groups. A free society cannot solve its basic economic problems unless free labor and free management can find the common denominators through good faith and understanding by which both can meet their joint moral and social responsibilities to the whole community. Collective bargaining must be based upon acceptance of and extension of the democratic processses in our industrial and economic life. Basic collective bargaining decisions must be based upon economic facts and not dictated by the use of economic power.

These are the basic factors that should influence our collective bargaining attitudes and in a large measure will control the destiny of free men in the challenging years that lie ahead. We must work for the complete destruction of the economic and moral double standards that certain industries bring to the bargaining table.

They gave their high-paid officials fat pensions when they didn't need them, while they denied pensions to working people who did need them. We have problems like the guaranteed annual wage. They pay the people who get more than they need by the year, and they pay the people who get too little by the hour. These are not just matters of economic justice to the worker, but they are matters of economic survival for a free society. That is why we are compelled to work and if need be fight for objectives such as the guaranteed annual wage, no matter how great the opposition. The future of peace and the future of freedom in the world in which we live cannot be made secure if we go on trying to divide up economic scarcity in the world. Freedom and peace are possible only if their future is made secure by the economics of abundance. We must fight the forces of monopoly and scarcity in their opposition to the expansion of our productive capacity and the full development of our material resources. We must create the maximum economic abundance and then translate that abundance into tangible human values. The world is going to judge America not by how many tons of steel we produce or what our material wealth is. America will be judged by the real standards by which a civilization should be judged. The real measurement of the greatness of a civilization is its ability to demonstrate the sense of social and moral responsibility needed to translate material values into human values, technological progress into human progress, human happiness, and human dignity. That is the job that we in the CIO are working on.

We are living in a period of great challenge. Never in the history of the world has there been such an aggregate of power mobilized against the cause of freedom. We in America, as citizens in the strongest of the free nations of the world, share a tremendous responsibility in this great contest.

Several months ago, I stood before the Republican Foreign Policy Committee in Chicago, and Senator Nixon, who was a member of that committee, asked the question, "Is there anything in the foreign policy of the Truman Administration that the CIO disagrees with?" He thought he had us over a barrel. And I answered the question thus—I said, "Senator Nixon, there are things in the foreign policy of the United States Government that we in the CIO disagree with, but in essence on its basic positions, we agree. We think that in some places the emphasis is wrong. We believe we need to do more on a positive basis in terms of Point Four, of helping people to help themselves. The essential difference between the CIO and the Republicans is that we criticize the Truman Administration foreign policy for its deficiencies and the Republican Party criticizes it for its virtues. That is a fundamental distinction."

There is a revolution going on in the world. The Communists didn't start the revolution. It is a revolution of hungry men to get the wrinkles out of their empty bellies. It is a revolution of people who have been exploited by imperialism and who are trying to throw off the shackles of imperialism and colonialism, and who want to march forward in freedom and independence. It is a struggle of the have-nots to get something for themselves. The Communists didn't start it. They are riding its back. What we have to do is to answer the Communist propaganda not with slogans; we must expose the hypocrisy of Communist propaganda which offers these hungry and desperate people the promise of economic security with a price tag.

We need to answer the reactionaries in Wall Street who play the other side of that Communist record. The Communists would have people trade freedom for bread and the reactionaries would have you believe that if you want to be free you have to be economically insecure. And we say to the Communists and the reactionaries, "You are both wrong. In the world that we are trying to help build, people can have both bread and freedom."

Man is an economic being and needs food, clothing, housing, medical care, and all of the other material needs, and we struggle to make that possible. But man is more than just an economic being. He is a social and spiritual being, and just as food is needed for the economic man so the spiritual man needs food, and freedom is the food of the soul. The great challenge in the world is to find a way so that men can so arrange their relationship of one to the other within a free society, and one nation to another in a free world, so that we can live at peace and harness the power of our advancing technology, develop our resources, and translate this abundance into a good life for everyone.

This struggle in the world between freedom and tyranny, between democracy and Communism, is a struggle for men's minds and their hearts and their loyalties. It cannot be won on the battlefields. It can only be won on the economic and social field in the struggle for human justice.

While we in the CIO support the building of military strength in our nation and with our allies in the free world, let us not forget that to win the hearts and minds of men we must move boldly ahead on the economic and social fronts in terms of the living standards of people, of their hopes and aspirations.

The shortest road for Communist propaganda to travel is through the wrinkles of an empty belly. One third of the people of the world are living on less than one dollar per week, and that is why they are the easy victims of Communist propaganda. Our job is not only to hold Communism, to stop aggression on the battle fronts, but to move ahead on the economic and social fronts.

We have a very practical decision. If we have the courage to take the price tag off our peacetime efforts, if we understand the forces at work in the changing world in which we live, if we grasp fully the fact that freedom faces a continuing crisis, and that Korea is merely a localized expression of a total world problem, then we shall understand and act in the knowledge that freedom's fight must be won on the economic and social fronts in the struggle for human betterment. I believe that history will prove that if we have the courage to carry out bold programs of economic aid to help people to help themselves, that the more young Americans we send abroad with medical kits and slide rules and textbooks as technical missionaries to work on the social and economic fronts, the fewer American boys we will need to send with guns and tanks and planes to fight on the battle fronts.

I want to conclude with one simple thought. What is the great challenge free men must face? It is not Communism; it is within ourselves. That is where the challenge lies. It is within free men, within a free society. I say we need, we must find a way, to tap the tremendous spiritual reservoir that resides within a free people and translate that power into constructive approaches to the world's problems. If we do that we can win the struggle for peace and freedom. The tragedy of the world has been that generation after generation, peoples all over the world have gone to war; they have sacrificed their finest young men on the battlefields of the world. Isn't there something wrong with free men when they can only find a sense of urgency in the negative terms of war?

You can get people marching and sacrificing and fighting for the negative ends of the war, and yet we haven't found the way to mobilize that spiritual power for the positive ends of peace. That is the great challenge. And I say to you in the CIO, in all humility, with a real sense of my own personal limitations, I pledge to you all that I have. I will do everything within my capacity to discharge this high office in a spirit of humbleness, in a spirit of teamwork with my associates, and I am confident that you and I, in discharging our joint responsibility in the years ahead, can make a contribution not only to our own membership, not only to our own country, but to free men everywhere. We can stand with them and work with them. We can march with them in building that brave new world we dream of, that world in which men can live in peace as neighbors, that world where people everywhere can enjoy a fuller measure of social and economic justice, a world that you and I and men of good will everywhere can shape in the image of freedom and in the image of justice and in the image of brotherhood.

The Guaranteed Annual Wage

Section of the opening address of the fifteenth constitutional convention of the United Automobile, Aircraft and Agricultural Implement Workers of America

Cleveland, Ohio
March 27, 1955

We will not go to the bargaining table just as a routine matter of another bargaining session. We are going there knowing that this is a crusade—a crusade to gear economic abundance to human needs. We plan to give management a little bit of the vision that we have. We would like to show them that great, new world that can be built if free labor and free management and free government and free people can cooperate together in harmony in harnessing the powers of America and gearing that power to the basic needs of people. We hope that they will grasp that vision which is essential to the leadership in this great world crisis. There is no limit to the great progress that we can make, because human progress is as unlimited as the creative genius of the free human spirit.

We are on the threshold of revolutionary technological development with the use of atomic power, with automation, and all the other things that can solve all the basic problems, provided we have the good sense to use this power.

Our union—I guess I can say this not boastfully but in all good conscience—no organization in America has worked more consistently, more courageously, more constructively in the practical fight for full employment and full production in peacetime than our union.

The guaranteed annual wage is an important move in achieving full production and full employment in peacetime.

I mentioned that our old-timers need greater security. That is a part of that job—better medical care, higher purchasing power—all of these things are geared to the basic question. How can we as a free people achieve full employment and full production in peacetime making the good things of life?

We don't say, we never have said—all the reactionary propagandists, notwithstanding—we have never claimed that a worker in the United States or a worker in Canada, is automatically entitled to economic security. We have no sympathy for a fellow who can get a job and doesn't want to work.

What we say is that while the worker is not entitled to automatic economic security, he is entitled to an opportunity for a good job at decent wages to earn that economic security.

When we fight for the guaranteed wage, we are not asking to be paid for not working. We just don't want our people to be penalized when they don't have a job through no fault of their own.

We have said at conferences in the past, and we have tried to formulate our economic demands in the light of three essential conditions.

First, our demands must be economically sound. They can't be based upon wishful thinking. They have to be based upon solid and sound economic facts.

Second, they have to be morally right. We have to fight for righteousness and justice.

Third, they can't be selfish demands that make progress at the expense of our neighbor. They have to be socially responsible. They have to reflect the basic needs of all people.

Our demands in 1955 meet those conditions. They meet those conditions on the basis of a careful and objective study. No one can deny the fact that economically we are in trouble in America. Nobody can deny the fact that economically Canada is in trouble because there is unemployment in these countries. In the United States we still have the equivalent of 5,000,000 unemployed. In Canada, their unemployment is even higher in proportion to the working force.

The other day even the Chamber of Commerce had to admit

that, and I read the headline in the *Washington Post*. It says, "Increasing National Production but Also Unemployment Is Forecast by the U.S. Chamber of Commerce."

Now, why the unemployment? We all know. We have said it many times. Everyone ought to understand it. We are in trouble in the United States, Canada is in trouble, because of the growing and serious imbalance between our ability to create wealth with our tremendous productive power and the inability of millions of families to consume that abundance because they lack adequate purchasing power.

Last year if we had utilized our economic resources and our manpower resources, the United States could have produced $40 billion more wealth.

Forty billion dollars means that every American family from Mr. Curtice of General Motors to the lowest paid sharecropper, every family could have had $850 more income.

In 1955 if you take the most optimistic projections of the little men of big business of the Republican Administration, we will underproduce $50 billion in 1955 compared to what we could do if we used our economy fully.

What does that mean? It means that every American family could have a thousand dollars more income.

When you lay that economic loss next to the cost of the guaranteed wage and higher pensions and medical care—the costs of these things are insignificant compared to the cost of the economic losses.

I don't know why the management groups in these small companies go along with the Republican program. I can understand why General Motors thinks the Republican Administration is doing a good job. When you make $1,645,000,000 you can't complain about that. You are doing O.K. But I will be doggoned if I can figure out why these little companies who are fighting for their survival are afraid to stand up and fight for the kind of tax policies, the kind of broad economic programs, that will give them a chance to survive. What did Studebaker get out of the last tax bill? General Motors got $219,000,000 in tax reduction. If Studebaker, Nash, and the small companies had made an effort to try to get sensible and sane economic policies, tax programs, if they had supported our efforts to raise personal exemptions from $600 to $800, we would have $4,500,000,000 of high-velocity purchasing power and that money in the hands of millions of American families would have created the market and the demand and Studebaker and Nash and Hudson and these other companies would have had a better chance of selling their products.

Frankly, I get discouraged sometimes when the management of some of these companies says, "Come to the bargaining table and help us meet our problem."

We will help them to meet their problem, but it is time they get realistic about the facts of life and forget their fight on the other front for the answers to some of these problems in America.

Now, when we talk about the guaranteed annual wage, we don't claim it is a cure-all. We don't say it is a panacea. We do say that it is one of the basic economic tools that free people need to use to bring about this dynamic balance between greater productive power and greater purchasing power. Nothing breeds unemployment like unemployment.

What happens in Michigan when the factory workers of Michigan alone in one year because of unemployment lose $640,000,000? What does that do? It means that workers can't buy $640,000,000 worth of goods and services. The workers who otherwise would supply and produce those goods and services don't have jobs, and then they lose their purchasing power, and this thing begins to spread and radiate further and further in our economy until we get into trouble. But if we had a guaranteed annual wage, the workers in Michigan who have been laid off would not have lost $640,000,000 in wages. Their income and their purchasing power would have been sustained, and therefore the negative impact of that on the economy would not have occurred. That is why we say that the guaranteed annual wage is not only a matter of economic justice to the worker, it is a matter of economic necessity to our whole economy in the effort to achieve full production and full employment making the good things of life for people in peacetime. Why can't we have full employment in peacetime? We ask a simple question and we demand an answer to this question. If we can have full employment in war why can't we have full employment in peace making the good things of life? We can. We have the know-how; we have the resources and we have the manpower. All we need to demonstrate is that we've got the courage and the will. That is precisely the element that we intend to supply in increasing measure at the bargaining table in 1955.

They say to us, "Is the guaranteed annual wage morally right?" I say that no demand in the history of collective bargaining has ever been more morally right than the guaranteed annual wage. Just look at industry. They meet the cost of every element of production by the year. They pay their taxes by the year. They pay the interest on their loans by the year. They pay their executives by the year. If they rent a building, they pay the rent by the year. If they have six months' production, they don't call the landlord and say, "Well, we just shut the plant down, we won't pay the rent for the rest of the year." They pay the rent twelve months every year. The only element of production that gets paid by the hour or by the piece and not by the year is the human equation—the most important equation in production.

If it is morally right to meet the cost of modern industry, pay your taxes by the year and your interest on these investments by the year, your executive salaries by the year, then we say it is morally right to pay the workers by the year, and in 1955 we intend to make it possible in our industry.

Where did this idea of paying workers by the piece or by the hour come from? Is this a sacred cow that we can't change? It came out of the early Industrial Revolution, and based upon the needs of our complex mass production economy, it is no longer adequate to meet our basic needs. That is why we need to change it.

We are going to the bargaining table and we are going there hoping and praying that our demands will be analyzed and the answers will be forthcoming based upon reason, based upon justice, based upon fairness, and based upon simple equity in terms of the economic factors involved in our collective bargaining program. We hope the answers will flow from the economic facts, and we hope it will not be necessary to use economic power. But we know that all the wishful thinking in the world will not change the sad record of collective bargaining. We know that time and again when labor went to the bargaining table with just demands, with fairness and equity and morality on their side, we were faced by calloused indifference on the part of management. Management had a double set of economic and moral standards. They had that on the pension fight and we had to use our power. We hope that that will not be the case. But this convention has to prepare for that possibility, just as the free world must be strong in a military way to meet the threat of communist aggression wherever it may raise its ugly head, when the free world builds military power. We don't do that because we are threatening war. We do that because the free world knows that it must negotiate from strength, and when we take steps to raise a defense fund of $25,000,000 we aren't preparing for a strike, we are just preparing to defend ourselves if we are forced into a strike. We are preparing to negotiate from strength just as the free world prepares to negotiate from strength.

We don't begrudge one penny that these corporation executives are paid. We know that when corporation management makes a contribution to the economic well-being of the country and to the economic progress of our country they are entitled to a just reward for their economic contribution. But we say that when workers make their contribution they, too, are entitled to just compensation for their contribution.

We are going to hear a lot about incentives, how the free enterprise system goes forward because management has these great incentives to make millions of dollars. We believe in free enterprise. We believe in individual incentives, but what we can't understand is the fact that management has a one-way street on this idea of economic individual incentives, and we said to them many times, and we are going to ask them this question again, we don't understand what kind of mental and moral gymnastics they are going to go through to say that if you are a corporation executive and you are making $400,000 a year

and you have the drive and the incentive to get $500,000 that
that is economically sound and morally right, but if you happen to be a wage earner and you are only getting $4,000
a year and you want $5,000 a year that is economically and mor-
ally wrong.

I say it is more economically sound, it is more morally right
for a worker making $4,000 to get $5,000 than for a corporation
executive getting $400,000 to get $500,000.

That is the thing we are trying to do.

I ask anyone—I say that we can look ourselves in the face
as brothers and sisters, that we can look management in the face,
and that we can face any person in our two great countries on
the moral issues of our guaranteed annual wage demand.

Take Mr. Curtice, the President of the General Motors Corporation. He probably is a very efficient executive. No one be-
grudges him a penny he gets. But in 1954 the General Motors
Corporation paid him very well. We don't object to that. What
we object to is Mr. Curtice denying our right, the GM workers'
right, to be paid well.

Mr. Curtice got $686,000 in salary and in bonuses.

We analyzed his salary on an hourly basis so we could under-
stand it. Based upon fifty-two weeks a year, 40 hours a week,
Mr. Curtice got $329 an hour. It would have taken the average
GM worker 150 years to earn what Mr. Curtice got in one year.

And when you look at the Chairman of the Board of Directors
of the General Motors Corporation, Mr. Sloan—now he had a
very modest salary. He is on sort of a semiretired basis. He got
a measly $48,600 in salary. But don't worry about how he met
his family needs, because he got $4,500,000 on General Motors'
stock which he owns. So that his hourly rate, if you take his stock
income and his salary together based upon 40 hours a week
fifty-two weeks in a year, Mr. Sloan had an hourly income of
$2,178 per hour.

Now I maintain no one will argue that each General Motors
worker ought to get as much as Mr. Curtice. No one will argue
that a GM worker, even in the skilled trades classification, ought
to get as much as Mr. Sloan.

But I say, based upon the standards of human decency and human morality, no one can say that any man is worth 150 times another man working for the same company. No one is that much better than the other fellow. And no one needs that much more.

When they gave 60 General Motors executives last year in salary and bonuses $12,600,000 divided up among 60 people, do you think that when those executives got that money, they bought one more quart of milk? Do you think that they bought one more pair of shoes for their kids? Do you think they called the doctor one more time? Of course not.

But you give the GM workers the guaranteed annual wage, you give the retired GM workers higher pensions, you give all workers higher purchasing power and they buy more milk and shoes and clothing and call the doctor when they need him.

That is why we say that the guaranteed annual wage and that your economic program is more than a matter of justice to the worker. It is a matter of necessity for the whole economy.

We say nobody can argue these facts. Nobody can argue the fact that when a corporation executive gets 150 times more in one year, that at least the worker is entitled to the basic necessities of life that will give him and his family that measure of security to which they are entitled.

Now, we can do all these things provided we gear the future of America and the future of Canada to the economics of abundance. We aren't trying to make a smaller and smaller economic pie. We're trying to find a way to make the biggest economic pie that science and technology and our resources make possible. And if we create that pie, then everybody can have more.

Basically what we are trying to do is to create the economic incentive so that management will be forced to make a plan for full production and full employment, so they will be forced by the very economic necessities to discharge their economic and social responsibilities in planning for full employment and full production in peacetime.

The Impact of Automation

Statement to the Joint Congressional Committee on the Economic Report

Washington, D. C.
October 17, 1955

I should like first of all to express my thanks to this Committee for the opportunity to testify on automation and to congratulate its members for calling these hearings.

One of the essentials of a strong and effective democracy is that we have leaders who attempt to anticipate situations which may arise and prepare in advance to deal with them. Too often in the past, nations have been surprised unnecessarily, by economic and social dislocations. In the eighteenth and nineteenth centuries, for example, the First Industrial Revolution brought untold hardships to millions of families in Great Britain, partly because Britain at that time lacked both the economic knowledge to understand and control the forces at work and the democratic institutions of government through which the people could have called attention to their needs. In our own country, had we understood the economic forces that were eating away at the base of our apparent prosperity in the 1920's, we surely would have been able to build safeguards into our economy that could have protected us from the collapse that followed.

In the spread of automation and the prospective large-scale industrial use of atomic energy—and the possible practical utilization of solar energy, as well—we are faced with mighty forces whose impact on our economy can be vastly beneficial or vastly harmful, depending on whether we succeed or fail in achieving economic and social progress that will keep pace with changing technology.

The willingness of this Committee to study these technological developments, and to look squarely at the potential problems they may create, gives hope that this time we will not be caught unaware. It gives us hope, too, that we may be able to foresee the threat of dislocations and take action in advance to enable us to enjoy the benefits of a new abundance, without first having to pay a heavy price in unemployment and human suffering.

We have been told so often that automation is going to bring on the "Second Industrial Revolution" that there is, perhaps, a danger we may dismiss the warning as a catch phrase, and lose sight of the fact that, not only the technique, but the philosophy of automation is revolutionary, in the truest sense of the word. Automation does not only produce changes in the methods of manufacturing, distribution, many clerical operations, and in the structure of business organization, but the impact of those changes on our economy and our whole society bids fair to prove quite as revolutionary as were those of the First Industrial Revolution.

Through the application of mechanical power to machinery, and the development of new machinery to use this power, the First Industrial Revolution made possible a vast increase in the volume of goods produced for each man-hour of work. Succeeding technological improvements—such as the development of interchangeable parts and the creation of the assembly line, which were essential to the growth of mass production industries —have led to continuous increases in labor productivity. But however much these machines were improved, they still required workers to operate and control them. In some operations, the worker's function was little more than to feed the material in, set the machine in operation, and remove the finished product. In others, proper control of the machine required the exercise of the highest conceivable skills. But whether the required skill was little or great, the presence of a human being, using human judgment, was essential to the operation of the machine.

The revolutionary change produced by automation is its tendency to displace the worker entirely from the direct operation of the machine, through the use of automatic control devices. No one, as far as I know, has yet produced a fully satisfactory definition of automation, but I think John Diebold came close to expressing its essential quality when he described automation as "the integration of machines with each other into fully automatic, and, in some cases, self-regulating systems."

In other words, automation is a technique by which whole batteries of machines, in some cases almost whole factories and offices, can be operated according to predetermined automatic controls. The raw material is automatically fed in, the machine automatically processes it, the product is automatically taken away, often to be fed automatically into still another machine that carries it automatically through a further process. In some cases the machine is self-regulating—that is, it is set to turn out a product within certain tolerances as to size or other factors, and if those tolerances are exceeded, the machine itself detects the variation and automatically adjusts itself to correct it.

The revolutionary implications of this new technology can best be understood by looking at a few examples of what is actually being done through automation today, in scattered parts of the economy.

The application of automation ranges all the way from individual automatic machines to virtually automatic factories.

An example of the first is an automatic lathe, produced by the Sundstrand Machine Tool Company, which gauges each part as it is produced and automatically resets the cutting tools to compensate for tool wear. In addition, when the cutting tools have been worn down to a certain predetermined limit, the machine automatically replaces them with sharp tools. The parts are automatically loaded onto the machine and are automatically unloaded as they are finished. These lathes can be operated for five to eight hours without attention, except for an occasional check to make sure that parts are being delivered to the loading mechanism.

A completely automatic plant is now producing mixed and ready-to-use concrete for the Cleveland Builders Supply Company. Operated from an electronic control panel, the plant can produce and load into ready-mix trucks any one of some fifteen hundred different mixing formulas that may be demanded. This plant uses no manual labor at any point in the process.

By a combination of teletype and radio, the control operator is informed as to the particular formula to be loaded into each truck as it arrives. He gets out a punched card, coded for that formula, and the automatic mechanisms take over. Specified amounts of the required materials are delivered by conveyors, in precisely the right quantities, to a mixing bin where they are automatically mixed and then loaded into the waiting truck. The control mechanisms even measure and compensate for any deficiency or excess of water in the aggregate (sand, coarse rock, slag, etc.) which goes into the mixer, and if the order calls for a dry mix, the materials are automatically routed through a dry spout.

The automatic plant has a capacity of 200 cubic yards of concrete per hour, as against 100 cubic yards per hour in the company's conventional plants.

An automatic two-way horizontal broaching machine for machining automobile cylinder heads has cut direct labor costs between 1949 and 1954 by more than all the technological improvements made in this process during the previous thirty-five years—and with an actual decline in the investment required.

In 1914 the Cincinnati Milling Machine Company would have used 162 machines, representing an investment of $243,000, to machine 108 cylinder heads per hour at a direct labor cost of 40 cents per piece. By 1949 it took 6 machines, representing an investment of $240,000, to turn out the same volume of production at a direct labor cost of 20 cents per piece. (The saving in man-hour requirements is much greater than indicated by these figures, when the increase in wage rates between 1914 and 1949 is taken into account.)

By 1954, however, those 6 machines had been replaced by a single automatic machine, representing an investment of only $230,000, for the same volume of production, and direct labor costs had been cut from 20 cents a piece in 1949 to 4 cents a piece in 1954—a reduction of 80 per cent in five years.

One of the important features of automation is that it can be applied not only to long runs of identical operations, but to fairly short-run jobs where instructions given to the machine have to be changed at the end of each job. This is made possible through the use of printed tape, punch cards, etc., on which the instructions are coded, and the machine is given a new set of instructions simply by changing the tape or card.

Minneapolis-Honeywell Regulator Company, for example, reports the development of a precision boring machine, used in aircraft equipment production, which can bore holes with an accuracy of one thousandth of an inch. Electronic signals from a tape move the blank metal back or forward, rotate it into position, and then turn on the boring mechanism to cut the hole exactly where it is desired. The machine is specially suited for medium-size production in lots of several hundred parts.

The use of automation is not restricted to manufacturing plants. Increasingly, so-called "electronic brains" are taking over the functions of office clerks, accountants, and other white-collar workers.

Stanford Research Institute has produced for the Bank of America an electronic computer which will do the jobs of many bank employees. When a check comes to the bank, an operator merely punches into the machine the amount on the face of the check. The check itself carries a code, printed in magnetic ink, which identifies the account number. The machine scans this code to identify the account. It then refers to its "memory bank," which contains information on thirty-two thousand separate accounts, makes sure there is enough in the account to meet the check (if there is not, a warning "overdraft" light is blinked at the operator's desk) and deducts the amount of the withdrawal from the account. The machine also checks up to make sure that there is no stop-payment order against the account. The whole operation takes approximately one second.

The transaction is recorded, first in a "temporary memory" bank, and is transferred later to a "permanent memory" bank. At the end of the month, the computer automatically calculates the service charge and then, connected to a high-speed printer which can print eight hundred characters a second, it prints the customer's complete monthly statement in less than five seconds. It is claimed that nine operators and one such machine can replace up to fifty bookkeepers.

Similar computers are being used to make up payrolls, to prepare insurance premium notices and record payments, to prepare telephone bills, to take inventory, to control the operation of electric power-generating plants, and for many similar purposes. One central computer to be installed by the Ohio Edison Company, for example, will simultaneously control the operations of thirty-five generators in nine plants scattered over an area of 9,000 square miles.

Even automation itself is being automated. One of the bottlenecks, in the use of computers, to which data is fed by punched cards, has been the time required to have the information punched on the cards by trained operators. Now the Burroughs Corporation has produced for the First National City Bank of New York an electronic device which "reads" the serial numbers on travelers' checks and reproduces them on punched cards at a rate of seventy-two hundred checks per hour, doing the work of ten highly skilled operators.

The great variety of applications shown in these few examples illustrates one of the most significant features of the new technology—its wide applicability. That is the real quality that makes automation a genuinely revolutionary force in our economy, rather than just another technological improvement.

It is technically possible to apply the feedback principle of automation, and the servomechanisms which implement it, to virtually every situation where human control of industrial processes is now used. The growing flood of new uses of automation indicates how quickly the economics of its application are being worked out.

One of the factors which has been responsible for the steadily increasing rate of productivity since World War II has been the enormous increase in research expenditures both by industry and by government. Alfred North Whitehead, the British philosopher, once said, "The greatest invention of the nineteenth century was the invention of the art of inventing." We might add that one of the great developments of the twentieth century has been to change inventing from an art to a standard business procedure. The research department is now a fixture in every important corporation, while the needs of government, especially in national defense, have added to the numbers of research workers, many of whose discoveries are readily applied to industry.

As a result, the flow of what may be considered "routine" technological innovations—new production methods, new materials and machines applicable only to specific processes or industries, and improvements in work-flow—has been greatly accelerated. Harlow Curtice, president of General Motors, noted recently that "new products, new processes are coming off the drawing boards of the engineers and out of the laboratories of the scientists at an ever faster pace."

This great expansion of industrial research and the flood of "routine" technological innovations it produces have been sufficient, alone, in recent years to boost the rate of rising productivity to the extent that past notions of what were "normal" productivity increases are already obsolete. Technological improvements of this sort, and on an increasing scale, can be expected to continue. By themselves, they would pose serious problems of adjusting our economy so as to provide sufficient purchasing power to absorb the steadily accelerating flow of goods which can be produced with every man-hour of labor.

Beyond these "routine" technological improvements, however, we are now confronted with the potentially explosive impact of automation, and we can be sure that this new technology, too, will grow by leaps and bounds.

In discussing the rapid advances of technology, David Sarnoff, Chairman of the Radio Corporation of America, stated in a pamphlet entitled "Fabulous Future":

The quantity of new powers and products and processes at man's disposal is important; but even more important is the *increasing speed* at which these things have come. It is not a case of continued increase but of continued *acceleration* of increase. We need only project the trend into the future to realize that we are merely on the threshold of the technological age.

Summing up the potential impact of the new technologies, Mr. Sarnoff says:

The very fact that electronics and atomics are unfolding simultaneously is a portent of amazing changes ahead. Never before have two such mighty forces been unleashed at the same time. Together they are certain to dwarf the industrial revolutions brought about by steam and electricity.

What is the attitude of the trade union movement, and specifically of the CIO, to this new technology of automation?

First of all, we fully realize that the potential benefits of automation are great, if properly handled. If only a fraction of what technologists promise for the future is true, within a very few years automation can and should make possible a four-day workweek, longer vacation periods, opportunities for earlier retirement, as well as a vast increase in our material standards of living.

At the same time, automation can bring freedom from the monotonous drudgery of many jobs in which the worker today is no more than a servant of the machine. It can free workers from routine, repetitive tasks which the new machines can be taught to do, and can give to the workers who toil at those tasks the opportunity of developing higher skills.

But in looking ahead to the many benefits which automation can produce, we must not overlook or minimize the many problems which will inevitably arise in making the adjustment to the new technology—problems for individual workers and individual companies, problems for entire communities and regions, problems for the economy as a whole.

What should be done to help the worker who will be displaced from his job, or the worker who will find that his highly specialized skill has been taken over by a machine? What about the businessman who lacks sufficient capital to automate his plant, yet has to face the competition of firms whose resources enable them to build whole new automatic factories? Will automation mean the creation of whole new communities in some areas, while others are turned into ghost towns? How can we increase the market for goods and services sufficiently, and quickly enough, to match greatly accelerated increases in productivity?

Finding the answers to these questions, and many others like them, will not be an easy process, and certainly not an automatic one. Even if the greatest care is taken to foresee and meet these problems, adjustments for many people will prove difficult and even painful. If there is no care and no foresight, if we subscribe to the laissez-faire belief that "these things will work themselves out," untold harm can be done to millions of innocent people and to the whole structure of our economy and our free society.

The CIO insists that we must recognize these problems and face up to them. But our recognition that there will be problems, and serious problems to be solved, does not mean that we are opposed to automation. We are not. We fully recognize the desirability, as well as the inevitability of technological progress. We welcome the potential benefits which automation can and should bring. But we oppose those who would introduce automation blindly and irresponsibly, with no concern for any result except the achievement of the largest possible quick profit for themselves.

When the First Industrial Revolution took place, no effort was made to curb or control greedy, ruthless employers. Businessmen took advantage of unemployment to force workers to labor twelve and fourteen hours a day for a pittance so small that not only wives, but children scarcely out of infancy, had to enter the factories to contribute their mite to the family earnings. The benefits which we today can so readily recognize as the fruits of the First Industrial Revolution were achieved only after decades of privation, misery, and ruthless exploitation for millions of working people.

Most of us find it difficult to believe that the Second Industrial Revolution—the Automation Revolution—can possibly produce similar results. But if vast social dislocations are prevented this time, it will be only because the combined social wisdom of private groups and government will be used to prevent them.

We now know that the greatest good of society is not served by permitting economic forces to operate blindly, regardless of consequences. We now know that economic forces are man-made and subject to controls, that the economic and social consequences of economic decisions can be foreseen, and when the consequences threaten to be harmful, preventive action can be taken. That philosophy is expressed, however imperfectly, in the Employment Act of 1946. We recognize today that it is not only possible, but necessary, for the government to analyze, to foresee, and to give direction to the economic forces that determine whether we shall have prosperity or depression.

Unfortunately, there are those who refuse to admit that automation poses any problems for individuals and for society as a whole. More unfortunately still, they are the very people who should be in the best position to foresee the difficulties that will have to be met, and in cooperation with government and the trade unions, to take action to meet them. Their spokesman is the National Association of Manufacturers. Their attitude has been all too clearly expressed in a pamphlet issued by the NAM entitled "Calling All Jobs." This pamphlet recognizes, and indeed elaborates on, the parallel between the First Industrial Revolution which ushered in the Machine Age and the Second Industrial Revolution which today is ushering in the Age of Automation. But with almost inconceivable blindness to the facts of history, the NAM completely disregards the misery and suffering that accomplished the introduction of the Machine Age, and dismisses all the protests of workers of that day as "unfounded complaints."

The workers of one hundred and fifty years ago who tried to smash the machines that had taken away their jobs had ample foundation for their complaints. They were wrong only in their methods. Their real complaint was not against the machines, but against the blindness of society which allowed the machines to be used as a means of ruthless exploitation.

We, in the labor movement today, have no complaint against the new technology of automation. We do not intend to let ourselves be misrepresented as opponents of automation. What we do oppose is the spirit of the NAM and those of like mind, whose views are expressed in the closing sentences of the pamphlet previously referred to:

Guided by electronics, powered by atomic energy, geared to the smooth, effortless workings of automation, the magic carpet of our free economy heads for distant and undreamed of horizons. Just going along for the ride will be the biggest thrill on earth!

We do not believe that any thinking person is prepared to accept the NAM's "magic carpet" theory of economics. Automation holds the promise of a future of new abundance, new leisure, and new freedoms, but before that future can be achieved there will be many serious and difficult problems to be solved. We do not believe that the American people or the Congress are prepared to "just go along for the ride."

Let us consider some of the specific problems that will have to be met. One of the major problems is that no one as yet has made a thorough study of what has been done in the field of automation, what is being planned for the near future, or what impact it has had or will have on our lives. As a result, an exhaustive list of the problems that automation will pose does not yet exist.

There are some problems, however, which can be foreseen. Obviously, there will be problems for the workers who are displaced from their jobs by automation. This is not merely a problem of finding a new job. One point on which most of the writers on automation seem agreed is that, by its very nature, automation will tend to eliminate unskilled and semiskilled jobs, while the new jobs it creates will be at a much higher level of skill. As one spokesman for the Ford Motor Company has put it: "The hand trucker of today replaced by a conveyor belt might become tomorrow's electronics engineer."

That sounds very nice, but it immediately poses the problem: *How* does the hand trucker become an electronics engineer—or a skilled technician? If automation destroys unskilled jobs and creates skilled jobs, means must be found to train large members of unskilled workers in the needed skills.

Another aspect of the same problem is that of the worker with a specialized skill who finds that his skill has been made valueless because a machine has taken over his job—such as the skilled machine operator displaced by a self-operating lathe or the book-keeper whose job is taken over by an electronic "brain."

You can easily see that if automation is going to displace any substantial number of workers in either of these two ways, we will need a carefully organized retraining program to give them the opportunity of acquiring the skills they will need. Such a program must take into account the needs of the workers, the fact that most of them will be mature men and women to whom the learning of new skills may not come easily, and that they have to live and support their families while they are acquiring these skills. The program will require not merely training facilities and expert vocational guidance. It will have to include provisions for training allowances to replace lost wages during the training period.

Without such a program, there may be a job as an electronics engineer for the hand trucker's son, but the hand trucker himself may have to join the ranks of the unemployed—one of a "lost generation" of workers who will have been scrapped as ruthlessly as so many items of obsolete equipment.

An alternative solution will have to be found in the case of older workers, not old enough for normal retirement, but too old to learn new skills or to adjust to the demands of the new technology. A single instance will be enough to point up the problem. This is from a report in the *New York Post:*

Then there are workers who can't keep up with automation. Such as Stanley Tylak. Tylak, 61 and for 27 years a job setter at Ford, was shifted from the River Rouge foundry machine shop to the new automated engine plant. He was given a chance to work at a big new automatic machine.

Simply, straightforwardly, he told his story: "The machine had about 80 drills and 22 blocks going through. You had to watch all the time. Every few minutes you had to watch to see everything was all right. And the machines had so many lights and switches —about 90 lights. It sure is hard on your mind.

"If there's a break in the machine the whole line breaks down. But sometimes you make a little mistake, and it's no good for you, no good for the foreman, no good for the company, no good for the union."

And so Stanley Tylak, baffled by the machine he couldn't keep up with, had to take another job—at lower pay.

This was a case where automation resulted in downgrading— not the upgrading so widely heralded by industry spokesmen as one of the fruits of automation. Yet, in one sense, Stanley Tylak was lucky. He at least was able to take another job. In many cases, there will be no other jobs available for a man in his sixties, or even younger. Perhaps if Stanley Tylak had been given more than just a chance to work at the new machine, perhaps if he had been given careful training for the job, taking into account the difficulties of adjustment to a new job at his age, he could have learned to do it even at sixty-one. But for those older workers who cannot adjust, I think we must be prepared to offer the opportunity of early retirement with the assurance of an adequate pension.

In some of our collective bargaining agreements, we have already laid the foundations for a system of early retirement which could help to meet such situations. But in the very nature of most private pension plans, the problem cannot be solved through collective bargaining alone. Industrial pension plans are based on the assumption that the worker, when he retires, will also be eligible for Social Security benefits. Much as we have improved the level of private pensions in recent years, a worker who is forced to retire before the age of sixty-five would find it impossible to maintain a decent standard of living on his industrial pension alone. I would strongly urge this Committee to consider, in formulating its recommendations, the need for earlier Social Security payments to workers who are forced into retirement before the age of sixty-five because technological changes have taken their jobs from them and their age makes it impossible for them to find other work.

The growth of automated factories can create problems of dislocation not only for individual workers but for whole communities. It is often cheaper to build a new plant from the ground up, so that the whole design of the buildings can be related to the industrial process, than to attempt to remodel an existing plant. In addition, corporations frequently seem to prefer to employ, on automated processes, workers who have had no experience with older methods. Thus, an employer whose only concern in his own profit may decide that it is to his advantage to build a new plant in a new location, perhaps hundreds of miles away—without any consideration for the old community.

Automation is not the only technological change which may produce such shifts in industry. The large-scale conversion of atomic energy into electric power, in quantities sufficient to supply the needs of industry, is now an assured possibility which will become a reality within relatively few years. A more far-reaching possibility exists in the direct conversion of energy from the sun, which has already been developed to the point of successful use in applications requiring small amounts of power. Such developments can provide limitless new sources of power for industry, but they can also produce severe dislocations and shifts in the geographical distribution of industries.

Many of the large industrial centers in our country today owe their location to ease of access to coal or other power sources. With the advent of new power sources, the advantages of such locations may disappear, and large-scale movements of industry to new areas may well take place.

Let me make it clear that we are not opposed to such changes when they are based on sound economic and social considerations. Such changes are part of the long-run dynamic economic growth, upon which the advance of prosperity depends. But it would be foolish to deny that changes of this sort will produce their own problems.

Special assistance will be needed to prevent the spread of distressed communities and there will be innumerable questions to be answered. When important industries move out of town, for example, what can be done to replace them with others? Should workers be encouraged to move to a new community, and if so, what help will they need in relocating themselves? When the movement of industry means a sudden burst of expansion for some communities, or perhaps the creation of brand new towns and cities, what help will they need in the way of housing programs and the building of schools, hospitals, and other community facilities?

Even today, there are scores of distressed communities in our nation, where hundreds of thousands of workers have been left stranded by shut-down plants, industry migration, closed coal mines, and curtailed operations of railroad repair shops. The impact of automation will possibly create additional pockets of substantial unemployment, even if high employment levels are maintained nationally.

Government assistance is required to aid in solving the pressing problems of such communities at present; government assistance has not yet been forthcoming, despite campaign promises that were made in the fall of 1952. Additional government aid will be needed in the future, as the new technology becomes widespread.

These are existing problems that result from the accumulation of "routine" technological change. Are we going to permit their multiplication and aggravation during the period of the widespread introduction of automation?

There is a tendency among management spokesmen, including some management-oriented economists, to dismiss these problems with the phrase, "mobility of labor." Workers who are displaced from their jobs in one community, so the argument runs, will simply move to another community where workers are needed and jobs are plentiful. Some have even suggested that proposals like the guaranteed annual wage, or other measures designed to cushion the shock of readjustment, are harmful because they interfere with the "mobility of labor."

As any study of real-life situations, like Professor Miernyk's *Inter-Industry Labor Mobility,* will show, for a substantial proportion of workers no real mobility exists. Because of financial obligations, family responsibilities, strong community ties, or simply because they are too old to hope to find new jobs, they continue to cling to their home communities.

In the long run, of course, the labor market *will* show a high degree of mobility because, in a stranded community, the older workers will eventually give up the search for nonexistent jobs and retire from the labor market, and few younger workers will move in to take their place. But that concept of "mobility" represents merely the use of statistics to camouflage the reality of a myriad of individual tragedies.

Even to the extent that labor is mobile, we know that such mobility can be achieved only at a price—the cost of retraining, the cost of moving and rehousing, etc. Those who consider that all of management's responsibilities can be made to disappear by invoking the term "mobility of labor" take it for granted that working people should be prepared to bear all the risks and pay all the costs of economic changes which destroy their jobs. Such an attitude is both irrational and irresponsible. As Professor Walter S. Buckingham of Georgia Institute of Technology has said:

There is no reason why labor should be more mobile, flexible and willing to assume the enormous risks of economic dislocation than the other components of production—capital, management and natural resources—which are to varying degrees organized, concentrated and immobilized. Indeed sacrifices made by other factors of production in participating in a competitive market are ordinarily much less than those made by labor. The worker has not his, or someone else's, money at stake, but his life, and his children's lives, on the auction block of the commercial market.

Although most of the needed help will have to come from governmental agencies, we should also give serious thought to the responsibility of business itself in attempting to solve these problems.

I have said that we welcome dynamic growth in our economy, even while we recognize the problems that such growth may bring. But we must not permit business to excuse irresponsible actions with the claim that, "this is part of the process of dynamic growth." The shutting down of a plant, the displacement of thousands of workers, the dislocation of whole communities cannot be justified simply because a corporation accountant can show that the potential profits to the corporation are greater than the direct costs reflected in the corporation's books.

In the program for a guaranteed annual wage, toward which the trade union movement has taken a long first step this year, one of our objectives has been to curb irresponsible action on the part of employers by requiring them to pay some of the social costs of policies which result in unemployment. In the same way, consideration should be given as to whether the costs of helping individual workers to adjust to the changes produced by automation should be borne by society as a whole, or whether some means should be sought to ensure that the employers will bear a share of the burden.

For example, if the result of automation is that a large number of workers in a plant have to learn new skills, I believe it is just as reasonable to expect the employer to pay the cost of retraining, including the payment of wages during the retraining period, as it is that he should pay the cost of building the new plant or installing the new equipment. When a plant is moved to a new locality, I believe the employer has a responsibility, not merely to retrain those workers who wish to move with the plant, but also to bear at least part of their cost of moving and new housing. These are just as much costs arising out of the employer's business decision as the business costs he now takes for granted.

This is primarily a matter for collective bargaining, but I feel the Committee should be aware of it. In our experience with employers—and it has been considerable—the one sure way of making them socially responsible is to make them financially responsible for the social results of what they do or fail to do.

The transition to the new technology will require a great expansion in our education system. As I have already noted, there seems to be general agreement that one of the results of automation will be a substantial raising of the level of skills required in automated factories and offices. That will require, in turn, a vastly improved program of vocational education to train young people in the new required skills, as well as to retrain the present working force for responsibilities in automated operations.

I want to emphasize, however, that it is not enough to provide merely the physical facilities—the schools, the teachers, the teaching equipment. It is equally necessary that students should have the economic means to delay their entry into the labor market so as to pursue their studies and training. Even today there are far too many young people dropping out of school before they should, simply because they and their families are not in a position to make the financial sacrifices that would be involved in their continuing at school. We need a greatly expanded program of financial aid to students through scholarships, and as the level of skill required in the factories of tomorrow rises, that need will be greatly intensified.

With the spread of automation, there will be a growing need for specialized semiprofessional technicians, as well as for professional engineers and skilled workers. The education system of the nation should be preparing now to meet these requirements.

I have made particular reference to the need for an improved program of vocational education because it ties in directly with the needs of automated factories and offices for workers with new skills. But we should not stop there. One of the benefits we should expect to gain from the great increases in productivity that automation makes possible is not only a reduction in hours of work—and I shall return to that subject in a few moments —but a reduction in the years of work. That reduction can be partly achieved by making it possible for more young people to continue their education in whatever field they choose and are fitted for. To meet the needs of our people, we require today far more teachers, doctors, nurses, and members of other professions than are now entering our schools to train for those professions.

We are dangerously short of engineers, especially at a time when in Russia the school system is being deliberately oriented toward the education of vast numbers of engineers as a necessary basis of further industrial expansion. Professional training apart, we should make it one of the major goals of our society

that every young person will have not only the physical opportunity but the economic means to gain the fullest education of
which he or she is capable.

So far I have been dealing primarily with the impact of automation on individuals and on local communities. But even
more serious consideration must be given to its possible impact
on the economy of the nation as a whole.

From the viewpoint of the national economy, the greatest
problem posed by automation is the threat of violent fluctuations
in employment and production during the period of adjustment
to the new technology. With the widespread introduction of
automation speeding up the potential output of goods and services, there is the possibility that the market may not grow fast
enough to sustain high employment levels.

I am not reassured by those who tell us that all will work out
well in the long run because we have managed to live through
radical technological changes in the past. Human beings do not
live long enough for us to be satisfied with assurances about the
long-run adaptation of society to automation. And while it is
true that radical technological improvements have been introduced in the past, it is well to remember that they were accompanied by vast social dislocations, recurring depressions, and human suffering. Most of us remember the depression of the 1930's
only too well, when the American people paid a heavy price for
the economy's failure to adjust to the introduction of mass production after World War I. We should now be thinking about
and planning for the transition period—the next ten years or so
—when the spread of automation may result in dislocations of
our society and in distress for countless individuals and communities.

Our economic needs will be rising in the years ahead. The
population, it is expected, will increase from approximately 165
million at present to about 190 million ten years from now. The
number of households will rise from about 48 million now to an
estimated 56 million in 1965. But the increase of economic needs
does not mean that these needs will be filled automatically.

Although automation is the use of automatic devices and electronic computers, there is no built-in servomechanism that will automatically adjust market demands to the rising output of goods and services made possible by the new technology. We are compelled to rely, instead, on our own wisdom or lack of it, and upon our private and public policies.

If the national economy expands with sufficient rapidity in the coming decade or two, along with the widespread introduction of automation, the problems posed by the new technology will be minimized and localized. But economic expansion does not arise simply because we desire it. Economic growth is the product of expanding markets that make possible the profitable utilization and further expansion of productive capacity.

Even under normal conditions, the national economy is compelled to expand on a continuing basis if high levels of production and employment are to be maintained. In a year when the civilian labor force is some 62–64 million, as in the recent past, the economy is burdened with the responsibility of providing over 3 million new job opportunities, when productivity rises 4 per cent and the labor force increases by some seven hundred thousand. In other words, we have to increase our purchases of goods and services by an amount equal to the output of over three million workers to absorb the increase in the labor force, as well as the displacement effect of rising productivity. The answer to such a burden is economic growth—a 5 per cent expansion of the nation's total output and consumption of goods and services, equal to the combined percentage increases in productivity and labor force.

It was substantial economic growth of that approximate magnitude—achieved through expanding markets—that gave us high levels of employment in much of the post-World War II period. But in 1949 and in 1953–1954, we saw how easily our economy can be shoved off balance—when markets fail to expand fast enough to absorb the rising output of an increasingly efficient economy.

These problems of attempting to maintain high levels of employment in the recent past will probably appear small by comparison with those that will demand our attention in the period ahead. One of the great challenges of automation is that it continues present difficulties in much more serious form.

There is sufficient evidence to indicate that automation will be spreading widely through the economy in the coming decade. Competition and the drive for reduced production costs are compelling the introduction of automated equipment. The *Journal of Commerce* of September 7, 1955, reported that a survey of twenty machine tool companies at the National Machine Tool Show "disclosed the belief that automation probably will make almost twice as much progress in the next five years as it has in the past ten."

"Demonstrated advances in productivity are amazing," is the way M. A. Hollengreen, President of the Machine Tool Builders' Association, put it to the *Journal of Commerce* reporter. "In case after case, new machines will do a job in a third, a tenth or even a fifteenth of the time formerly required. Advances in machine tools have never been as rapid as they have been in the past five years, and most members of the industry expect the pace to be stepped up considerably in the next half-decade."

Productivity is already increasing at a faster pace than in the long-run past. In commenting on recent productivity increases in manufacturing, the August, 1955, issue of the *Federal Reserve Bulletin* states that "output per manhour has risen somewhat more rapidly over the past two years of recession and recovery than the average post-war rate of about 4 percent a year."

In other words, man-hour output in manufacturing industries, which had been rising at an average annual rate of about 3 per cent in the long-run past before World War II, rose to an average yearly rate of approximately 4 per cent after the war and to somewhat more than 4 per cent in the past two years.

As a result of the sharp productivity increases of the past two years, employment has lagged considerably behind the improvements in general economic conditions. This is particularly true in manufacturing. In September, 1955, there were six hundred thousand fewer wage and salary workers employed in manufacturing industries than in September, 1953 (17.5 million two years ago in September, 1953, by comparison with 16.9 million in September, 1955).

Automation—in addition to the more conventional improvements in machines and work flow—will be increasing the rate of the national economy's rising man-hour output still further. Instead of average annual productivity increases of some 3 to 4 per cent, the annual rate of rising man-hour output in the national economy may reach 5 to 6 per cent or more. With a civilian labor force of 70 million, 5 to 6 per cent annual increases in the economy's man-hour output would make it necessary to add about 3½ million new job opportunities each year, merely to absorb the possible displacement effect of rising productivity. Another way of stating it is that annual productivity increases of 5 to 6 per cent in the coming decade will be capable of displacing about 3½ million or more employees each year, if the national economy fails to expand, along with the rapid improvements in productive efficiency.

The problem grows still greater when we consider that the labor force will be increasing at an accelerating rate in the period ahead. And the accelerating growth of the labor force will require the addition of yet more new job opportunities each year, if high levels of employment are to be maintained.

The average annual growth of the civilian labor force at present is some seven to eight hundred thousand, according to government estimates. In two or three years, the expansion of the labor force will be accelerating—when those who were born since 1939 start looking for jobs (after taking account of probable increases in both school attendance of youngsters and retirement of the aged). The size of the labor force, according to Census Bureau estimates, will be expanding at a rising rate in the coming ten years, at the same time when automation and other technological changes will probably be pushing productivity increases above the rates of the recent past.

The civilian labor force, which has been growing at an average annual rate of about 1 per cent in recent years, will probably be rising at annual rates of 1.2 per cent to 1.6 per cent in the coming decade. The accelerating growth of the labor force in the years ahead will probably necessitate the creation of some 800,-000 to 1,250,000 new job opportunities annually, if high levels of employment are to be maintained. And this requirement is in addition to the necessity of the economy to prevent the disemployment each year of some 3½ million or more workers, when productivity rises 5 to 6 per cent annually.

There is a possibility, therefore, that in the years ahead, the national economy will have to provide about 4½ million or more new job opportunities each year to absorb both the increases in the labor force and the displacement effect of rising productivity. To do so, the national economy's markets will have to expand more rapidly than in the recent past, when an average yearly 4 to 5 per cent rise of the nation's total output was generally sufficient.

With the labor force growing 1.2 to 1.6 per cent a year in the coming decade, and man-hour output possibly increasing some 5 to 6 per cent or more each year, the economy's output of goods and services have to expand by some 6 to 7 per cent or more annually, if high levels of employment are to be maintained.

There are those who tell us that this problem should be of no concern to us. An expanding electronics industry, they tell us, will automatically absorb workers who may be displaced from factory and office employment.

It is true that the electronics and machine tool industries that produce automation equipment are expanding. But productivity in these industries is rising rapidly, with the introduction of labor-saving devices, new materials, and automated equipment. These industries, too, are being automated.

A Department of Labor study states:

Electronics output in 1952 was 275 percent higher than in 1947 but was produced by only 40 percent more workers. . . .

Output per manhour (in the electronics industry) may rise even faster during the next few years as a result of improvements in manufacturing techniques. . . . These trends toward "automation" may result in the greatest reduction in unit manhours in the industry's history during the next few years.

General Mills, Inc., the breakfast food producer, for example, has announced that it has put on the market a fully automatic machine for the production of electronic equipment. Called "Autofab," this new machine, it is said, will assemble, in a little over a minute, the same number of multiplepart electronic units that now takes one worker a full day to assemble. It requires only two workers and a supervisor, and has a capacity of more than two hundred thousand assemblies a month, operating forty hours a week.

I do not believe that we can complacently put our faith in the expanding automation equipment industries to provide the large number of required new job opportunities to maintain high levels of employment in the coming transition decade. Nor do I believe that the transition period to the era of the new technology will be accompanied by rapid and large-scale job-producing secondary investment—sufficient to be an adequate shock absorber. There is no assurance whatsoever—and there can be none—of automatic and immediate adjustments to the widespread introduction of automation.

Automation is a new technology with the possibility of economy-wide displacement effects; its major requirements are equipment and power from industries whose productivity is rising at sharp rates. The new technology, for that reason, cannot be compared to a new product, such as the automobile whose widespread introduction was, of necessity, accompanied by secondary investment in road construction, oil, rubber, steel, and glass.

Another factor that must be taken into consideration is that the productivity of capital is rising along with the productivity of labor. In some of the illustrations of automation I have given here, it is noted that while the automatic machines cost more than those they replace, the increase in cost is less than the increase in productivity. That is to say, the investment *per unit of production* is actually less than that of the replaced machines.

This is in line with a long-term trend. Recent studies, published by the National Bureau of Economic Research, show a fairly steady rise in the productivity of capital investment ever since World War I.

The rising productivity of capital as well as of labor makes it more important than ever that consumer markets expand rapidly.

There are those who try to tell us that there is no cause for concern, because increased productivity will automatically result in lower prices. The fallacy of this view is that automation finds its major field in the "administered price" industries, such as the automobile industry, where lower costs more often lead to higher profits than to reduced prices. For example, the Ford Motor Company has announced that it expects to make a record profit this year. Yet rather than pass a share of that profit along to consumers in the form of lower prices, Ford has actually announced price increases on its 1956 models.

Then there are the optimists in the sales departments and the advertising agencies who seem, quite honestly, to believe that we can sell anything we can produce if business will just put enough high pressure behind its advertising and selling campaigns. They seem to think that consumer purchasing power will be created automatically.

Only a little thought on the subject should be enough to convince anyone that consumer purchasing power will not be raised automatically. It will not be raised unless the benefits of increased productivity are passed along to the mass market of consumers through such measures as increased wages, reduced prices, and increased expenditures by government in such fields as education and housing, as well as improved government programs in such areas as social security and health. Increases in consumer purchasing power will arise, not from reliance on nonexistent automatic forces, but from the effort of private groups and government.

I do not believe that people who seek out untenable reasons for complacency about the potential problems posed by automation are serving any socially useful purpose. Neither do I believe that one need be unduly pessimistic. I am firmly convinced that our economy can adjust to the challenge of automation, if we use our foresight and the combined wisdom of private groups and government. It is wise social policies by private and public groups that are called for, rather than either smugness or pessimism.

As I have already indicated, one major and rather obvious requirement for an orderly economic adjustment to the new technology is the continuing rapid growth of consumer markets, along with the economy's ability to produce a rising volume of goods and services. In the coming decade of transition to the widespread use of automation, emphasis will have to be placed —even more so than in recent years—on the need for consumer markets to grow rapidly.

A basic cause of the depression of the 1930's was our inability to realize during the 1920's that while increasing productivity creates the possibility of expanding production, it must be accompanied by rising purchasing power so that consumers can buy the additional goods and services which can be produced.

Increased man-hour output without growing markets is a formula for depression. Without customers for the mounting output that will be made possible by the widespread use of automation, mass unemployment will be inevitable.

I can assure you that organized labor will in the future, as in the past, do all in its power to maintain an expanding mass consumption base for the national economy. But the consumer purchasing power needs of the coming decade will require, to a greater extent than in the past, that business accept collective bargaining and the right of workers to continuing improvements of their living conditions.

Rapidly growing consumer markets, however, require more than price reductions and union gains in wages, guaranteed wage plans and fringe benefits. They likewise require federal, state, and local tax structures that will provide expanding consumer purchasing power, especially among the millions of low- and middle-income families. They require, too, an adequate unemployment compensation system for unemployed workers, and an improved Social Security system for retired workers, and a generally liberal monetary policy that will encourage small business, farmers, and consumers to expand their investments in plant, equipment, homes, and consumer durables.

The needed rapid growth of consumer markets will require

further increases in the statutory minimum wage. According to the staff report, prepared for the Senate Labor Committee, which investigated the minimum wage, the increase from 75 cents to $1.00 which comes into effect next year will not be sufficient to take into account the combined effect of the increase in the cost of living and increased productivity since the beginning of 1950, when the 75-cent minimum became law.

In a period of sharply rising productivity, it is a national disgrace that a country as wealthy as ours should still have a considerable number of workers earning no more than a bare subsistence. The $1.00-an-hour legal minimum wage, effective March 1, 1956, should be revised to $1.25 without delay, and coverage under the law should be extended. As a matter of public policy, we should adopt a program designed to increase statutory minimum wage levels, substantially faster than increases in productivity, until they shall have reached a point where we need no longer be ashamed of them.

An important step toward minimizing potential social dislocations during the coming decade of transition to the new technology would be the reduction in length of the workweek.

In the past, the rise in man-hour output has made it possible to increase both leisure and total output. Rising productivity at present—and the more rapid increases expected in the coming decade—make possible further increases in leisure.

The reduction of the workweek to thirty-five or thirty hours in the coming decade can be an important shock absorber during the transition to the widespread use of automation. It can both reduce the impact of sharp rises in output and increase the manpower requirements in industry and commerce.

The past reduction of the workweek to forty hours, and the prevalence of paid vacations and holidays, have brought a share of the fruits of industrial progress to wage and salary earners in the form of increased leisure. These proud achievements of organized labor and the New Deal have contributed to the growing importance of leisure-related activities—such as educational, recreational, and cultural activities, do-it-yourself, gardening, sports, and vacations.

The further reduction in the length of the workweek, below

40 hours, in the years ahead will probably result in a stimulus for additional leisure-related activities—additional interest in education, museums, libraries, parks, sports and resort centers.

The thirty or thirty-five-hour workweek, the 2½ or 3-day weekend, extended vacations, early retirement for older workers, and increased schooling for young people—these are some of the possibilities that arise out of the anticipated rapid increases in productivity during the coming decade. But we will not achieve these possibilities without planning for them and working for them.

In many industries, we will be able to achieve a further reduction in the workweek through effective trade union organization and collective bargaining. But the increased leisure which automation makes possible will not be enjoyed by all groups of Americans, except through legislation to shorten the statutory workweek under federal and state laws. Here is an area in which a continuing study of industrial conditions and the effect of automation on employment can be particularly valuable as the basis for recommendation to Congress for legislative action.

In the same way, we will not achieve early retirement under the Social Security Act, or increased vocational training, or improved educational opportunities for young people without government guidance and action.

One of the fruits of automation, which we should welcome, is the opportunity it gives us to meet the present and growing social deficits in health, housing, schools, highways, natural resources, and other public services. Through increased productivity, our economy can meet the cost of these long-delayed measures, without strain—and their achievement will help, by creating new jobs, to ease any necessary adjustments in employment.

But I hope we will not wait until unemployment has become a serious problem before we make a start. Millions of new homes, at least a million new hospital beds, hundreds of thousands of added school classrooms will be required within the next few years, simply to meet the needs of a growing population for adequate housing, health and educational facilities.

The rapid productivity increases that automation makes possible should enable us to devote increasing attention to social welfare and public services. Such activities should be viewed as a means of strengthening the fabric of our society, rather than as mere antirecession devices.

The maintenance of high levels of employment nationally is the major requirement to reduce the size and nature of the possible problems posed by automation. Nevertheless, the dynamic changes of the transition period—even with high levels of employment generally—will probably be felt by some groups of workers and businesses. For them, the impact will be harsh, and some forethought by private groups and government must be given to devising means of assistance.

Many small business firms, as well as workers, may find themselves in distress during the period of transition to the new technology. In some industries, automation equipment may be so expensive—and the required output so large—as to make its use prohibitive by small or medium-sized firms.

Small business has been hard pressed in the past two years. Business failures rose sharply in 1954. They remain high now, despite the general improvement in economic conditions. Last June, there were 914 business failures, by comparison with 965 in June, 1954, 817 in June, 1953 and 671 in June, 1952.

Small and medium-sized business has not shared in the recent prosperity of the giant corporations.

The Quarterly Financial Reports on United States Manufacturing Corporations, issued jointly by the Federal Trade Commission and the Securities and Exchange Commission, show that between the first quarter of 1953 and the first quarter of 1955, manufacturing companies, with assets of $100 million and more, increased their sales by $2.2 billion; their profits before taxes went up by $450 million, and their profits after taxes by $591 million.

In the same period, the sales of all other manufacturing corporations declined by $2.5 billion, their profits before taxes fell by $578 million, and their profits after taxes were lower by $102 million.

These figures have the closest bearing on the economic questions posed by automation. For the most part, it is the large companies that will be in the best financial position to scrap old equipment and old plants, and replace them with new automated machines and automated plants, thus increasing still more the margin of efficiency which they enjoy over their smaller competitors.

It is possible that relatively low-priced electronic computers will be available for smaller firms. It is also possible that some types of multiple-purpose automated equipment will be available for medium-sized plants whose products are mixed. But in industries where a great volume of identical products are made—as in the automobile industry—the required output for profitable operations may be so great, and the cost of the equipment may be so high, as to make it difficult, if not impossible, for small firms to purchase automated machines.

Government policy should be aimed at assisting small business firms to maintain their existence. A generally liberal credit policy —with low interest rates—is an essential part of such programs to enable small businesses to obtain funds for investment in expensive automatic machinery. Long-term government loans, at low interest rates, for industrial and commercial expansion, should be made available to small and medium-sized firms. Government procurement policies should aim at getting work on government contracts to smaller businesses. The antitrust division of the Justice Department should be instructed to be more vigilant than it has been in the recent past in the effort to eliminate monopolistic practices in industry.

Automation may bring with it the danger that big firms will grow even bigger, while small and medium-sized competitors are squeezed against the wall. The danger must be minimized by government policies and actions to assist small business and prevent trends toward monopoly.

Automation has been hailed as the "Second Industrial Revolution." But no radical change in technology can take place without parallel changes in the economic structure.

It is within our power to see to it that these economic and social changes take place in an orderly and evolutionary manner —toward improved standards of living and social welfare, an extension of leisure and new horizons of individual opportunities for educational and cultural achievements. Such evolutionary changes in the coming decade will require forethought, planning, and guidance. If we permit the new technology to follow its own blind course, directed only by the selfish interests of those who would utilize it for their own immediate profit, our free society may be subjected to dangerous disruption in a world beset by international tensions.

We cannot permit any weakening of our national strength nor any undermining of our social fabric. The Communists are only too willing to assist in such an endeavor. We should take advantage of the rising productivity that automation makes possible to increase our national strength and improve living standards at the same time.

High levels of employment and rapid economic growth must be achieved in the period ahead. But those goals can be attained only through growing markets that will expand rapidly, along with the economy's rising productivity. A positive government effort is required to provide the expanding markets that are the basis for economic growth.

Organized labor is doing its part, through collective bargaining for higher wages, extended vacations and holidays, guaranteed wage plans, improved pension and health-welfare plans. There is no need to defend these social gains won by unions for millions of working people; they stand on their own merits, and rising profits generally indicate that business has been able to pay for them. But the power of big corporations to administer prices has tended to dilute some of the benefits of these improvements.

A national approach is needed to help make certain that the benefits of automation will be shared among all groups in the population. A Congressional inquiry into the price policies of giant corporations, for example, is long overdue—to place the spotlight of public attention on the failure of the dominant corporations to pass on to consumers the benefits of rising productivity.

There is need, too, for a more equitable distribution of the tax burden, an adequate unemployment compensation system, improved Social Security benefits, a higher legal minimum wage and reduced legal workweek, protection of farm income, improved educational facilities, financial aid to students, an extended program of hospital and road construction, and natural resources development.

We in the CIO do not pretend to have the answers to all the problems posed by automation. We are quite sure, in fact, that no one can have all the answers at present. Not nearly enough is known yet about the current achievements of automation, the planned progress of automation, or the precise impact that automation will have on productivity, on employment, and on the national economy.

No one in industry or government has yet gathered together in one place enough information about what is happening in the field of automation to have the full story. Individual companies know what they are planning or already have done, and corporations manufacturing automation equipment may know what their customers are doing, but there is still the job of putting this knowledge together coherently.

I hope that in these hearings, the Committee will ask representatives of various corporations, who come before it, to answer specific questions about what their companies have done and intend to do in the way of introducing automation, and the impact of automated equipment on manpower requirements.

I would urge that a continuing study of the social and economic impact of the new technology be made, either by members of the staff of this Committee or by some government agency to which the Committee might recommend that the task be entrusted.

Through these hearings and a continuing study, we should find out just how much displacement of manpower in industry has already resulted from automation, to what extent the displaced workers have been absorbed into other jobs with their own employer or with some other employer, the impact of such displacement on older workers, how many displaced workers have been able to find other jobs, how many are unemployed, how many displaced workers have retired from the labor market, and how adequate are the incomes of those who have retired.

We should find out to what extent displaced workers tend to move into jobs like their old ones, and to what extent they are forced to accept lower-paid jobs requiring less skill.

From these hearings and future studies, we should find out to what extent the introduction of automation, by firms which are able to expand their share of the market, has resulted in the disemployment of workers in other companies that have not been able to make the investment in automated equipment. For example, it has been said of the auto industry that automation in Detroit has resulted in unemployment in South Bend. Some employers may be able to tell this Committee that they have been able to maintain, or even increase their employment in spite of automation. But that is only half the answer, if expansion on the part of such employers has resulted in unemployment in other plants and in other communities.

A thorough study should be made of the industrial movements which may be anticipated over the next several years—the industries and geographical areas most likely to be affected, and the problems that will probably be created both for workers and for their families, and for the affected community.

Particular attention should be concentrated on the prospective rate of productivity increases as a result of automation and other technological advances. This information is essential if we are to have an idea of the required increases in consumer purchasing power and the possibilities for a rapid reduction in the length of the workweek. It is likewise essential if we are to be able to plan private and public policies intelligently for continued economic growth and the maintenance of high levels of employment.

The results of these hearings and ensuing studies should lead to positive recommendation from this Committee to the Congress. Such recommendations should cover the problems of displaced workers, industry migrations, stranded communities, small business and education requirements. Above all, such recommendations should promote national economic policies, designed to expand consumer purchasing power, with sufficient speed so that we shall be able to buy and consume the vast flood of goods and services made available by automation. Such policy recommendations should be aimed at taking full advantage of the opportunities presented by rapid productivity increases—to improve federal, state, and local facilities in health, housing, education, natural resources, and other fields of public activity.

We must do all in our power to make sure that the potential abundance of the new technology will be used with social wisdom to improve standards of living and welfare and to provide increased leisure for all Americans.

These are great tasks. In the years that lie immediately ahead, we shall have to undertake these tasks, because the new technology confronts us with a tremendous challenge. If we refuse to accept that challenge, if we fail to solve the problems that will probably crowd upon us, we may be forced to undergo shattering economic dislocations that could threaten our whole economy and our free society.

If we accept the challenge of the new technology, if we use foresight and act wisely and vigorously, we can help to usher in an age of abundance and freedom, the like of which the world has never known.

Closing Address at the final convention of the Congress of Industrial Organizations

New York, New York
December 2, 1955

We have had two days in which together we have relived twenty years of hard struggle, twenty years in which we have had the high privilege of serving the free labor movement, twenty years in which we have enjoyed the warmth of friendship, the great leaders like Philip Murray and Sidney Hillman, Van Bittner, Allan Haywood, John Brophy and Adolph Germer, and many other people, and the warmth and fellowship of millions of rank-and-file American workers. We have made the friendship of trade union people all over the world. We have established the CIO in its proper place and proper role in the American community. This has been a rich experience. We can be proud of our contribution. But as we go forward, let us be strong, but let us be humble. Let us demonstrate great courage but never let us be arrogant. Let us understand that they who have power have responsibility in proportion to that power. Let us build the power of the American labor movement as great as the expanding multitude of our membership will reflect that greater power. Let us use it wisely, tempered with justice, tempered with human understanding, tempered with the knowledge that when God made man He made each of us in His image, but He made each of us different, that what we need is unity, not conformity, not unity that regiments the human spirit and enslaves the human soul, but the unity of a free society that draws its power out of the unity of diversity, not conformity.

Let us go forward with our banner high in the knowledge that our cause is just, in the knowledge that free men in common dedication will mobilize that spiritual power in the world against which the forces of greed and selfishness and totalitarianism cannot prevail. Let us go forward and remain true to the things that we believe in and true to ourselves, with high faith in our purposes, with high faith in the values that we believe in, and with high faith in ourselves.

If we do that, as I know that we shall, we shall share in the great human satisfaction that having been called to duty we performed that duty well, that having had an opportunity to serve our fellow man we subordinated ourself in total dedication in the pursuit of the advancement of the interests and well-being of our fellow man.

There is no greater calling than to serve your brother. There is no greater contribution than to help the weak. There is no greater satisfaction than to have done it well.

I say to you this is not the end. This is part of that great historic struggle that goes on as long as hope beats within the human breast—that hope for a better tomorrow, that hope for a better world, that dream that mankind can fashion a world in which man's inhumanity to man can be ended, and which the great power of creation which God gave us can be used by man to create a better world—a world in the image of the things that the Prophets talked about, that the poets dreamed about, that the philosophers sketched with their broad strokes.

This is one of those glorious hours. We are fortunate to be blessed, each of us in his own humble way, with our little place on the page of history, and to share in this kind of great historic decision. Millions of people have been denied that kind of opportunity. Let us pray we shall be worthy of it.

Let us go forward with courage, with humility, with dedication. Let us make the most of the new opportunity that the new beginning presents us with. Having done these things, we will contribute, we will help build with our fellow workers in America and our fellow workers in the world, and with men and women of good will everywhere, a wonderful new world society in which the teachings of the great religions can be applied in the everyday life in man's relationship to man. Let us never forget that he who would serve God must prove that he is worthy by serving man. This is our pledge. This is the great challenge. I believe that we shall be worthy of that challenge and I pray that God may make us strong in our faith, that He may sharpen our vision, that He may raise our sights, and that the days that lie ahead shall be days in which together we shall labor in the broad vineyards of American democracy and in the broader vineyards of the world, in which peace, freedom, social justice, and brotherhood must be given meaning and purpose.

And so I say to you, not as the president of your union, but as a human being, thank you for having enriched my life, for my having had the privilege of associating with you. Let us go forward together and build more strongly the instruments of social justice, the tools with which we can build and the weapons with which we must fight the good fight for the good life.

Atoms for Peace

A Separate Opinion to the Joint Congressional
Committee on Atomic Energy, submitted as a member
of the Panel on the Peaceful Uses of Atomic
Energy

January 25, 1956

I joined the report of the panel because I am in agreement
with its general conclusions and recommendations and because
I feel it was motivated by a high sense of duty and public interest on the part of the members of the panel. However, I advised
the panel that I wished to exercise the usual privilege accorded
to members of such advisory groups in submitting on my own
behalf a separate statement of views concurring with the report
in general but differing in conclusions and emphasis on particular
points.

The chairman of the panel, Mr. McKinney, said he interpreted
the assignment of the panel as requiring it to report only a con-
sensus of the members' views. Accordingly, he declined to include
my statement as a part of the panel's report to your Committee.

I therefore had no alternative but to send my separate views
to you directly and request that, in accordance with customary
procedure in advisory committees of this kind, the Committee
incorporate them in its records as an integral part of the panel
report and include them in any report to Congress or other publication which the Committee may make of that report.

The points which I wish to emphasize are as follows:

In the cold war—in freedom's struggle against the forces of
Communist tyranny—in the struggle for the hearts and minds
of men—speed, all possible speed, in harnessing the atom to
man's peacetime needs—can be decisive.

Access to low-cost nuclear power may prove the key to the

economic development of backward areas and make possible
the liberation of millions of people from poverty, hunger, ignorance, and disease. America's leadership is essential if we are
to block the Communists in their efforts to forge poverty into
power.

Our success in harnessing the atom to lift the burden of poverty and disease from hundreds of millions of the world's people
living in hunger and ill-health would establish America in a position of moral leadership against which Communist propaganda
would be impotent.

Harnessing of the atom for peaceful purposes will give us the
tools with which to wage freedom's most effective propaganda to
these people—the propaganda of the democratic deed. Failure
on the part of America to pursue the peaceful harnessing of the
atom with maximum speed, determination, and dedication may
prove to be the Achilles' heel of the cold war.

We shall not give leadership to other people if we refuse to
exercise it in our own behalf. The fact is that the United States
is failing to demonstrate the outstanding leadership in releasing
atomic energy for peaceful purposes which it demonstrated in
putting the atom to work for war.

We are not moving with speed and determination to convert
atomic energy into an instrument of peaceful progress. Our program for developing atomic energy as a source of electric power
is moving too slowly.

For many years after the war no really significant beginning
was made to apply the atom to peaceful uses. Finally, one year
ago, AEC invited private enterprise to submit proposals for
participating in the development of atomic reactors for the generation of electric power. But no private power reactors are
now under construction and none has completed the initial
stages of design.

The one large-scale reactor now building is the AEC demonstration reactor at Shippingport, Pennsylvania. Apart from this
government project, the sobering fact is that, today, ten and a
half years after the end of the war, America's peacetime atomic
power program has not advanced beyond the drawing boards.

The head of the AEC reactor division states that as of today there is no certainty when, if ever, private industry will build and operate a power reactor.

The British government recently announced that its first full-scale power reactor will begin to deliver electric current on October 17, 1956. Soviet Russia claims to have a small-scale pilot model delivering electric power now. Japan's atomic energy commission has been assured by the General Electric Company, according to press reports, that it can build a full-scale power reactor for that country to deliver power within three years at a cost competitive with existing power rates in many areas of the United States.

The need to develop atomic energy as a practical source of power for use in the United States is urgent. There are power-hungry areas in our country today. There are other areas where the high cost of power retards economic progress and is encouraging the flight of industry to other parts of the country.

Total power requirements in the United States will expand at a tremendous rate over the next twenty-five years. We shall need nuclear power to meet those requirements. I cannot accept the comfortable assurance that our conventional fuel resources will meet all our power needs for another twenty to twenty-five years. Nor will I rely upon the Federal Power Commission's consistently conservative forecasts of power requirements as reflecting the true growth potential of our economy or the increasing needs of the American people.

No power ceiling should be imposed upon the normal and necessary expansion of our economy. Of that we must make sure. We must develop every source of energy we have, including atomic energy.

To meet the challenge and to realize the opportunity of the peaceful uses of atomic energy, we must mobilize all our forces and enlist the active participation of every segment of our economy. We must make full use of the capabilities both of government and of private enterprise. Only by drawing upon the special contributions of each can we make satisfactory progress toward our objectives—fortifying the strength of our nation, advancing the welfare of our people, and discharging our world responsibilities.

The technological barriers ahead of us are formidable. Enormous investments are required. The financial risks are great. But all these difficulties can be overcome by a united, determined, and coordinated effort.

It would be tragic to destroy this great opportunity for national achievement and world leadership by dissipating our strength in ideological warfare over the respective roles of government and private enterprise. That is a sure-fire formula for standing still here in the United States while the rest of the world moves forward in the practical application of atomic energy to human needs.

The opportunities for government and private enterprise to make their special contributions in this new field will arise out of the particular problems encountered at each stage of development. Both will have a vital part to play throughout, but the character and degree of their responsibilities will change as we make progress in mastering the new technology.

The early research and experimental phases of the program are primarily the government's responsibility, it is generally agreed. The development and construction of small-scale power reactors is also primarily a government responsibility, according to the panel report.

As to the next stage of the program, I question whether the present AEC policy of placing prime responsibility on private utility companies to provide risk capital for the construction and testing of full-scale demonstrations reactors is sound. I share the point of view that the productive know-how and managerial skill of American private enterprise can make an important contribution to this phase of development, providing, however, the government takes the initiative and assumes the financial risks involved in the construction and testing of these full-scale reactors. Building these first full-scale power reactors is an extension of the research and experimental work which only the government is capable of performing under present circumstances. Accordingly, I suggest that the AEC policy of placing primary reliance on private enterprise at this stage of development be subjected to early review and reappraisal by the Joint Committee.

Once the practical possibilities of atomic energy have been demonstrated, a realistic and attractive opportunity will have been created for private enterprise to engage in the new atomic industries and develop their full potential. When this stage is reached, the government is obligated to guard against monopoly control in the new industries, and to make sure that consumers are protected by effective competition in the sale of nuclear power and other atomic services. Both publicly and privately financed electric utility systems should engage in supplying nuclear power to the public just as in the past they have supplied power generated from conventional energy sources.

Further elaboration will be given to each of these five general observations, followed by points I wish to emphasize on the subjects of manpower and training, and hazards and protection.

When Senator Clinton P. Anderson (D., New Mexico) appointed the panel on March 26 of last year, he said:

Other industrialized nations, besides the United States, are pressing to become leaders in the manufacture and sale of atomic power plants for export. Around the winners of this race, underdeveloped, power-hungry nations may group themselves in new satellite orbits, far different from present alliances.

We dare not ignore this challenge. As the strongest of the free nations, America's responsibilities of world leadership require that the achievement of maximum progress in the peaceful uses of atomic energy be dealt with as a matter of highest national priority.

We must help make it possible for the hungry and desperate millions of the world to develop their economic and human resources so they may win economic security and material well-being without political or spiritual enslavement. Recent Soviet offers of economic assistance to Egypt and Middle East nations, and the increased economic aid promised by Soviet leaders during their recent Asian tour, testify to the increasing emphasis that economic penetration will play in Soviet foreign policy in the new phase of the cold war.

Speed may prove to be the very essence of survival. The free world cannot win the cold war except as it succeeds in winning to freedom's side the vast majority of the uncommitted people of the world.

If less than our best effort would result in the Soviet Union's gaining the initiative and capturing the position of leadership in the field of nuclear power, then this potent weapon of economic penetration would be used to enslave further millions of people and could dangerously shift the center of world balance to the jeopardy of the free world. Only with the initiative and leadership securely in the hands of America and the free world can we be certain that nuclear power will be used as an instrument of economic liberation rather than a weapon of political enslavement.

The seriousness of the challenge that we face in maintaining leadership is reflected in a story in *The New York Times,* dated January 24, 1956, which reported as follows:

The prospect of Soviet leadership in nuclear energy development by 1960 is causing concern among United States specialists in the field.

Should present plans be realized, the Soviet Union will have atomic electricity plants with greater capacity than the United States and Britain combined in 1960.

The new Soviet Five-Year Plan calls for completion by 1960 of atomic energy plants with total capacity of 2,000,000 to 2,500,000 kilowatts.

I support the report of the panel which recommends that "the United States call a series of regional conferences of bilateral partners for the immediate establishment of realistic goals for the installation of atomic power abroad. And that the United States announce that it is prepared to furnish the nuclear fuel, provide the necessary technical assistance, and permit contracts for the installation of at least one million kilowatts of atomic generating capacity outside the United States at as early a date as possible, hopefully by 1960."

The panel then notes: "Such a [foreign] program would parallel and possibly exceed the capacity installed during the same period at home."

While supporting the panel's recommendation that America must lead in providing assistance to friendly nations in the development of nuclear power, I think it is dangerously unrealistic to expect America to achieve and maintain a position of leadership in the world if we are not in a position of leadership at home. American leadership in the world contest must rest upon and be a reflection of a highly developed and advanced nuclear power industry in America. I am at a loss to understand how America can be in a position of technological leadership in building nuclear power plants in underdeveloped countries if we have not advanced the level of our technology by building a nuclear power industry in America.

As an interim measure the panel proposes that the foreign nuclear power program be carried out by bilateral agreements between the United States and other countries.

I wish to emphasize in addition the special responsibility that devolves upon our government in the forthcoming conference where twenty nations will make plans to establish a special atomic agency in the United Nations. The United States should take the lead in urging that this UN atomic agency provide practical fulfillment of the "atoms for peace" proposal which President Eisenhower made to the world in his appearance before the UN Assembly in December, 1953. The inspiration and the rallying point which he provided for forging the positive instruments of peace brought new hope into the hearts of men. His bold initiative placed a solemn obligation upon our nation to do all within its power to fulfill the pledge he made and to justify the hopes which he called forth.

Full participation of the atomic "have-not" nations in the policies and programs of the UN agency is imperative and should be provided for. The international atom-bank, which was the

core of the President's proposal, should be entrusted to this
agency. It should have powers of inspection and control adequate
to prevent diversion to military use of the fissionable fuels and
by-products thus dedicated to peaceful uses.

I believe that the present state of development of peaceful
uses of atomic energy in the United States fails to reflect the
urgency which our domestic needs and our responsibilities of
world leadership demand. Let's look at the record.

In January, 1955, the Atomic Energy Commission asked for
proposals by interested parties or groups to participate with it
in the development and construction of large-scale nuclear power
reactors. Two such proposals are now under negotiation with the
AEC. Two other proposals to proceed independently were received and are in negotiation with the AEC on the issuance of
licenses. Two other participation proposals submitted were not accepted by the AEC as a basis for negotiation.

On October 10, W. Kenneth Davis, director of the AEC reactor division, publicly stated:

There is one aspect of this search for development contractors
that is most important; we would like to have new contractors get
into the business. The expanding program badly needs more contractors.

No private construction of power reactors has begun. No firm
construction contracts have been signed. None of the private
proposals has reached the end of the first five stages which,
according to the director of the AEC reactor division, must be
completed in order to test the commercial feasibility of full-scale
power reactors.

Because of the many difficulties to be overcome and the financial risks involved, we are told by this AEC official that
there is today no definite assurance how many privately financed
full-scale reactor projects will be carried to completion, or
whether any of them will.

Thus, while a beginning has been made, progress is lagging.
In contrast to our record in the United States, Great Britain
has launched an extensive power reactor program which, within

five to ten years will take over a considerable part of the burden of meeting that country's power needs. It has announced that power from its first full-scale reactor will go on the lines October 17 of this year.

There is no question that interest in putting nuclear power to work is lively in Soviet Russia, in western Europe, in Japan, and in other countries. With the same degree of interests and urgency in the United States, our unquestioned superiority in technology and resources could quickly restore our country to the position of leadership which rightfully belongs to us.

The world's first chain reaction of uranium under human control was set off by the United States in December, 1942. Two and a half years later we detonated the first atomic bomb. In that short interval, experiment, discovery, plant construction, demonstration, development, production, and practical results followed each other at a pace unparalleled in the history of the world.

This was under the urgency of a world war. The government mobilized our energies to achieve the goal regardless of cost. We cannot expect development of the peaceful uses of the atom to proceed at that pace. But it cannot be disputed that the little progress which has been made toward peaceful application of the atom in ten and a half postwar years is much less than we should have accomplished with the great scientific, technical, and material resources available to us.

One reason for the slow start we have made in developing nuclear power appears to be the view held by some that there is no urgent need for a new source of energy in the United States. Another cause of delay can be found in the excessive, overheated and, in my judgment, unwarranted controversy that is given so much attention in official circles today—the issue as to the proper roles of government and of private enterprise in carrying out projects of national concern. I express my views on this question in the sections below.

There is unquestionably real and urgent need for the additional power which atomic energy will give us just about as soon as we make up our minds and commit our resources to its development as a commercial source of electricity.

The fact is we could use nuclear power today in many power-hungry and high fuel-cost areas of the United States if the technology of producing it were far enough advanced to bring costs down to the levels that we have every reason to believe possible.

Estimates given to the panel on the declining capital and fuel costs of nuclear power that are to be expected as development progresses suggest that it will become a competitive source of power in many areas. Indeed we can safely assume, I believe, that before too long nuclear power will begin to bring to some areas of the United States the same stimulating effects on business prosperity and employment opportunities that low-cost power has brought to the Tennessee Valley and the Pacific Northwest. I am attaching copies of a working paper which I submitted to the panel on cost estimates of nuclear power in comparison with conventional power costs.

The urgency of our need for nuclear power will intensify as total power requirements of the United States increase. Energy needs of this country have grown rapidly in the past and will grow more rapidly in the future. Sixteen years ago each man-hour of a production worker in manufacturing required 4.6 kilowatt-hours per man-hour. Today the requirement is 7.8 kilowatt-hours per man-hour. Fifteen years from now, according to *Electrical World,* it will be 14.1 kilowatt-hours. No one today can even begin to estimate how much the automation of production processes may increase the consumption of power per man-hour. Rapidly expanding uses for the light metals, especially in military applications, can create large new demands for power.

Reliable estimates of our future power needs show that in the next twenty-five years we probably shall have to add five times as much new capacity to the nation's installed generating capacity as the total capacity we have created over the past fifty years. From 115 million kilowatts today we shall need to expand to approximately 600 million by 1980. This is the forecast given to the panel by an industry group brought together to advise on this question.

A second and lower forecast of power requirements is also included in the panel report. This shows a need for only 360 million kilowatts by 1980. The panel concludes that actual requirements probably will fall somewhere between these two widely divergent forecasts.

Whereas the forecast of 600 million kilowatts by 1980 is based on a forecast issued by *Electrical World,* the lower forecast was made by the Federal Power Commission. The industry group that advised the panel would not accept the FPC forecast as a reliable basis for anticipating our future power requirements and it was supported in this by industry members of the panel's power seminar. The past record proves that the Federal Power Commission's forecasts of power requirements have consistently failed to anticipate the expansion of power consumption that has actually occurred. For example, the Federal Power Commission's estimate for the southeastern area of the United States for 1955 was 57 billion kilowatt-hours while actual power use in this area (excluding AEC consumption) was 110 billion kilowatt-hours, almost double the FPC forecast for 1955 and 32 per cent higher than its forecast for 1970. I do not think Federal Power Commission forecasts should be taken into account in appraising our future power needs.

A fivefold increase in power supply in twenty-five years presents a tremendous challenge. We should enthusiastically welcome the opportunity which the advent of nuclear power gives us to meet that challenge.

The necessary expansion of our dynamic economy must not be restricted or limited by a power deficit. Adequate power resources are essential for the economic growth that is needed to meet the possibility of war and to fulfill the opportunities of peace. The need to prepare today to meet tomorrow's requirements is an urgent and compelling one.

There are two other reasons why the need for nuclear power is urgent. The panel was advised that some informed observers question the capacity of our coal industry to meet competitively the enormous requirements that will be made upon it by the anticipated increase in electric power generation.

The other reason is the tremendous hunger of our economy, both in peacetime pursuits and in military operations, for liquid and gaseous fuels. There is no indication that our dependence on these fuels, especially for motive power, will decline. There is every reason to expect a large increase in demand.

The supply of liquid and gaseous fuels is exhaustible. The ultimate supply of atomic energy would appear to be almost inexhaustible. Every unit of oil or gas that can be replaced by atomic energy in the generation of electricity is, from a national point of view, money in the bank. This will be true of coal also when we decide, as we undoubtedly will, to develop the technology of converting coal into liquid fuels.

The big task before us is to achieve major technological breakthroughs in the construction and operation of full-scale demonstration power reactors, the fabrication of fuel elements and the reprocessing of spent fuels. Only by doing these things on a full-scale basis will we begin to find solutions that will lead ultimately to an efficient atomic power industry. Demonstration power reactors of all the promising types must be built, operated and put to the test.*

The AEC program for getting us through this development phase is to turn the primary responsibility over to electric utility companies, or groups of them, who in turn call upon manufacturers to contribute designs and build the components. While the

* W. K. Davis, director of the AEC division of reactor development, described in a speech on October 10, 1955, the nature of the full-scale development problem:

"The plain fact is that today we do not know how to do many of the things required for economically competitive power in the United States. . . .

"The construction of large prototype, or demonstration, reactor power plants is a very necessary step for a variety of reasons. For example, many features of power reactors simply do not scale up in a wholly predictable fashion. Therefore it is necessary to go essentially to full size to get certain technical data. In addition, it is impossible to estimate the cost of components, the cost of construction, or the cost of operating a power reactor with sufficient accuracy without building one. Until some of the steps are actually taken one simply cannot have a reasonable estimate of power costs in the new nuclear field.

"It is also necessary that someone build the first generation of fullscale nuclear power plants—a generation that will be relatively expensive—so that there will be the cheaper second, third, and following generations. The first prototypes of any power reactors will be expensive. The second will be simpler by virtue of experience gained with the first. Simpler and cheaper manufacturing methods will be learned and the expanding volume will still further reduce costs."

AEC will furnish information, assist in research and development, make nuclear fuel available at low rentals, reprocess spent fuel, and lend considerable financial assistance, it still requires private participants to take the basic risk and gives priority to proposals which impose the least financial burden upon the government.

AEC policy thus seeks to achieve two purposes at once: to promote the development of nuclear power, and to transfer to private enterprise a major part of the initiative and responsibility.

The panel report recognizes that it may not prove possible to achieve these two purposes simultaneously. It recommends that, in the event industry does not take on the full risks and burdens which the AEC has assigned to it, the AEC should construct a full-scale demonstration reactor of each major type and bring atomic power to a point where it can be used effectively and widely on a competitive basis.

In support of the panel's recommendations, I urge the Joint Committee to institute early inquiry in order to determine how far and how fast private enterprise can and will assume the full risks and burdens of getting us over the hump and on to the highroad of practical nuclear power.

I make this supplementary recommendation because so much evidence has come to light that indicates private enterprise cannot reasonably be expected to shoulder so much of the burden in this development phase. Tremendous capital investments and development expenditures are called for. The chance of incurring major losses through unsuccessful design or early obsolescence are considerable. Neither the AEC nor the manufacturers of reactors and components can give a utility system entering this field the kind of safety standards, performance guarantees, and other assurances which bankers financing a private venture normally require. The AEC will contribute substantial financial and other assistance, but the basic risk remains with the private participants.

The serious shortage of engineers and scientists trained in this field is another barrier to widespread participation of private industry in this development work. I shall discuss this question in a later section.

Another serious deterring factor with respect to private enterprise carrying the prime responsibility relates to the matter of classified information and national security. The panel properly recommended that "the Commission remove all reactor technology from the 'restricted data' category, including such areas as fuel element fabrication and processing techniques, leaving specific military applications of such technology to be protected in so far as national security is involved, by the defense classification system."

This delicate matter of national security versus free accessibility to secret data is a further factor discouraging private construction of full-scale demonstration reactors in this stage of the program.

The panel accurately reports that "no administrative agency can even give a guarantee that a private citizen has all the information needed for decisions and actions." For example, a private group might use the information available from the AEC to plan and build a reactor which already has been made obsolete by new information in reactor technology which the AEC cannot make available because it is in the restricted military category. Under these circumstances only the scientists, engineers, and technicians working on government projects can have free access to all of the latest data since they are working on both the military and the peacetime phases of the reactor program.

Manufacturers of equipment in this field have shown a great interest and undoubtedly have a vital contribution to make, but their experience and inventive qualities are brought into play only as they are engaged to join in the actual construction of a full-scale demonstration reactor. If the initiative in such construction is left in the hands of the private utilities at this stage of the program, the manufacturers' creative contribution will not be fully realized.

The utility companies are not powerfully motivated to develop new sources of low-cost power. The policies of state regulatory commissions assure them a fair return on their investment whether they expand or not, whether they increase power use through rate reductions or hold it back by keeping rates high. The incentive to them is rather to occupy the nuclear power field in order to hold it against the nonprofit public power systems. This is the motive ascribed to them by a dispatch to the *Wall Street Journal* from the "atoms for peace" conference at Geneva, August 22, 1955:

Officials of the companies which make reactors say frankly that most of their utility company customers have no early expectation of cutting costs by building atom plants; their primary motive is to stake this out as an area of private rather than public power.

The attempt by the AEC to transfer prime responsibility to private enterprise at this time appears to be premature. If, as a result, we continue to encounter serious delay in nuclear power development, we shall be guilty of pursuing a doctrinaire "free enterprise" approach to a problem which, at least for the present, is essentially national in purpose and scope and involves risks and losses of a magnitude which only government can reasonably be expected to incur.

The development of large-scale reactors is, essentially, an experimental operation—as fully experimental as the construction of the small research reactors for which the AEC is assuming the full responsibility and cost. If it is economically sound and proper for the government to bear the burden of primary research in building the small experimental reactors, it would appear to be equally sound and proper for the government to carry the major responsibility and risk in the second phase of experimentation—the building of full-scale demonstration reactors.

This view of the problem is confirmed by the views expressed by Gordon Dean, former Chairman of the AEC, in his book, *Report of the Atom,* published in the fall of 1953:

To help create the technological climate needed for further rapid progress, it is quite evident to me that the government, through the Atomic Energy Commission, must continue to play a significant and leading role in reactor development, not only for military purposes, but for general power purposes as well.

In close association with industrial groups, whether public or private, the Commission must, therefore, design and build and operate the forerunners of the large reactors which will some day feed appreciable quantities of electricity into the utility networks of the country.

Further indication that the government is better equipped than private enterprise to advance the development program can be found in the speed with which the AEC demonstration reactor at Shippingport, Pennsylvania, is being built, in contrast to the slow progress of private projects. Admiral Hyman Rickover, who built the reactor for the *Nautilus* and is in charge at Shippingport for the AEC, made this statement last December about that project:

We started constructing this plant in May of this year (1955). We expect to have it done in 1957. So you see that we are designing, developing, manufacturing, constructing and building an atomic power plant in generally less time than it takes to build a conventional power plant.

We do the utility companies no service by asking them to accept burdens which in view of all the unknowns in the present state of atomic technology they cannot finance as sound or normal business ventures. We do them no disservice when we ask the government to recognize the national importance and scope of the task at hand, to carry the basic risk of this full-scale reactor development, while affording the designing and manufacturing segments of private enterprise full opportunity to make their valuable contributions to the program.

The ingredients of the present situation do not add up to a formula for progress. If we want useful civilian atomic energy as soon as we can get it, both for domestic use and for international purposes, something must be done, starting immediately, to solve and overcome the many important technological problems that stand in the way.

Only bold initiative by government can accelerate needed progress and get full-scale reactors in operation so that the time lag between theory and practice can be minimized. Only when the government has completed both phases of this basic research work of completing and getting into operation both the model reactors and the full-scale demonstration reactors can we expect to get the influx of private risk capital and the resulting full impact of the dynamic qualities of individual initiative essential to carry the program to higher levels of development.

I hope that the ideological barrier will not be raised against my recommendation that the Joint Committee examine the AEC development policy with a view to putting the AEC to work building demonstration reactors, as the 1954 Act already authorizes it to do.

Neither government nor industry can do this job alone. It was the blending of the special contributions of each that provided the genius which gave America the atomic know-how to produce the first bomb. At this stage of our national atomic effort, nothing could be more tragic than to split our forces by engaging in a sterile and senseless fighting of ideological windmills. Our free enterprise system is not being challenged in America. If it were, less than 1 per cent of the American people would support such a challenge, for the American people understand clearly that our free economy motivated by individual initiative and enterprise has given them a higher standard of living than any other people enjoy. We must approach this problem free from preconceived prejudices or fixed theoretical or ideological positions. We need to make judgments on a sane and sensible basis as to how best we can, as a free nation and a free people, get the job done.

As the operation and testing of full-scale demonstration reactors begin to show how nuclear power can be produced on a commercially competitive basis, realistic and valuable business opportunities will arise.

Electric utility systems, both private and public, will then find it feasible to finance their investments in the generation and distribution of nuclear power as new capacity is required to serve areas where such power can be supplied at lower cost. This will create an expanding market for the manufacturers of reactors, fuel elements, and other components, and for others who equip themselves to perform the various service operations required by the new industry, such as fuel element fabrication and the reprocessing of spent fuels.

At this stage of development the declaration of Congress in section 1 of the 1954 Act deserves emphasis; namely, that it is the policy of the United States that "the development, use and control of atomic energy shall be directed so as to . . . strengthen free competition in private enterprise."

To make sure that this purpose is carried out, the attention of the Joint Committee should, in my opinion, be directed to three considerations that bear directly upon it.

One is the policy with respect to patents. Both to prevent monopoly and to encourage progress the Joint Committee should give consideration to a simpler and more expeditious procedure than section 153 of the Act now provides for the cross-licensing of all essential patents, so that the application of past discoveries and the stimulation of new ones will invigorate the atomic industry in the same way it has invigorated the automobile and radio industries. Atomic energy is a basic resource of the American people, developed for them at their expense by the government, and it must be put to the widest possible use in advancing the public interest.

The antimonopoly provisions of the 1954 Act also deserve the consideration of the Joint Committee. Section 105 of the 1954 Act permits the AEC to use revocation of license as an antimonopoly procedure only after adjudication of the facts in an antitrust proceeding. Thus this remedy is available only if court action is instituted and only when such action has been successfully concluded. This is taking action after the damage is done, usually long after, and it is likely to prove ineffective because of the delay. I suggest that the Joint Committee give consideration to amending the 1954 Act so as to give the AEC authority to take action when the danger is clear and such action is necessary, to prevent by revocation of license the consummation of monopoly control.

The third consideration I call to the attention of the Joint

Committee in connection with this Congressional declaration is the necessity for making competition possible in the sale of nuclear power.

Electric utility companies are not competitive enterprises. They are, and must be, local monopolies, franchised by state authority to serve defined areas and protected from competition within those areas. Their rates are set by state authority at levels calculated to provide a return on investment sufficient to attract the capital required to continue to serve the needs of their customers.

Long experience with electric power rates in the United States has demonstrated that the only effective competition which brings lower rates to consumers is the competitive yardstick that is applied to public power projects. The power policy of the United States government, and of state governments, has long recognized the right of the people to develop their power resources for their own benefit, acting through their federal, state, or local governments.

Experience has also demonstrated that the competitive rates of public power can stimulate greater consumption of electricity, speed up industrial progress, increase job opportunities, and raise the living standards of workers, farmers, and all consumers. It has also been demonstrated that electric utilities which, because of this competitive yardstick, sell power on a low-rate high-use basis find their own prosperity advancing along with that of the communities they serve, thus demonstrating the truth of the principle that there can be more prosperity in sharing abundance than in dividing scarcity.

No exceptional and artificial barriers should be erected against nuclear power. It should be permitted like any other power, where the people so elect, to fulfill its promise of bringing lower costs to areas where power rates are high. The estimates of future nuclear power costs given to the panel indicated roughly that nuclear power publicly produced could speed up by some ten years the relief from high power costs which nuclear power may be expected to bring.

The 1954 Act permits only limited application of the national power policy to the field of nuclear power. It does not allow the AEC to engage in the production or distribution of nuclear power for commercial use. This erects an exceptional and artificial barrier against nuclear power. If it stands, the full benefits of this new source of power will be denied to industry, workers, farmers, and consumers generally.

I suggest that the Joint Committee give consideration to amendment of the 1954 Act to bring it into harmony with national power policy by authorizing the AEC directly, or through a specially designated agency or division, to produce nuclear power for its own use, and to transmit, or arrange for the transmission of, such power to load centers, and to give nonprofit electric systems first call upon such power for sale to consumers at lowest possible rates.

The acute shortage of highly trained scientific, engineering, and specialized technical personnel is the most serious limiting factor in every phase of the program of applying the atom to peacetime uses. This is not a short-run problem. Failure to take effective and adequate steps now to make both a qualitative and quantitative solution will put in serious jeopardy our domestic economic growth and progress and will strip us of the ability to meet the responsibilities of world leadership.

Admiral Lewis L. Strauss, Chairman of the AEC, recently stated that America's colleges and universities are providing less than half of the people required in the fields of science and engineering in all classifications and that we are training less than one-third of the scientists and engineers needed in the field of atomic energy.

I believe that insufficient attention and urgency has and is being given this problem of assuring an expansion of our highly trained manpower base. The AEC program is being seriously delayed because it cannot get needed scientists, engineers, and technical personnel. Private industry by the attraction of high salaries is robbing the AEC of key scientific and engineering personnel and is depleting our already inadequate faculties of colleges and universities. The practice of robbing Peter to pay Paul has already inflicted an inestimable price in delaying our progress in harnessing the atom to man's peaceful needs. Only a realistic approach to our problem of training and education through expanded facilities, larger and adequately paid faculties, stepped-up scholarship programs, better apprenticeship courses, and other such measures can overcome this serious and costly manpower deficit. It must be recognized that the tax structure of both state and local governments and the financial problems of private schools make substantial federal aid to education essential if we are to remove the roadblocks and make our school system adequate to the challenge and equal to our needs.

I am confident that, as a free people, we can find a formula to provide federal aid to education without federal control. We need to reduce the size of our classes and to give greater attention to gifted students. We need to give greater attention to the curriculum of our secondary schools for they form the basis on which our higher schools of education build. Speaking in Cleveland in December, 1955, Admiral Strauss stated: "Our atomic progress will be determined primarily by the numbers of young people who study science and mathematics in our high schools and go on to college to become scientists and engineers."

We are losing precious and irreplaceable time for every year we fail to provide educational opportunities to facilitate to the fullest the growth and development of our youth. This loss cannot be recaptured. It is an asset gone forever.

The extension of human knowledge and the training of adequate numbers of competent scientists, engineers, and technicians can be decisive in freedom's struggle against the immoral forces of Communist tyranny. The seriousness of our national educational deficit is reflected in the fact that in 1955 American universities and colleges graduated twenty-seven thousand engineers and scientists, while it is reported that the Soviet Union graduated thirty-four thousand students in these fields. A reliable educator reports that the Soviet Union has approximately three times as many students in the fields of engineering and physical sciences enrolled in their higher schools of learning than does the United States and that the Soviet Union is doing a comparably qualitative job of training.

If these reports are true, this is a frightening and dangerous situation, for the struggle between freedom and tyranny is both real and for keeps. It is already clear that the Soviet Union is prepared to send scientific and technical personnel to foreign countries for purposes of economic penetration and subversion in greater numbers than we can afford for our program of economic aid and liberation from poverty.

Dr. James R. Killian, Jr., President of the Massachusetts Institute of Technology, as reported in *The New York Times,* January 24, 1956, recognized that Russia has outstripped the United States in the output of scientists and engineers. *The New York Times* reported that Dr. Killian urged the government to draft a master plan for maintaining the nation's technological lead in the face of swift Russian gains. Dr. Killian proposed a scientific commission for giving direction and velocity to our technological advance. He stated that the safety of the free world depended "increasingly on that combination of science, engineering, and industry which we call technology." Dr. Killian further noted Russia's long-range planning, her short lead time from idea to finished production, the percentage and monetary awards accorded her scientists, and her budget for her technological projects.

The shortage of highly trained scientific and technical personnel will continue to be the most serious retarding and limiting factor both in our domestic progress and in our ability effectively to carry out our responsibility of world leadership. Here again bold and imaginative action is needed by the federal government in cooperation with state and local governments in the field of education.

As a practical step in overcoming our educational deficit and manpower shortage, I would like to suggest that Congress give consideration to the creation of a broad and comprehensive system of federal scholarships to be awarded to students on a competitive basis. Such scholarships would be granted on condition that, upon the completion of their education and training, students would be obligated to serve wherever their training and skill was most needed. If their services were needed to help overcome the teacher shortage or the manpower needs of the AEC's military or peacetime atomic programs, they would be obligated to serve whenever assigned for a period of one year greater than, and in lieu of, the period of their normal military service. If their services were needed in the implementation of our foreign aid program, they could be assigned anywhere abroad for a period equal to, and in lieu of, the period of normal military service. Such a scholarship program would expand our trained manpower base and would enable tens of thousands of young Americans to develop the capabilities more effectively to serve their country and the cause of human freedom.

I believe that such a scholarship program would inspire thousands of our young people with a sense of democratic idealism and devotion and would afford them an opportunity to make a positive contribution in freedom's peaceful struggle against the forces of Communist tyranny. Such a program would enlist thousands of America's youth as technical missionaries in the struggle against man's ancient enemies—poverty, hunger, ignorance, and disease—and would strip the Communists of the opportunity of forging human desperation and poverty into power.

In the struggle for the hearts and minds of millions of yet uncommitted people in the economically underdeveloped portions of the world, the more young Americans we send to help as technical missionaries with slide rule, with textbook, and with medical kit to work in the pursuit of peace, the fewer we might need to send with guns and flame-throwers to resist Communist aggression on the battlefields.

Workers in atomic energy in installations exposed to ionizing radiations far above levels normally received from the natural environment must be protected by the adoption of federal standards fixing safe maximum limits of exposure, both on a short-time and cumulative basis, requiring full use of protective devices, and constant use of recording devices to accumulate the record of each worker's exposure, with the facts of that record available to the worker as a matter of right.

Compliance with these federal standards should be made a

condition of AEC licenses for the use of nuclear materials, with revocation of license available as a penalty for noncompliance.

Justification for high safety standards and their strict enforcement in this field derives from the unusual nature of the hazards incurred by workers exposed to radiation over a period of years. In addition to the more easily identified injuries resulting from brief exposure to severe radiation, the injury that can result from moderate overexposure continued for many years may not become apparent until long after the damage has been done.

Experts in the field state that shortening of life by a period of years may result; the victims will die of the usual causes that other people die of but they will die earlier.

Other experts report that genetic mutations adversely affecting the offspring of overexposed individuals may transmit undesirable human characteristics through many generations.

These are, or certainly should be, matters of grave concern for a nation that is about to enter into the age of the peaceful use of the atom in a large way. They should not cause hysteria. They do not require us to discard the atom as a too hazardous instrument for employment in industry, medical therapy, or research. But they do compel us to ascertain just as quickly and as surely as we can what the real hazards are, and, from the beginning, to exercise an excess of precaution until more is known about the hazards and how to guard against them.

This much is known already that justifies great concern about the course we are now following. We know, in the first place, that the National Committee on Radiation, acting under the auspices of the United States Department of Commerce, recommends maximum permissible exposure of 300 milliroentgens per week for persons under forty-five years of age, 600 milliroentgens for persons over forty-five. We know, in the second place, that the AEC has adopted a much more exacting standard than 300 milliroentgens per week for the protection of workers in its atomic installations. It has been publicly stated, for example, that the average exposure of all Hanford and Oak Ridge workers in 1949 was held down to 4 milliroentgens per week, as contrasted with the 300 figure permitted by the Department of Commerce. Weekly average exposure of the ten most highly exposed workers at Oak Ridge in 1949 was only 80 milliroentgens per week.

G. Hoyt Whipple, who was invited to discuss this subject at the Nuclear Engineering and Science Congress in December, 1955, asserted that workers subjected for a working life of thirty years to the maximum permissible exposure promulgated by the Department of Commerce would incur the risk of having their lives shortened, on the average, by three years. This, according to Whipple, is almost double the reduction of life span resulting from cancer that thirty-year-old males can anticipate, and more than three times the average number of years that will be subtracted from their lives by accidents of all kinds.

If every individual in a generation, Whipple's figures indicate, were subjected to an exposure of 65 to 130 milliroentgens per week over a working life of thirty years, the mutation burden of the next generation would be twice that which would normally occur.

Whipple recommended that the government standard promulgated by the Department of Commerce be reduced from 300 milliroentgens to 30 milliroentgens per week.

I do not doubt that almost any statement made today concerning the life-shortening and mutation effects of ionizing radiations can, and probably will be disputed. I have recited the above statements that have come to my attention not by way of proof, but to give my reasons for believing that the protection of workers in atomic industries must be given immediate and exhaustive study by unions, by Congress, by the government agencies concerned, and by industries which expose workers to atomic radiations. I hope that the Joint Committee on Atomic Energy will take the initiative, through hearings of its own or by other means, to ascertain the facts so that adequate standards to safeguard workers will be established and to remove unfounded fears that might impede progress.

India, the United States, and the Free World

Address before the Indian Council on World Affairs

New Delhi, India
April 5, 1956

My visit to India is the fulfillment of a long cherished dream. I have come to see and learn of your great achievements in building a new India. Word of your village development programs has inspired people everywhere as the most promising example of mass democracy at work in the world. Your River Valley Development Programs are the largest and boldest in the world. Your five-year plan is a practical demonstration of democratic economic planning at its best. I want to see these great and impressive economic achievements, but most of all, I want to meet and learn to know the people of India better so that I can in some small way help in building and enriching the friendship and understanding between the peoples of our two great countries.

In 1947, when you raised your flag of independence, millions of Americans shared the joy of your successful struggle for political freedom. Since that day, the American people have been inspired by your sense of devotion and dedication in your heroic effort to solve the problems of India through democratic methods which recognize the worth and the dignity of the human individual.

India and America have much in common. Both of our nations were born out of the sweat, the tears and the sacrifice of the common struggle to throw off the chains of colonial domination. Both of our nations were conceived and dedicated to the proposition that all men are created equal. Each of our nations contributed to the world and to the ages, two of the world's great moral giants, Gandhi and Lincoln. In an age of nuclear giants, we need more than ever a rededication to the human and moral values of both Gandhi and Lincoln, for neither peace nor freedom can be made secure in a world of nuclear giants and moral pigmies.

It is universally recognized that man has mastered the weapons of total self-destruction and that the H-bomb has made peace a condition of survival. To end war and to banish forever man's inhumanity to man, we need to develop a moral force in the world greater than the power of the H-bomb.

We live in the most challenging period in human history, for the same scientific and technical know-how that gives us the H-bomb and the weapons of total self-destruction also provides us with the tools of economic abundance. These new tools of economic abundance, if used constructively and morally to satisfy man's needs, his hopes, and his aspirations, can usher in an unprecedented period of human progress and human betterment.

The great challenge before us is to find a way to use the bright promise of science and technology in massive retaliation against poverty, hunger, and social injustice in the world.

For the first time in human history, mankind has the tools with which to master his physical environment. For the first time, we have the tools of economic abundance with which to eliminate poverty, hunger, ignorance, and disease—the ancient enemies which have plagued the human family throughout the ages.

As we satisfy man's basic economic and material needs of food, clothing, and shelter, we shall be able to devote greater time, energy, and resources to facilitate man's growth as a social, cultural, and spiritual being.

The greater dilemma in the world grows out of the developing moral and cultural lag between man's progress in the physical sciences and his lack of comparable progress in the human and social sciences.

We need to match our developing scientific, technical, and production know-how with a comparable human social and moral know-why.

With the harnessing of the atom to peaceful uses and other

scientific developments, the possibilities of human progress and human betterment appear to be as unlimited as the creative genius of the free human spirit. As this knowledge of mankind's new and productive tools spreads throughout the world, millions of hungry and desperate people are awakening to the realization that they need not live in poverty and misery.

Abraham Lincoln, in his profound wisdom, said that "America could not endure half slave and half free." In the world in which we live, peace and human freedom cannot endure with the world half well fed and half starving—half enjoying high material standards of living and the other half eking out survival on a subsistence diet.

The free labor movement of the world, which unites 53 million workers in Asia, Africa, Europe, South America, and North America in the family of the International Confederation of Free Trade Unions, is a great force for peace and freedom. Free labor understands and acts in the knowledge that the struggle for peace and the struggle for human freedom are inseparably tied together with the struggle for social justice. Free labor understands the social dynamics of our changing world. We understand the struggle of those who are hungry in their search for bread—of those who are oppressed in their search for freedom. We have geared our struggle not to be a negative program of anti-Communism but rather to a positive program for social justice. We believe that it is not enough to fight against the things that we oppose—we must fight with equal courage and equal dedication for the things that we believe in.

Free labor believes that no power on earth can stop the revolutionary forces that are loose in the world as men search for freedom and economic and social justice. There can be no doubt that the hungry will find bread. The question is will they find bread with freedom, with both national freedom and individual freedom? Winning national independence and political freedom is the first and an essential step toward winning individual freedom.

It is not enough, however, to substitute home-grown oppression for foreign oppression. Unfortunately, some national revolutions have won political independence but not political freedom for the individual.

India is the great hope of Asia and your revolution is the great lesson for other people who seek to win both national independence and individual freedom.

I worked in the Soviet Union as a worker in the Gorki automobile plant for eighteen months, and as a worker, not a tourist, I traveled over eighteen thousand miles throughout the Soviet Union including the Soviet Republics of Central Asia and Siberia. I worked with and I know and learned to love the Russian people. They shared the same hopes, the same aspirations, and they dream the same dreams as other people. They have made great progress in developing an industrial nation. No one can deny the fact that the people of the Soviet Union have gained a measure of economic progress and economic security. But no one who has lived and worked with the people of the Soviet Union can deny the harsh fact that while they have won more bread, they have not won more freedom.

Gandhi, with his sensitive appreciation of human and spiritual values, understood the tragic price that the people have paid for industrial progress. Gandhi said, "As I look to Russia . . . the life there does not appeal to me. To use the language of the Bible, 'What shall it avail a man if he gains the whole world and loses his soul?' It is beneath human dignity to become a mere cog in a machine. I want every individual to become a full-blooded, fully developed member of society."

The Communist way, in the Soviet Union or in the Chinese People's Republic, inevitably subordinates the worth and the values of the individual. On the other hand, India is committed to the democratic way which makes the worth and the dignity of the individual paramount.

We who are dedicated to the democratic way believe that we can so organize and develop our economic resources that it will be possible to provide bread for man's stomach without putting man's spirit in chains. It is this dedication to winning both bread and freedom that brings into sharp contrast the basic difference between the democratic and totalitarian approach to industrial development.

Viewed in the broad context of the human and democratic values that we as a free people cherish, India and America have a great deal in common. It is, however, both natural and understandable that between free independent and democratic nations, there can be differences. Democratic nations must seek and find unity in diversity, while Communists achieve unity through conformity.

In light of these broad principles, I should like to review briefly certain aspects of United States foreign policy.

First and foremost, the people of India need to always keep in mind that the American people are sincerely dedicated to the cause of peace. They want to work with men of good will everywhere in building a just and lasting peace. The question of peace transcends all other issues in the minds of the American people.

The other day, I heard an Iowa farmer complain bitterly about the low price he was receiving for his corn and hogs. But after complaining about his loss in income, he concluded that the important thing was that his son was still driving a tractor in peace rather than a tank in war.

The most popular speech President Eisenhower has made since he took office was his Atoms for Peace address before the United Nations in the spring of 1953 when he proposed that we harness the wonders of the atom for man's peaceful needs and that we work out a program to share these blessings with all people everywhere.

To understand America's position, it is necessary to review our actions following the last war. At war's end, when you in India were in the final phase of your struggle for political independence, America demobilized 15 million men and reduced its armed forces to almost extinction. David Lilienthal, the great administrator of our TVA system, who was in charge of our atomic progress, presented to the United Nations the United States' proposal for a system of universal control and inspection so that the power of the atom could be used to uplift mankind and not to destroy it. The Russians rejected this proposal and refused to agree to any system of effective control and inspection. This repeated rejection of an effective system of controls blocked the peacetime development of the atom and ushered in the nuclear arms race.

In 1948, despite the assault and the overthrow of Czechoslovakian democracy and the continuance of full Soviet military mobilization with two hundred divisions under arms, the American people still hoped for an understanding and America did not rearm.

A series of provocations culminating in the unprovoked aggression against South Korea finally shocked America into the cold war and the arms race. Because of these political realities, the American people have supported policies of military preparedness as a necessary means to meet the threat of aggression wherever it may raise its ugly head.

While I, like most Americans, have supported this policy of military preparedness, I have insisted, however, that military preparedness is but the negative aspect of a dynamic foreign policy. I believe that the struggle between freedom and tyranny is essentially a struggle for men's minds, and their hearts, and their loyalties, and that such a struggle cannot be won with military power but rather by a positive peacetime program of economic and social construction.

I believe, particularly, that freedom's struggle in Asia will be won primarily in the rice fields and not in the battlefields. Like many Americans, I have felt that United States foreign policy in Asia has placed undue emphasis upon military power, military pacts, and military alliances. This overemphasis on military power has, in my opinion, tended to trade reliable democratic friends for doubtful military allies.

As a step in the direction of achieving a proper balance in our foreign policy, I have recently submitted a proposal calling for the creation in the United Nations of a World Fund for Peace, Prosperity, and Progress. Under this proposal:

1. The people of the United States through their government would commit themselves to contribute to a World Fund a sum equal to 2 per cent of the gross national product of the United

States for a period of twenty-five years for the purpose of helping peoples of the economically less developed nations to help
themselves in developing their own economic resources and raising their standards of living, their standards of health, and their
standards of education.

This contribution by the United States would be made uncon-
ditional and without regard to contributions to the World Fund.

2. To give substance to and build upon the Geneva spirit,
the United States would request the USSR to make a similar
commitment to the World Fund for Peace, Prosperity, and
Progress, equal to 2 per cent of the gross national product of
the Soviet Union for a period of twenty-five years. All other nations able to contribute to the World Fund would also be urged
to contribute within the limits of their resources.

With both the United States and the USSR participating in
such a proposal, we could usher in an era of peaceful competitive
coexistence with each of our two social systems having an opportunity in terms of peacetime values to demonstrate its worth.
Thus the people of the world would have an opportunity to
measure political propaganda against practical performance.
Such a contest would demonstrate which economic and social
system could build and make available the most efficient nuclear
reactor for man's peaceful use rather than which could build the
most devastating nuclear bomb for man's destruction. In such
a contest of peaceful values, I am confident that the democratic
world has a margin of superiority, for only in an atmosphere of
freedom can the creative genius of the human spirit find full
expression.

3. The World Fund would be administered through the United
Nations either through existing special agencies or through the
creation of special new agencies so that the broadest possible
multilateral approach can be made to the problem of economic
and social construction.

4. America would commit itself to share its food abundance
with countries suffering from serious food shortage in a world
half fed and half starving. This sharing of our food abundance
over a long period, until the economically less-developed areas

of the world can adequately increase their own food supply, would, I believe, release a spiritual force of human solidarity which would be of greater power than all of the H-bombs in the stockpile.

Provisions could be made to ensure that the distribution of America's food abundance would be used to raise and improve the diets of needy people under arrangements that would not dislocate the economy of any country that exports grains or foodstuffs.

5. A scholarship program would be created for the purpose of training engineers, doctors, and technicians as America's contribution to a United Nations Technical Task Force to be used in helping people to help themselves develop their economic resources. I have been saying for a long time that I believe the more young Americans who are trained to join with other young people in the world to be sent abroad with slide rule, textbook, and medical kit to help people help themselves with the tools of peace, the fewer young people will need to be sent with guns and weapons of war.

6. I have proposed that United States economic aid be made available to every free and independent nation without any political strings whatsoever. Aid should be made available both in loans and outright grants on the basis of need, giving equal consideration to nations who choose to remain unaligned and those who choose to join alliances. I have admired the passion with which India has jealously guarded its political independence. India has pursued a policy of nonentanglement and nonalignment with other powers much like the policy outlined by President Washington in his Farewell Address and pursued by the United States at a time when we had just won our independence. Just as you sometimes are unable to understand United States policy, many Americans have not clearly understood your policy and the fundamental distinction which you make between your position of being unaligned and a position of neutralism. While India is unaligned, it certainly is not neutral on the great moral issues on which men and nations must take their stand.

7. I have further proposed that economic aid be made available immediately through the special agencies of the United Nations, through SUNFED, through the Colombo Plan, or through such other multilateral agencies created for this purpose.

Now you may well ask whether the American people will ever support such a comprehensive, long-range economic aid program. I can only say to you that in the American labor movement and in the ranks of forward-looking Americans in all walks of life there is growing recognition that the economic imbalance in the world must be quickly rectified as a necessity dictated by elementary human justice and as a precondition to enduring peace based on mutual respect. The American people have the will and the sense of moral obligation to take the price tag off our efforts at waging the peace, but unfortunately some of our political leaders are timid in exercising the leadership that the situation demands. I wish to assure you that this excessive emphasis on military preparedness does not reflect the heart of America. Americans are not military-minded. They want world peace above all and they know that peace must be built upon justice. Americans are, in short, predisposed by all their traditions to believe in international cooperation in its truest sense—which means a willingness to share generously so that all nations of the world may face each other as self-reliant, truly independent equals.

When the Gallup Public Opinion Poll asked recently whether food surpluses should be given to other nations, 82 per cent of the American people immediately responded affirmatively.

President Eisenhower's recent foreign aid message in which the sums requested reached nearly five billion dollars indicates that even now the level of our foreign aid spending is not too far below what I am advocating. The difference, of course, between present outlays and what I have proposed is that we are now caught up in a world atmosphere of suspicion and so therefore nearly 85 per cent of the foreign aid budget that the Administration is requesting will go to military purposes. If events justify a continuing relaxation in our fear of military aggression in the world, I am confident that this unfortunate military emphasis will give way to a realization that the real enemies we all face are poverty, hunger, disease, and economic despair.

With overemphasis on military preparedness molding certain of our policies in Asia, the true image of America has become beclouded in the world. Take the current case of India's rightful demand that Portugal withdraw from Goa as the British and French have already relinquished their colonial pockets in your country. All Americans can readily understand the rightness of your cause because the entire American national tradition begins with our own revolution against colonialism. I want to say as unmistakably as I know how that the American people are with you in your support of the Goa freedom movement. It is our failure to keep military considerations in their proper perspective which makes it necessary for me to stress this clarification. The United States and Portugal both belong to the system of defense cooperation against aggression which has been fashioned in Europe. The American people overwhelmingly support this defense system but I am sure they do not want their Secretary of State to permit this relationship with Portugal in Europe to distort American policy in Asia. Many Americans have been urging Secretary Dulles to place the United States on India's side against Portuguese intransigence in Goa so that the heart of America and the policy of the American government will be in unison.

This year America celebrates the one hundredth anniversary of the birth of Woodrow Wilson. Last week, a national public opinion poll published the results of its survey among the American people to determine how many would support Wilson's principle of self-determination for all peoples. The public opinion poll indicated that more than 80 per cent of the American people supported the principle of self-determination and agreed that the United Nations should create machinery for conducting elections in countries seeking self-determination. The poll of the American people related to the right of self-determination of people living both in countries controlled by nations friendly to the United States and in countries controlled by the Soviet Union. The American people are in full sympathy, and support the struggle of all people to be free, whether they struggle in Asia or Africa to free themselves of the old colonialism of European powers or whether they struggle to be free from satellite control of the new Communist imperialism.

The very day that the nations of Asia, Africa, and the Middle East gathered at the Bandung Conference marked the 180th anniversary of Paul Revere's famous ride which sounded the alarm that launched the American Revolution. For 180 years the American people have been conquering a wilderness, building a nation, and struggling to fashion a free society in the image of the principles of the Revolution. During these years, millions of people of all races, of all creeds, all colors from all over the world came to America as the land of promise. They labored in the vineyards of America at the practical task of giving substance to the principles that all men are created equal and that all are endowed with certain inalienable rights, among those being life, liberty, and the pursuit of happiness.

While much progress has been made toward the fulfillment of these dreams, there still remains serious unfinished work before the principles of the American Revolution of equality and justice for all are universally applied.

It is with sadness that I must report in all truthfulness that racial discrimination and bigotry still remain as ugly scars on the face of American democracy. In no aspect of American life is there such a serious moral gap between American democracy's noble promises and its ugly practices as in the field of civil rights. Millions of Americans, however, feel that this goal of achieving racial equality is a matter of compelling urgency and must be dealt with as an issue of highest priority on the agenda of American democracy's unfinished business.

Great strides have and are being made to square America's practical performance with its noble promises. During the past eighteen months the Supreme Court, the highest court in our land, has ruled that the practice of providing separate and equal school facilities violated both the letter and the spirit of the Constitution, and the Court has ordered that all schools must end segregation in education.

The present turmoil in certain sections of the South is a reflection of the great progress which America is making in the field of civil rights. The activities of extremist white racial groups who are resisting the implementation of the decisions of the Supreme Court represent the final desperate struggles of these racial bigots who see the handwriting of history on the wall.

Change always brings problems, but in this case the problems are a reflection of great progress in the direction of achieving racial equality and first-class economic and political citizenship for all Americans, regardless of race, creed, or color.

In the North, schools have been integrated for many years. In the South, as a result of the Supreme Court decision, many schools have already been desegregated. Other forms of segregation are under strong attack and the ugly and immoral forces of discrimination and segregation are in retreat on many fronts. Millions of American Negroes, through their participation and membership in free trade unions, have won higher wages and economic security and other benefits of equal job opportunity.

A tangible illustration of the great progress that has and is being made to win equality for all people is reflected in the marked change which is taking place in Detroit, Michigan, the headquarters of my union and one of the great industrial centers of America. In Detroit, we had the tragic experience of race riots in the early period of the war. Today, in the same Detroit, a Negro has been elected to our national Congress from a Congressional district which is predominantly white. Another Detroit Negro citizen has been elected to a judgeship in the highest local court by an overwhelming majority even though the Negro population in Detroit is but 20 per cent of the total population.

These are the signs of progress and more progress is in the making because American Negroes and millions of American white citizens are on the march against racial discrimination and intolerance.

In Montgomery, Alabama, the Negro population is struggling against the practice of discrimination on the community transportation system. Here Negroes are effectively waging a struggle of passive resistance in keeping with the spirit of Gandhi. This is not strange, for Gandhi himself first tasted the bitter experience of racial discrimination on his first train ride in South Africa as a youth. American Negroes have adopted the methods of struggle developed and used so effectively by Gandhi in the struggle for Indian independence.

The Reverend Martin Luther King, Jr., the leader of the struggle of passive resistance against the bus company in Montgomery, Alabama, reflected Gandhi's great influence when, following his arrest, he said:

. . . We have known humiliation, we have known abusive language, we have been plunged into the abyss of oppression, and we decided to rise up only with the weapon of protest. It is one of the greatest glories of America that we have the right of protest.

If we are arrested every day, if we are exploited every day, if we are trampled over every day, don't ever let anyone pull you so low as to hate them. We must use the weapon of love. We must have compassion and understanding for those who hate us. We must realize so many people are taught to hate us that they are not totally responsible for their hate. But we stand in life at midnight; we are always on the threshold of a new dawn.

Just as the moral and spiritual power of Gandhi won in India, so American Negroes shall win in America, and they shall take their place as free and equal citizens in the family of American democracy. America, like every other country, has had to face problems, but fortunately in a democracy in contrast to a totalitarian form of government, there are ways and means for making one's protest heard. There are procedures for correcting grievances and there are democratic means for winning justice.

The struggle against racial intolerance and racial discrimination and bigotry must be waged everywhere in the world wherever such immoral and ugly practices exist. We must learn to judge people, not by their color or race or creed, but rather by their worth as human beings. Racial equality should be established as a matter of simple justice and simple human decency. Each of us needs to understand that human freedom is an indivisible value and that in truth no one is really free until all men are free. If we are to protect our own individual freedom we must fight to make freedom universal for all men. When the immorality of racial intolerance denies the people of South Africa their freedom, a part of your freedom and a part of my freedom dies in South Africa.

The test of our courage and the test of our faith in freedom will be found not in the convenience of compromise, but in the challenge where the controversy is sharpest. Let us always bear in mind that freedom in the world in which we live is not a luxury but a tool to build with and a weapon to fight with.

Despite the many problems in our troubled world, I have unlimited faith in the capacity of free men to win through. The great challenge before us is to find a way to get people and nations working together in the positive and rewarding tasks of peace as they have repeatedly joined together in the senseless and destructive waging of war. I believe that free men united in common dedication can find answers to our complex and challenging problems.

In the great task of mobilizing the spiritual resources of the world for peace, India has made and can continue to make an important contribution and provide a powerful inspiration because of the great tradition of Gandhi and the consuming passion and determination of the Indian people for freedom and independence.

If the peoples of great nations can work, sacrifice, fight, and die together because they share common fears and common hatreds in war, why can we not find a way to tap the great spiritual reservoir that lies deep within each of us and get people and nations working, sacrificing, and building together in peacetime because they share common hopes and common aspirations. If we shape our policies in the image of our common faith instead of our common fears, I am confident that men of good will everywhere can march forward together, and together they can build a better tomorrow fashioned in the image of peace, in the image of freedom, in the image of justice, and in the image of human brotherhood.

Labor's Witness

Statement to the Senate Subcommittee on Privileges
and Elections

Washington, D.C.
October 9, 1956

*Following herewith is the complete text of the entire afternoon
session of the Subcommittee. During this session, Mr. Reuther
amplified his prepared statement in response to questions from
the Chairman, Senator Albert Gore, Democrat of Tennessee;
Senator Carl T. Curtis, Republican of Nebraska; and the Special
Counsel to the Subcommittee.*

SENATOR CURTIS: Mr. Reuther, do you have, do you publish,
a document called "The Voting Record of Congressmen and
Senators"?

MR. REUTHER: I gave a member of the staff of your Committee the copy which I think Senator Gore has just handed you.
It is a mimeographed voting record of the last Congress, dealing
with the votes in the Senate and the votes in the House. It is
just coming off the mimeograph machines and will be made available to a limited number of our leadership. It is not for mass
distribution.

SENATOR CURTIS: And they, in turn, publish it by other means?

MR. REUTHER: Well, if a local union gets a copy of this, and
they care to reproduce the section dealing with the voting record
of the Congressmen in the areas of their membership, that is, of
course, a matter which they can make judgment on.

SENATOR CURTIS: Now, Mr. Chairman, the reason that I ask
for this—I see that this voting record for Senator or Representative has a certain list of issues or bills included, and that after

143

the Senators' or Representatives' name, there is a "W" or a "R" indicating that they voted right or wrong.

Also, I want to call attention for the record that COPE's voting list likewise is a publication that says that a Congressman or Senator voted right or wrong on an issue.

I have here the ADA list voting record, and they use not an "R" or a "W," but a plus or minus, and a plus indicates a vote which ADA believes to be in harmony with liberal policies.

I call that to the attention of the Committee, Mr. Chairman, for the purpose of refuting any notion that the publication of a voting record is an educational, unbiased, informational service.

It is political service, intended to elect and defeat candidates, and as one member of this Committee, I am going to insist that it be so treated in reports.

Now, Mr. Reuther, will you secure for this subcommittee all the issues, beginning with the first of September and running through the election on November 6, all the newspapers of the local units of UAW or the shop papers that are issued by all local units on the state level or regional, or district level, and provide them for this committee?

Mr. Reuther: I should be most happy to try to cooperate. Some of the local unions just have little mimeographed throwaways. The printed ones, I think, we can get without too much difficulty.

But I hope you will also get all of the political propaganda put out by the NAM and the manufacturing groups.

Senator Curtis: I will not ask you to provide it.

Mr. Reuther: We would be glad to cooperate on that, though, too.

Senator Curtis: Now, you, this morning, came out for a limitation of five dollars on contributions. Are you acquainted with one Roy L. Reuther?

Mr. Reuther: I am. He happens to be my brother.

Senator Curtis: Did he in 1954 hold any position in a union?

Mr. Reuther: He did. He was on the staff of the UAW.

Senator Curtis: According to the Congressional Quarterly,

in reference to the 1954 election, Roy Reuther—I can't read the middle initial—is reported to have contributed five thousand dollars to the campaign of Senator Barkley of Kentucky. Is that a correct report?

MR. REUTHER: It is not. The UAW made such a contribution, but not Roy L. Reuther. He may have transmitted the contribution, but the contribution was the contribution by the UAW.

Roy Reuther does neither have the resources nor the inclination to make a five-thousand-dollar contribution.

SENATOR CURTIS: How about the reported contribution that he gave to the Democratic National Committee of one thousand dollars in the same year?

MR. REUTHER: I think you will find that that was a contribution of the UAW, and the method of purchasing some Jackson Day Dinner tickets; again, Roy Reuther's name was only associated with it because he, perhaps, transmitted it. This is just bad bookkeeping, that is all.

SENATOR CURTIS: Bad bookkeeping on the part of the Congressional Quarterly people?

MR. REUTHER: On the part of the people who submitted the records that, I suppose, the report you are talking about was based upon.

Roy Reuther has never made such a contribution either to the National Democratic Committee or any Senatorial candidate in any election, because he doesn't have that kind of resources.

SENATOR CURTIS: And that was UAW funds?

MR. REUTHER: That is correct. They were voluntary funds. They were contributions made up of voluntary dollars we received from citizens and from members of our union. They were not organizational contributions.

We have been very careful to make contributions in national elections or to the National Democratic Party only from voluntary dollars.

SENATOR CURTIS: Do those voluntary—was that money raised in Kentucky?

MR. REUTHER: Some of it was; it could have been. You must

remember that all of the money that we raise in terms of voluntary dollars, while it may come into COPE, comes from the several states. In Illinois, it comes from the people in Illinois; in Ohio, it comes from people in Ohio.

When we send it back, it is the same money except that we merely put it together in a central office of COPE in order to work out a more realistic distribution, based upon the needs of candidates.

SENATOR CURTIS: All right. I have covered what I wish in regard to these voting records as being campaign documents. Now I want to talk about radio programs. Are you familiar with the Guy Nunn show now running in Michigan and surrounding states?

MR. REUTHER: I am familiar with the radio program which our union established some years ago, which is a public service.

SENATOR CURTIS: Now, that program—

MR. REUTHER: May I finish the answer?

SENATOR CURTIS: No, I just asked you whether you were familiar with it.

SENATOR GORE: You would not mind him, if he has something further, to answer?

SENATOR CURTIS: All right, go ahead.

MR. REUTHER: I was merely trying to point out, Mr. Chairman, that we established these radio programs some years back. They have nothing to do with campaigning as such; that we spend as much money on these radio programs in nonelection years as we do in election years, so that this is not an election-year proposition.

SENATOR CURTIS: All right. Who pays for Guy Nunn's program called "The Eye Opener" that is broadcast in the early morning?

MR. REUTHER: The UAW pays for those broadcasts.

SENATOR CURTIS: Out of which funds?

MR. REUTHER: We pay for them out of organizational funds.

SENATOR CURTIS: In other words, dues money?

MR. REUTHER: That is correct. Just like General Motors pays for their national broadcasts.

SENATOR CURTIS: Did they pay for the Guy Nunn "Eye Opener" program that was broadcast on September 20, 1956?

MR. REUTHER: We pay for all of the "Eye Opener" shows.

SENATOR CURTIS: Out of dues money?

MR. REUTHER: Out of organizational money.

SENATOR CURTIS: Where do those programs originate?

MR. REUTHER: Well, they originate partially in Detroit. I am not sure exactly how much time is used locally, but the program is geared to permit local people to come in on a portion of the show. It is a thirty-minute radio program. The major portion originates in Detroit, but each locality can take over a portion of the program to discuss purely local matters or report on local developments or local union news and things of interest.

SENATOR CURTIS: What is the name of the station where Guy Nunn speaks from?

MR. REUTHER: CKLW.

SENATOR CURTIS: And that is in Canada?

MR. REUTHER: That is a station in Windsor, Ontario, which is across the river from Detroit.

SENATOR CURTIS: Any particular reason why these broadcasts originate outside the United States?

MR. REUTHER: No reason at all, other than we were able to get time there both on radio and television, where we had great difficulty getting it.

You must remember that sometimes we can't even buy an ad in the Detroit papers, and they control some of the radio and television stations. This is something else that bears investigation.

SENATOR CURTIS: All right.

MR. REUTHER: So it is a matter of convenience.

SENATOR CURTIS: I have here a copy of that "Eye Opener" program, broadcast at 6:15 A.M., on September 20, 1956, which was paid for out of union dues by Republicans and Democrats alike, and they had to pay it or lose their jobs.

MR. REUTHER: Well, I challenge that, of course. Senator Curtis, you are entitled to your prejudices, but you are wrong on this one.

SENATOR CURTIS: All right. This program, I have listened

to it as well as I have read it. After an opening, it brought in the voice of Adlai Stevenson, and Stevenson's voice is carried for some time.

Among other things, he said:

"Responsible union leaders have proposed programs for industrial rehabilitation and aid to the distressed areas.

"The Democratic platform endorses these proposals. Senator Paul Douglas of my state, and other Democrats, have already introduced bills in Congress to establish such programs.

"I know that when Congress reconvenes they can, with the White House endorsement that they have lacked so far, be enacted into law."

Then, in this same program which presents the voice, the arguments of one candidate, it goes on and has something to say about Mr. Stevenson's opponent, and I am quoting now, I believe, what appears to be the words of Guy Nunn:

"You know, there is one big issue in this presidential campaign that the Republicans are not talking about, openly at any rate. As a matter of fact, the Democrats are pretty quiet about it, too. But the people, voters all over America, are talking about it and thinking about it plenty. That issue is the state of health of President Eisenhower.

"Last year the President had a very serious heart attack. Early in June of this year he underwent emergency surgery for a severe illness.

"The Republican medicine men, Leonard Hall and others, insist that the President is now in better shape than he was before his heart attack and before the ileitis operation," and so on.

Now, the point is, I do not think the American people are being fooled. Regardless of whether or not the Congress needs to revise the laws in defining political contributions, the facts are that those things are political advertising carried on to elect candidates and to defeat other candidates.

There again, as one member of this Committee, I am going to insist that they be so reported.

MR. REUTHER: May I comment on that?

SENATOR CURTIS: Briefly. [Laughter] My time is limited to forty-five minutes. I listened to you all morning.

MR. REUTHER: I am willing to stay longer than you are.

SENATOR CURTIS: All right. We will come back at five o'clock.

SENATOR GORE: Let us see what happens.

MR. REUTHER: Mr. Chairman, this really resolves itself down to a very simple but very fundamental constitutional matter. I do not object or quarrel with Senator Curtis' right to his opinion. This matter is before the courts. On every occasion on which they have been asked to rule upon this basic constitutional matter, they have ruled that any group has a right to free expression.

Now, you can question a fellow's judgment on whether what he said on the radio was good, whether it fooled anybody, or whether it didn't fool anybody, but that is really not the question.

The question is, does a person have the right to express himself?

Now, we are labor unions. We buy radio time and we express our point of view on the issues, as we have a constitutional right to do.

We express our preference on the candidates, as we have a constitutional right to do.

When *Life* magazine, which is a corporation, endorsed President Eisenhower, as it did in the last issue, they have a right to do that constitutionally.

When the *Detroit News,* which is a corporation, does the same thing on the front pages, they have a right to, and we have the same constitutional right as a trade union to put out our publications, to buy radio time, to buy television time, to express our point of view on the issues and our preference on the candidates.

Until the Supreme Court of these United States, which has always held that we have that right, changes that, we are going to continue to exercise that right whether Senator Curtis thinks it is proper or improper.

SENATOR CURTIS: All right now, Mr. Chairman—

MR. REUTHER: Because this is a fundamental matter of constitutional liberties, and the right of freedom of speech. This is what is involved here, and if Senator Curtis wants to talk about spending workers' money who are involuntarily boxed in, as he would put it, and they will lose their jobs if they don't contribute, I am prepared to talk about that sensibly and based upon what the facts are.

SENATOR CURTIS: Now, let us get the record straight. No one has raised the question or am I proposing on my part to restrict free speech or in any way limit or criticize any group or individual or organization from political campaigning.

I do raise two questions in regard to this: One is that when they engage in political campaigning, to call it such and so report it.

MR. REUTHER: Would you say that *Life* magazine is engaged in political activity when they endorse candidates in a six million circulation magazine, subsidized by second-class mailing privileges? Are they engaged in political action?

SENATOR CURTIS: Listen, you are not questioning me.

MR. REUTHER: I would like to have your opinion. I would like to be enlightened about this matter.

SENATOR CURTIS: No, you are not—

MR. REUTHER: Are they, or aren't they?

SENATOR GORE: Well, a member of the Senate is not required to respond to questions.

SENATOR CURTIS: No, I do not.

MR. REUTHER: I would just like to know, Mr. Chairman, Senator Curtis' point of view.

SENATOR CURTIS: Well, I think you know it quite well. You are one of the most influential members of the Democratic Party.

MR. REUTHER: I am not a member of the Democratic Party.

SENATOR CURTIS: You come in here with an array of aides and legal counsel and your own television setup and your own motion picture setup the likes of which have never been seen in the history of the Congress.

MR. REUTHER: Well, we can't get you people to come on our station, so we figure we will make a movie and put it on. [Laughter]

SENATOR CURTIS: You come here with all this array—

MR. REUTHER: Will you come on our stations?

SENATOR CURTIS: You come here with all of this—yes, I appeared before your program once.

MR. REUTHER: I am asking, will you come on our television and radio programs? You substituted for Senator Goldwater the other time, maybe you will do it now.

MR. MAZEY [Secretary-Treasurer of the UAW]: We would like to ask you some questions, Senator Curtis.

SENATOR CURTIS: I see. We will talk about that at a later time (laughter) but you are with the CIO-AFL merger—

MR. REUTHER: Right.

SENATOR CURTIS: It represents the greatest merger in our industrial history. It represents the greatest economic force, and, as I say, your appearance here in all of its kingly splendor has never been equaled in the history of the Congress.

MR. REUTHER: You dazzle me; you dazzle me.

SENATOR CURTIS: You are the man that makes or breaks presidential aspirants in the Democratic Party.

MR. REUTHER: You are now flattering me, and I don't like that.

SENATOR GORE: Most people do. [Laughter]

SENATOR CURTIS: I ask merely that if a broadcast is a political broadcast that it so be reported. If I have said anything at any time that would indicate that I wanted to interfere with free speech or the right of expression, I certainly never intended it.

MR. REUTHER: Your bill, we think, does that, Senator Curtis.

SENATOR CURTIS: I beg your pardon?

MR. REUTHER: We believe that the practical aspects of your bill would be to limit our right to freedom of expression.

SENATOR CURTIS: No. I think you people are approaching this from a very reactionary point of view. [Laughter] The most sacred thing in this country is the right of the individual, and he may be in a minority or only one, but if he has to work under conditions of compulsory union membership so that the minute he stops paying his dues he is out of a job, that money should never be used to champion political causes and candidates in which he does not believe.

It is forcibly taking his money away. It is totally disregarding the rights of minorities as well as individuals, and I think the practice is most reactionary.

Now, I want to ask you something else.

MR. REUTHER: May I address myself to that question, because that is the nub of the problem?

SENATOR CURTIS: I didn't ask you a question.

MR. REUTHER: Except that you throw out a lot of things here that are untrue.

SENATOR CURTIS: Oh, no.

MR. REUTHER: And then you don't give a person a chance to answer it.

SENATOR CURTIS: I didn't throw out anything untrue.

MR. REUTHER: I can prove they are untrue if you will give me a couple of minutes.

SENATOR CURTIS: Oh, no.

MR. REUTHER: I can do it in less time than that if you give me a chance.

SENATOR CURTIS: No, you can't.

MR. REUTHER: Why don't you give me a chance?

SENATOR CURTIS: You have had all your chance.

MR. REUTHER: But you are making speeches and then say it is not a question. You say workers get discharged. You say they are captives; you say we are abusing the rights of the individual minority if there is only one worker, and I can prove to you that that is not true if you will give me a couple of minutes' time.

SENATOR CURTIS: I do know—

MR. REUTHER: If you won't give me time then I will have to find another way to let the people know.

SENATOR CURTIS: I do know that when the UAW takes dues money and carries the voice of Adlai Stevenson in a favorable light and carries criticism of President Eisenhower, that that is using their money against their wishes and contrary to their individual views of some of them, and it is overriding the rights of minorities and, furthermore, I believe it is in violation of law.

MR. REUTHER: Well, I would like to answer by saying that,

first of all, it is not a violation of the law, nor does it violate any basic human relationship between free men. I would like to direct your attention to a communication sent out to every one of our local unions, which was reproduced in *The United Automobile Worker* so that every member of our union received a copy in his home, saying that if any member disagreed with what we were doing with our citizenship funds in the way of political activity, that individual worker could notify us, and that money would be diverted to some public charity, or nonpartisan group, such as the American Heritage Foundation, or some similar group.

Now, that simply means this: Although what we are doing is adopted by a unanimous decision of the union at its various levels, if that one individual worker you are talking about feels that the expenditure of these citizenship funds is for purposes contrary to his desire, he can request that the ten cents earmarked in that citizenship fund will go to the American Heritage Foundation, the Heart Fund, or any other such group.

SENATOR CURTIS: He still has to support your union to hold his job.

MR. REUTHER: He has to help pay for—

SENATOR CURTIS: To have a union shop.

MR. REUTHER: He has to help pay for the cost of collective bargaining, but he does not have to help pay for politics; that is the thing you are arguing about.

SENATOR CURTIS: No, I am not opposed to unionism, but I think that if any union is going to spend money for political purposes or going to divert money to other groups that that union ought not to be allowed a union shop. It should be a voluntary association.

MR. REUTHER: Do you know what votes we have in our industry for the union shop? Do you know that eighty-eight thousand Ford workers voted for the union shop, according to the NLRB, as compared to one thousand? That in General Motors, when we got our final modified union shop, there were less than 1/2 of 1 per cent of the workers outside of our union? You would have people believe that we drove them in with clubs.

Senator Curtis: Oh, no.

Mr. Reuther: They came to be liberated. We liberated the workers in this industry. We didn't enslave them. A little insignificant minority that wouldn't pay a dime for anything wants a free ride. They want their fellow workers to pay for the cost of arbitration and medical doctors, and so forth.

Senator Curtis: The discussion here isn't whether a union shop is good or not.

Mr. Reuther: What is the discussion?

Senator Curtis: The discussion is if you have compulsory union membership clauses that you shouldn't use that money for political purposes.

Mr. Reuther: May we put this in the record, Mr. Chairman? This is the letter that, if I had time, I would read, because it says in simple, understandable language that if a member of our union feels that there is an improper use of his ten cents, this citizenship money that we are talking about that is used for political activities, if it is not being properly used, he can notify us and we will divert his contribution to whatever public charity he indicates.

Now, that meets completely the charge that Mr. Curtis has made. I have another letter I would like to put in. It is from a Republican member of the New Jersey State Legislature. He happens to be the president of one of our local unions, with five thousand members; he happens to be the Republican who was designated by President Eisenhower to be a member of the White House Conference Committee on Education. He is a very prominent Republican, making speeches all over the country for the Republican Party, and his letter gives lie to these people who are trying to slander our union in order to try to undermine the confidence of our membership.

I would like to put this in the record since Mr. Curtis won't let me read it.

Senator Gore: Mr. Curtis, I don't believe, has declined to let you read that specific letter.

Mr. Reuther: May I read it, Senator? I think it is of general interest to everyone. It is a very short letter.

SENATOR CURTIS: It isn't in response to any question I have asked.

MR. REUTHER: But it has a bearing on your charges.

SENATOR CURTIS: Now, listen, you misconstrue my charges. I haven't attacked unionism nor the union shop.

What I am talking about is taking people's money forcibly and turning it over to the Democratic Party and Democratic candidates.

MR. REUTHER: We are not doing that.

SENATOR CURTIS: Well, I think you are.

MR. REUTHER: You can be wrong on this as you are—

SENATOR GORE: The two letters will be printed in the record, and if, after Senator Curtis has concluded, the witness desires the letter to be read, I would be delighted to let him read them.

MR. REUTHER: That is quite agreeable.

SENATOR CURTIS: Are you familiar with the publication called "Local 600 Ford Facts?"

MR. REUTHER: I am, sir.

SENATOR CURTIS: I want to read a paragraph from the October 22nd issue, 1955. It says:

"The Wayne County CIO Council has endorsed John Dingell in the Democratic primary election in the Fifth Congressional District to be held on November 8, 1955. Approval is requested of the Council for concurrence in the above endorsement and also to authorize the local officers in line with past procedure to incur and pay the expenses in connection with said election."

What I want to ask you is, who comprises the Wayne County CIO Council?

MR. REUTHER: The Wayne County CIO Council is the central body of the CIO unions in the greater Detroit area which, essentially, makes up the County of Wayne.

Each local union, each UAW local, each Steelworkers local, each Clothing Workers local, each Rubber Workers local, all of the CIO-affiliated unions have direct representation on the central body from each of its affiliated local unions.

SENATOR CURTIS: Now, what does this mean, "in line with

past procedure to incur and pay the expenses in connection with said election?"

MR. REUTHER: Well, I think I can explain that this way:

First of all, the people in that Congressional district have a meeting and they make the decision in the form of a recommendation to the central body of the Wayne County Council.

The Wayne County Council then votes to approve the recommendation that comes out of the Congressional district, and after the Wayne County Council does that, then the local unions having membership in the Congressional district involved— in this case I think it was an election because of the death of Congressman John Dingell, Senior—act upon the recommendation of the Wayne County Council, and this action on the part of Local 600 was merely to authorize the local union to do the normal things of getting out material, advertising the campaign, trying to get people interested in the campaign and doing what they could in that respect to try to get people to support that candidate, expressing themselves on the issues and expressing their preference on the candidates.

SENATOR CURTIS: And the expense is the expense in connection with that?

MR. REUTHER: That is right. It means if they printed a leaflet in the plant in which they said that "young John Dingell was running and that his father had a good record and we know that he would do the same kind of a job in terms of the basic interest of working people, then we urge you if you live in this Congressional district to support his candidacy."

It means authorizing that kind of an expenditure.

SENATOR CURTIS: Now, what is a candidate committed to if he has your endorsement?

MR. REUTHER: He is committed to do nothing more than to follow the dictates of his own conscience and his good judgment in voting for the kind of legislation that will enable America to provide the things we need, and to meet the challenge it faces in the world.

We do not in any way ask for patronage; we do not in any way ask for commitments. We vote for people because we believe they stand on the right side of issues, and we hope that they will have the integrity to carry out the kind of leadership in Washington that will give America a good clean government for all the people.

We didn't get anybody on the Cabinets when we used to win the national elections, and we didn't ask for anything.

SENATOR CURTIS: Now I want to read from the ticker tape of one of our wire services of February 16, 1956, a statement in reference to or a statement of Representative Don Hayworth, Democrat of Michigan.

"Representative Don Hayworth, Democrat of Michigan, said he had been threatened with loss of CIO labor union support because he voted against a Democratic bill to restore rigid farm price supports.

"He called a news conference to make the announcement. He said the threat was raised six days ago at a meeting at Lansing, Michigan, attended by many CIO union leaders and six members of the Ingham County Democratic Committee.

"Hayworth said he turned down the labor officials' demand that he reverse his position. He said that would have meant breaking a promise he made during the 1954 campaign that on farm legislation he would vote the way a majority of the farmers in his District wanted him to vote."

Mr. Reuther, were you present at that Lansing meeting to which Don Hayworth refers?

MR. REUTHER: I was not.

SENATOR CURTIS: Then I won't ask you anything about that.

MR. REUTHER: All I can say is that he has our endorsement in this election, despite the fact that he didn't change his vote, and he should not have changed it. He was voting his conscience. He was carrying out a commitment made honorably, and anyone who tried to force him to change it was wrong.

I think the proof of the pudding is in the eating. We are supporting him this time and he didn't change his commitments.

SENATOR CURTIS: Now I have an article here from the October 6th issue of the *AFL-CIO News*, this year.

MR. REUTHER: Pardon me; what was the date of that, sir?

SENATOR CURTIS: October 6th. It says:

"New York unions waging vigorous campaigns.

"New York. Some of the state's largest unions are waging vigorous campaigns to elect the Stevenson-Kefauver-Wagner ticket.

"To list them all would be impossible. To select a few is to give a general idea of what the many are doing.

"The Ladies Garment Workers, always active in political campaigns, has launched its community captain program to spur registration. The ILGWU program is coordinated with COPE's and dollars are coming in better than ever before.

"The Brotherhood of Electrical Workers has played an active role, devoting time and effort to boosting the team.

"Throughout the state, the Auto Workers are making registration drives. In addition, UAW has a giant trailer which tours the state in advance of flying visits by Wagner, Governor Harriman, and Senator Lehman."

May I ask how that is financed?

MR. REUTHER: The trailer?

SENATOR CURTIS: Yes.

MR. REUTHER: I presume it is one of the trailers we have in the East for organizational purposes.

It is being used in the registration drives and trying to get people aroused about the issues. That is paid for out of organizational funds. That is a part of this right of free expression, just using the truck and sound equipment to help do it.

SENATOR CURTIS: I just asked who was paying for it.

Then I read this sentence where it says, "throughout the state the Auto Workers are working on registration drives."

How is that paid for?

MR. REUTHER: Registration drives?

SENATOR CURTIS: Yes.

MR. REUTHER: As I said earlier this morning, we are encouraging our people to do everything humanly possible. I showed you the ads we ran in papers throughout the United States. We are spending as much money as we can afford. We are trying to mobilize as much manpower as we can mobilize to try to achieve the highest maximum registration on the part of citizens in this country so that they can discharge their citizenship responsibilities.

Our only apology is, as I said this morning, that we aren't able to do more.

SENATOR CURTIS: Now, has any labor group or any labor educational group, gotten out a publication concerning the President's health?

MR. REUTHER: Not to my knowledge; and I think if they do they are making a very serious mistake, both in terms of what I think are just ethical standards as well as political tactics. To my knowledge, nothing like that has been done, and if I were asked about it, I would do everything in my power to stop it.

I think that there are things floating around America which just shouldn't be floating around. The President repudiated this little comic book the other day put out by the Republicans, but it is still being mass-distributed in Detroit. I think that that is wrong, and if anybody else does that sort of thing, that is equally wrong as far as I am concerned.

SENATOR CURTIS: Now, this Guy Nunn program, is that paid from a special radio account or from an educational account, or what is that paid from?

MR. REUTHER: I think that that is paid out of the general funds of the union, its organizational money, its dues money.

SENATOR CURTIS: What is your editorial fund? What is that?

MR. REUTHER: Well, our constitution, Senator Curtis, earmarks five cents of each member's monthly dues, and that is to pay for our monthly publication, called *The United Automobile Worker*.

That is a special fund that covers the costs of the publication of our house organ.

SENATOR CURTIS: Do you have a few copies of that with you?

MR. REUTHER: No, but I can make copies available.

SENATOR CURTIS: And is that distributed to your members?

MR. REUTHER: That is mailed to the membership each month.

SENATOR CURTIS: Does the UAW endorse somebody for President?

MR. REUTHER: Well, I told you this morning that we had

what we called an election year conference on September 15th at which we had approximately three thousand local union officers from thirty-six states; and after discussing the issues all day, they voted by secret ballot, with the press there watching the ballots being cast and voted; they voted 97½ per cent for Stevenson and Kefauver, less than 1 per cent for Eisenhower and about 1¼ per cent for no endorsement at all.

So the UAW has made an endorsement by this broad rank-and-file leadership conference with representatives from thirty-six states.

We thought this ought to lay to rest this whole idea that these things are all dictated from the top down by the powerful labor bosses.

SENATOR CURTIS: Well now, from this editorial fund, that you publish this paper with, do you advance the cause of Stevenson and Kefauver, the Stevenson-Kefauver ticket?

MR. REUTHER: We will report, as I think we have already done in the last issue, the results of this conference and the reasons why.

SENATOR CURTIS: I mean the columns and the material carried?

MR. REUTHER: This is the case that Mr. Murray tested when the *CIO News* endorsed a candidate, I think, in Maryland, and this case went to the Supreme Court, and the Supreme Court upheld our constitutional right to do just the same as *Life* magazine is able to endorse Mr. Eisenhower.

SENATOR CURTIS: I am not questioning anybody's constitutional rights to say anything they want to. I want to live in a country where we can criticize anybody, the umpire or the President of the United States or anybody else.

MR. REUTHER: The Supreme Court happens to be the umpire in this case, and they ruled in our favor.

SENATOR CURTIS: Yes. But I do think that political expenditures should be in conformity with the law, and I do think they should be reported.

MR. REUTHER: We tell you what we are spending here and

we aren't running away from this. Under the law we are permitted to do this.

SENATOR CURTIS: I think not, Mr. Reuther.

MR. REUTHER: The Supreme Court ruled in the Murray case that what the CIO had done was proper.

It ruled in the case of the radio time purchased by the Painters Union in Connecticut that it was proper.

The Judge of the District Court in the case of the UAW ruled it was proper; and the Supreme Court will rule it is proper because this is a fundamental matter of freedom of speech, and whenever anyone attempts to tamper with that, you tamper with it as it relates to labor, and at that point you begin to eat away the basic right of all of the American people, because freedom of speech is an indivisible value. You cannot have it excepting I have it; I can't have it unless you have it, and you cannot begin to infringe upon our right to free speech without destroying the basic rights.

SENATOR CURTIS: Mr. Reuther, that is a convenient smoke screen to charge you with wanting to interfere with your right of free speech. What I am trying to say is that if someone buys radio time and lauds one candidate and criticizes another one, that it ought to be reported as a political expenditure.

MR. MAZEY: Maybe you ought to call Fulton Lewis, Jr., before this Committee.

MR. REUTHER: Fulton Lewis, Jr., does this every day, and he has a right to. *Time* magazine has a right to; *Life* magazine has a right to. If you will ask them to report those expenditures— you figure out what it would cost to get an endorsement in *Life* magazine, with a six million circulation, and have them report it as a political expenditure. You have no argument with me, but you cannot look the other way when big business does it, and look in this direction when we do it.

I stand for one standard of political conduct in America, not two standards.

SENATOR CURTIS: Well, no one is finding any fault with that.

MR. REUTHER: Well, is Mr. Luce coming down here to be

asked why he didn't report that *Time* magazine and *Life* magazine endorsement?

SENATOR CURTIS: You are responsible for the conduct of the UAW, and that is what we are talking about now.

MR. REUTHER: Yes, but are you going to get the other people in?

SENATOR CURTIS: According to your testimony here I can see no reasonable interpretation but what there are many political activities that are paid out of union funds, dues, money, in violation of the statute, and contrary to the wishes of at least a minority, and I think a much bigger minority than you realize, of your members.

MR. REUTHER: Well, I can say, Senator Curtis, that when the membership of our union received this letter, as each member did, if what you say is true, there would have been a tremendous avalanche of workers saying, "I want my money diverted to some charitable organization."

Mr. Chairman, I would like to report that we only received one letter from more than one and a half million members, and if this large minority was in a state of revolt, that we are told they are, certainly more than one worker out of a million and a half would have made his wishes known.

This particular worker wrote in and asked that his money be turned over to the American Heart Foundation, one member out of one and a half million.

I wish Mr. Curtis could have stayed for this letter, and I would like to read it now, if I may, Mr. Chairman.

SENATOR GORE: I think in fairness to Senator Curtis that it should be recognized that he was operating against a deadline. I am sure he was not reluctant to hear the letter.

MR. REUTHER: I understand.

SENATOR GORE: It was a matter of time, and the Chairman will be pleased to hear you read the letter now.

MR. REUTHER: Thank you. This letter is the result of the fact that the Chairman of the Republican State Committee in the State of Michigan, Mr. John Feikens, has been carrying on a continuous running battle with our union, in which he has willfully, we believe, misrepresented the facts.

He has tried to make it appear that we are spending or we were spending all of our income and all of our money for political activities, which is not the case, and this letter was directed to Mr. Feikens to try to clarify this particular situation.

SENATOR GORE: Mr. Reuther, when you say "willfully," I think you must recognize that there is not a real opinion—it is a matter of disagreement. No member of the Senate in my years of service will willfully misrepresent anything. He may have a different opinion.

MR. REUTHER: I am talking about Mr. John Feikens.

SENATOR GORE: Oh.

MR. REUTHER: I am talking about Feikens, the Chairman of the Republican Committee in the State of Michigan whom we have given the facts to, and who just ignores them and goes on his horse misrepresenting the facts.

This letter was directed to Mr. Feikens on October 4, 1956, by a fellow Republican who has been working with Mr. Feikens.

Now, this person happens to be the President of Local 300 of our union. His name is Thomas Lazzio, and he is a member of the Legislature in the State of New Jersey, a Republican member, for five years.

He is very active in Republican politics. He has been speaking all over the country for the Republicans, and he was the appointee of President Eisenhower on the White House Committee on Education, and here is what he wrote Mr. Feikens:

"Dear Mr. Feikens:

"I recall having spoken to you about a matter which has disturbed me, accordingly I rechecked this procedure thoroughly.

"You questioned the legality of the use of our COPE moneys. I want you to know that I am firmly convinced that there is no misuse of these funds.

"As the president of UAW Local 300, comprising a membership of some five thousand office workers and engineers, it is in my experience to know that both the method of raising money for our Citizenship Fund and the manner of expending this money is carried on in as high a democratic fashion as I have ever witnessed.

"You might know that our Citizenship Fund in the Local Unions was established by an overwhelming democratic vote at a regular legislative conference held by our unions. The money expended from these funds is spent in a democratic manner with the majority making the determination of the direction of this expenditure. There is no bossism in the UAW.

"I have been a Republican member of the New Jersey State House of Assembly for the past five years. I can vouch for the fact that during this time no political pressure of any kind has been placed upon me by my organization. The UAW not only preaches democracy but effectively practices it. As a member of my union, I have gone along with the will of the majority in matters of political expenditure because I firmly believe that if we are to maintain an effective democratic union the wishes of the majority must be heeded. I can attest to the fact, however, that as an individual I have been given complete freedom to run as a Republican and to solicit votes and aid to the Republican Party without hindrance of any kind.

"Moreover, I want to attest to the fact that the voluntary COPE dollars which are collected in our union are collected on a purely voluntary basis without any degree of coercion or intimidation, and to my knowledge these moneys so collected are the only ones employed in general elections. The Citizenship Funds are used primarily for registration and for political education to the end that we make better citizens of our members.

"I wanted to get these remarks off to you for the very simple reason that I am proud of the organization to which I belong. I am proud of the democratic manner in which it is run and I am desirous of reaffirming that which I said to you during our conversation while I was in Detroit speaking for the Republican Party.

> "Very truly yours,
> "Thomas Lazzio, President,
> "Local 300, UAW"

Now, there is just no question about it that Mr. Feikens is deliberately trying to twist the facts, and the simple facts are

that while the decision to spend these moneys is made democratically by the members, we have even gone beyond that by
saying that even after the democratic decision to expend these
funds is made, if one single member feels it is improper he can
have his ten cents sent to some charitable organization.

SENATOR GORE: This Mr. Lazzio is President of Local 300,
UAW, according to this letter?

MR. REUTHER: That is correct.

SENATOR GORE: What part did you have in bringing about his
election as president of the local?

MR. REUTHER: Well, I don't vote in his local union, but I
might say that I have enjoyed a very friendly and personal relationship with him, and certainly inside of our union there has
never been any friction.

If a member in his local union said to me, "If you were a
member of Local 300 would you vote for this person for the
presidency of the local?" I would say, yes, emphatically I would.

SENATOR GORE: Well, did you, in fact, exercise influence in
bringing about his election as president of the local?

MR. REUTHER: Well, I don't interfere in local union elections.
I mean, this is a matter where the local people elect their own
officers, but certainly I am in favor of him being the president
of that local because he has done a good job.

SENATOR GORE: Is it a practice of yours to interfere with the
election of local union officials?

MR. REUTHER: No, that is a matter of local autonomy. The
only time that we have intervened in local situations is where
there have been known Communists in leadership, and that is
contrary to our constitution, or where a few racketeers wormed
their way into our union.

In Patterson, New Jersey, in this same city but not in this same
local, in Local 669, that is, the production workers in Curtiss-
Wright, there were some gangsters who got in control of that
local union.

We moved in and we kicked them out.

SENATOR GORE: How did you move in?

MR. REUTHER: Well, we tried them before our convention.

What happened there, Senator Gore, we had constitutional procedures—this was some years back—whereby, when a person was tried by the local union, he was tried by his peers, and they elected a trial committee and he had to be found guilty by two-thirds of the membership.

We had the facts on these crooks, these gangsters, who were tied in with the numbers racket and some very evil and ugly people, and we tried them locally, but they intimidated the workers.

The workers who stood up and argued against them had their tires slashed when they came out of the parking lot that night, or their wives were threatened, and the result was that all the evidence proved these fellows were crooks, but the local membership was so intimidated it was fearful to vote against them, and the result was they came out of the local with a verdict of not guilty.

We then took this case to the convention. There were twenty-five hundred delegates. It was in 1949 in Milwaukee, Wisconsin, and we tried these gangsters before the twenty-five hundred delegates.

We gave them the floor. We tried them right there, and we found them guilty and we kicked them out of our union.

SENATOR GORE: Who was the judge?

MR. REUTHER: The twenty-five hundred delegates made the decision, at the convention, but then the courts in New Jersey put them back in our union, but we kept working at it, and now we have got the membership to the point where they are still in the union but they are out of leadership.

SENATOR GORE: Well, do you or do you not believe in local autonomy of your local unions?

MR. REUTHER: Oh, absolutely. As I said, we do not interfere in local autonomy except where there is a known Communist and where they are racketeers. We will not tolerate either Communists or racketeers in our union, and at that point we, as the International body, could conveniently hide behind local autonomy.

We have a responsibility to keep our union clean of racketeers and crooks and Communists, and we move in, but in each case where we move in at the International level, the International Executive Board doesn't have the authority to take action.

We have to pick a trial committee. For example, we would take the three-thousand-odd names of the delegates at our last convention. We would pick out fifty people, who then are a jury panel.

The defendant can strike ten names, and we can strike ten names, and the remaining, the top people, become the jury, and then after that decision is made it still goes to the convention for final review.

So this is not a matter where the leadership has the power to kick people out. We haven't got the power to do that, but we do have the responsibility for moving in to keep our union clean if in a local situation a bunch of gangsters get control and, therefore, intimidate the membership, and the membership cannot free itself from the gangsters' control, and we are responsible for moving in and we do move in.

It is one of the great shames of the labor movement that it has taken us too long to get around to cleaning labor's house and kicking these crooks out and putting them in jail where they belong.

SENATOR GORE: These representatives who came to your meeting in September, at which you made the political endorsement, were selected locally?

MR. REUTHER: Yes, they were the officers and committee members elected democratically by each of the various local unions, and it was a proportional representation. The big local had more representatives than the smaller local.

SENATOR GORE: Then, is it a fair summary of your position that in the absence of subversion or criminality you believe unqualifiedly in local determination and autonomy?

MR. REUTHER: Absolutely; and I think I can say that in our union we have been criticized because we have too much democracy. We have never been criticized because we have too little.

SENATOR GORE: Would you say that you would take the same position with respect to the people of a given Congressional district or state?

MR. REUTHER: Absolutely. I have no right to tell the people in Congressional district X who they ought to have. That is their business, and we don't even remotely think of telling them. They make that decision.

I said this morning the only decision which I had participated in—though I have been an officer now for twenty-some years in our union, and I have been president for more than ten, the only decision in which I have participated was the question of the national candidates. I have not gone into the states in terms of gubernatorial candidates or the Congressional candidates. That is a matter worked out in each state, and we accept the decision of the people in the district or in the state.

SENATOR GORE: Well, when you make a large financial contribution to the campaign of a given candidate for governor or Congress or for the Senate in a state other than that in which you have citizenship, is not that an attempt to interfere with the untrammeled right of the people of that state or district to exercise their own right of selection of their own officers and representatives without undue interference from without?

MR. REUTHER: Well, if the membership in the State of Illinois endorses Senator Paul Douglas, as they did in the last election, we have a large membership there—I think we are, perhaps, the largest trade union group in the State of Illinois—now, if the membership there makes the decision and then says to us, "Now, we have sent you so much money and COPE so much money, we would like to get some of that back now to help on this," I don't think that is wrong.

Or, supposing we send them a few more dollars than they send us? If there is big money in there from industry and the fellow who is running has a hard row, it seems to me that the decision that this turns on is who made the first decision, was it hand-picked from the top down or did the people at the local level make the decision?

In our case the people at the local level make the decision. We do not make that decision.

I have not participated in a single meeting in which they selected a Senatorial candidate or Congressional candidate. I have participated in the question of the decision of the Presidency and the Vice Presidency.

SENATOR GORE: You understand I raise no question whatever about the right of the members of your organization who are citizens of a state to fully exercise and vigorously exercise their right of citizenship. The more vigorous they are, the better.

I really cannot see anything wrong with that proportion of the political fund which the membership of that state has contributed being used in that state.

I cannot go with you that last step, however, when you attempt to justify one wrong by another. The two do not make a right.

I certainly would concur that there is some equity involved when large funds are being expended from one particular economic source to encourage the offsetting thereof by funds from another source.

However, I still cannot arrive at a right being made by the two wrongs.

It seems to me that we must preserve, if we are to have truly representative government, as inviolate as it reasonably can be preserved, the right of people within a given jurisdiction to elect their own officers and representatives without undue influence from without.

MR. REUTHER: I am in complete sympathy with the point of view which I know you share because I heard you discuss this very ably the last time I appeared before the Committee on the gas bill, but I think you have got this kind of problem, which disturbs me greatly, as I know it does many other people who are concerned about the future of American democracy.

Here we have an imbalance in the political situation where four families contributed more in 1952 than the one and a half million members in my union. That is with all the hard work we put in, still four powerful families contributed more money.

Where did that money go? It didn't go to the Congressional district where they lived.

The DuPonts live in Delaware, at least part of the year; but that money went all over America.

If you will look at the big oil interests, just check and see what is happening in the campaign of Senator Wayne Morse out in Oregon, and you will find out how much money is going there from the oil industry and its powerful financial groups, so you have got this imbalance.

And I say, Senator Gore, you cannot correct that except by limiting the size of the contributions. You get it down to five dollars so that the Rockefeller family can give five dollars per voter in a Senatorial campaign, and you will not have to worry about how much of that crosses state lines because the volume will be so reduced in terms of the impact of wealthy families or any other group that it will not constitute a threat to the integrity of American democracy.

It is the volume of this thing that creates the problem, and I say that politics has got to be practical, too. You cannot save democracy in a vacuum of idealism. You have got to be motivated by idealism, but you have got to also be fighting the hard problem of practical politics.

In helping to build the union, I was motivated by sheer idealism because I believe in what I am doing. But do you think we could have organized the auto industry in an idealistic vacuum when we were fighting paid thugs and gangsters hired by these powerful corporations, who broke into people's homes and shot us and did other things?

We had to fight back, and we have built a decent little world now out of a social jungle, and the same thing is true in politics.

In the City of Detroit we had a very corrupt situation. In 1937, Richard Reading ran for Mayor of the City of Detroit.

Who was he supported by? By the same newspapers that write these scurrilous editorials against our union, by the same powerful financial people, by the same respectable Republicans.

They supported this man—it is all in the record—and he ran on a pledge to drive our union out of the City of Detroit.

Well, he didn't succeed. Senator Ferguson sent him to prison, along with the Commissioner of Police.

Now, he was the candidate of the respectable people who were fighting the CIO. He was the candidate of big business and big money.

Now, what did we do? Did we have to yield to that corruption where politics and the underworld were in the same gang? We fought it, but if you had said to us, "But they are wrong. You can't get some balance in this thing by helping the fellow who is fighting against that," we never could have cleaned it up.

This guy would still be in the City Hall playing with the gangsters and the underworld. This is not some dramatic speech. This is a matter of record. Richard Reading stayed in Jackson Prison until he was ready to die, and they released him a few months before he died; and Mr. Fromm, the Commissioner of the Police Department, was in prison with him because this is the way it was all tied together.

Go back and see what the editorials of the *Detroit News* were about Mr. Reading when he was running. You will find they were just like this, and they were against us and with him.

And we had to fight. We were motivated by idealism, by decent human values that we had to fight or otherwise we couldn't have survived.

Go back and find out what Harry Bennett did. I mean, these are the facts of life; and I agree with you, your motivations are a thousand per cent right, I am sympathetic with what you are talking about. But the way to correct it is to put a five-dollar limitation upon this so that the DuPonts and the Rockefellers can send five dollars to Arizona, but they can't send five thousand dollars.

SENATOR GORE: It seems to me that there is the basic threat to popular government, when roughly 1 per cent of the people finance 95 to 98 per cent of our political campaigns—we need to reform our system. Were it not for the interlocking and complex relationships between the Federal Government and the states, I would very readily say to you and to the public that I would favor an absolute prohibition against any monetary contribution to any campaign for federal office.

I am sure that it can be put into effect. Of course, you know that former President Theodore Roosevelt favored something along this line.

MR. REUTHER: I would favor that, too.

SENATOR GORE: But this Committee is engaged in the serious study of election reform, and we will have further hearings in January, and it may be that we will invite you back.

MR. REUTHER: I think the tax credit which we have proposed, Senator Gore, on the five-dollar contribution will create the kind of incentives where we can broaden, really, the great financial base upon which American politics must rest. Get more and more and more people to contribute smaller amounts, and the parties and the candidates will get adequate financial help, but they will get it from a lot of little people rather than a few big people.

I think that approach, the tax credit, would be a tremendous incentive. We would lose a few dollars in federal revenue, but that would be a very small price to pay for the fact that American democracy would be stronger and healthier.

SENATOR GORE: I am prolonging this interrogation more than I desired that I should, but I do want to ask about one other thing, and then the Special Counsel will have a question or two.

To what extent do you send into a given state with an election contest employees of the UAW? I am talking for the purpose of political organization. My question now does not relate to registering. So far as I am concerned, the activities of your organization and the activities of Ford Motor Company—I heard a letter the other day in which Mr. Henry Ford had written throughout his large organization urging people to register and be prepared to vote—are laudable.

But I am asking a question not about the use of employees to encourage registration, but the organization of political rallies, organizing support, hauling voters to the polls, the use directly of employees who are paid directly from UAW funds for the purpose of political activities per se.

MR. REUTHER: As I said this morning, we get our staff people to try to make their contribution in the whole broad field of political activities as a part of their normal activities and normal functions, and you will find that most of our people are working where most of our membership live and work because that is where their normal activities and normal responsibilities take them; and you will find that that is what we are doing.

For example, I am doing my job, I still do my collective bargaining job, and take care of the other problems of administering our union, and yet I make a speech on political activity, on the issues and candidates, whenever I get a chance.

If I am before a local meeting or some convention or some labor organization I make my speech. Well, the staff members conduct themselves essentially in the same manner.

MR. MOORE [Special Counsel to the Subcommittee]: Mr. Reuther, if the pending case in the Supreme Court of the United States, if in that case, it is held that 610 is unconstitutional will it not also be that that section is a dead letter so far as corporations are concerned?

MR. REUTHER: It seems to me that the Supreme Court, if it rules—it may just refuse to rule, but if it rules—

MR. MOORE: If you have a square holding—

MR. REUTHER: Yes.

MR. MOORE: [Continuing]—on the unconstitutionality.

MR. REUTHER: I think very strongly that this whole question of free speech is something that you cannot infringe upon as it relates to any group and that, therefore, the President of the General Motors Corporation could, if he felt that the candidate that he was hoping would get elected, could be helped, he could make a public speech and so forth, I do not in any way want to interfere with the right of anyone—

MR. MOORE: The president of General Motors or any corporation can do that now, may he not?

MR. REUTHER: Sure he can.

MR. MOORE: Just as you can.

MR. REUTHER: And they do it much more subtly than we do. We, I think, just do it open and aboveboard, and we don't try to fool anybody.

MR. MOORE: What is your position with respect to the constitutional guarantees in so far as it applies to you and to individuals and to corporations?

MR. REUTHER: I think corporations are not individuals, we all understand that.

MR. MOORE: Yes.

MR. REUTHER: Certainly, with respect to the right of any corporation official to act and express himself as I expressed and act as president of my union, I would expect to give them the same rights and privileges that I enjoy. I would not want to infringe upon that right in any way.

MR. MOORE: Well, is this a fair statement: That if this section of the law is held unconstitutional would it, in your opinion, be proper, then, for labor unions to expend dues money directly for political purposes?

MR. REUTHER: No.

MR. MOORE: As distinguished from voluntary contributions?

MR. REUTHER: No, I am still willing to make the distinction between the exercise of free speech with respect to issues and the expression of preference on candidates, and to do that with organizational money, but to maintain the distinction with respect to contributions of federal candidates, doing it out of voluntary money, but I would still say that the long-range answer to the problem is a limitation on contributions. That is the answer.

MR. MOORE: I have just one other question. You mentioned, I believe, in your testimony the use of radio and TV facilities in Windsor, Canada. Are there any other outside the continental United States?

MR. REUTHER: No. CKLW is the only station. They used to have a studio in Detroit, too. They still have an office there. The only reason it is over in Windsor is because of some of the international regulations in placing the station. We didn't go over there so we could operate from a foreign base or anything like that. That is just nonsense.

It is a Greater Detroit station. Our difficulty was we couldn't get time on the Detroit stations, plus the fact we get a better rate over there. The other stations in the little network that we have put together are all in the United States. I don't know how many stations there are, seventeen or eighteen.

MR. MAZEY: We have thirty stations.

MR. REUTHER: Do we have that many?

So CKLW is the only one, and we use it for no other reason except convenience, and we made a better arrangement in terms of the rates.

MR. MAZEY: We couldn't buy time on the other stations in Detroit, that was the basic reason.

MR. MOORE: Mr. Chairman, we do have from counsel for the UAW a copy of the brief that has been filed in the Supreme Court of the United States which, I assume, sets forth fully your position, and we do have it for the files.

This is an area that certainly is a very engaging one from the point of view of counsel. However, in view of the time, I think we would have to desist.

SENATOR GORE: Thank you, gentlemen.

The Future of American Education—A Labor View

Address before the National Council for Social
Studies of the National Education Association

Cleveland, Ohio
November 23, 1956

I would like to think out loud with you about some of the
many complex and compelling problems that we face in this
very troubled world of ours. All of us have been overwhelmed
by the potential catastrophe with which we are faced because of
developments in the Middle East, and the more recent and
tragic developments in Hungary.

I think all of us need to understand that—literally—we stand
with the human family on the rim of hell, and that the H-bomb
has finally provided mankind with the weapon of total self-
destruction. And yet, while we stand on the rim of hell and face
that possible catastrophe, we stand at the same time on the
threshold of what promises to be man's greatest opportunity for
human progress and unlimited human betterment, because the
same scientific and technical know-how that has made it possible
for man to create the H-bomb has also given mankind the most
productive tools with which to create economic abundance.

So this is the great challenge—do we permit mankind to
plunge somehow over the rim of hell, or do we find a way to
face the future together, so that we can use these productive
tools to improve and enrich human life?

I believe that this is perhaps the most challenging period in
the history of the human family, because, for the first time, mankind has the tools with which to master his physical environment.
For the first time, mankind can feed, clothe, and house the human family, and take care of man's basic economic and material

needs. Having found the way to satisfy man's economic needs, we can begin, as a civilized people, to devote more time, energy, and resources to enabling man to grow as a social being, a cultural being and a spiritual being.

This is the beginning of the realization of the higher aspects of human civilization. Whether we shall live to achieve those higher aspirations, or whether we will plunge over the rim of hell, depends in a large measure upon what we do in the field of education, for what we do in this field will determine the equipment we give each generation to deal with these new, complex, and challenging problems.

The struggle in the world, throughout its many, many thousands of years, essentially has been a struggle between peoples and between nations to divide up economic scarcity. People struggled for a bigger share of the world's meager resources. Today, we no longer face that problem. That's why yesterday's concepts are no longer sound as they relate to tomorrow, because we live in a period of opportunity. Instead of struggling to divide up economic scarcity, we can cooperate in the creating and the sharing of economic abundance.

Here in America, we possess the most productive economy in the world, and we have been blessed as no other people have with great material resources and productive power. Moreover, we have a great heritage of freedom and democratic tradition. Because of all this, we face a great responsibility as the strongest of the free nations of the world. What we do in America will determine the direction in which the world will move.

I believe that we need to evaluate, not only the broad responsibilities that America must assume in the period ahead, but the special responsibilities that American education must assume. Those obligations and responsibilities must be shaped in the image of the new and challenging dimensions of war and peace in this atomic age. The H-bomb has now made peace an absolute condition of survival, and unless we maintain peace the human family cannot survive. We need to recognize, therefore, what the crisis in the world is, what its source is, so that, understanding it, we can deal with it.

The crisis in the world is not economic, military, or political; essentially, it is a moral crisis. It is a reflection of man's growing inhumanity to man, which finds its most horrible expression in the total destruction now made possible by the H-bomb. I believe our problem is a reflection of the fact that there is a growing and most serious moral and cultural gap between the progress we have made as a people in the physical sciences, and our lack of progress in the human and social sciences. We know much better how to work with machines than we know how to live with people.

This growing lag between our know-how in the physical sciences and our failure to make comparable progress in learning to know and understand and work with people, confronts us with a very serious dilemma. The problem will not be made easier, because all of the pressures are in the direction of intensifying it. We are today on the threshold of the second phase of the Industrial Revolution, during which human knowledge in terms of physical sciences is moving forward at an accelerated rate. This means that we need to give greater and greater attention to the social and human sciences.

If you have time while you are here in Cleveland, take an hour and go through the new Ford engine plant near the airport. There you will see automation which symbolizes this second phase of the Industrial Revolution.

I went to work in the automotive industry back in 1927. At that time, it took us about twenty-four hours to take a rough engine block as it was cast in the foundry and to machine that block, ready for assembly. And that was a simple model-T Ford engine. We kept making progress. We cut it down to 18 hours, and then 14 hours, then 12, then 9 hours. If you'll go through the Cleveland Ford engine plant, which is fully automated, you will see a Ford V-engine, 8 cylinders—a very complicated piece of mechanism—in which the rough castings are automatically fed into this automated line, and in fourteen and six-tenths minutes later, it is fully machined, without a human hand touching it. You will see the machine bore the engine cylinder, and the boring bar go back in place with an electronic eye measuring the diameter of the bore. If it is not the right size, an electric impulse in the brain of the machine makes an adjustment on the tool which makes another cut. When that cut is finished, it measures it again, and if it's the right size, it goes on to the next operation. Not a single hand touches that.

Is that good or is that bad? The people who invented that machine will not make that decision. That is not a mechanical problem. That is a human problem, and the answer will not be found in a laboratory dealing with the know-how in the field of the physical sciences. The answer must be found in the human and social sciences, and in the capacity, the ability, and the morality of a free society to gear the wonders of these great machines to the common good, so that all may share in a better, richer, fuller life, so that having satisfied our material needs, we can all have more time and more opportunity to grow intellectually, spiritually, and culturally into better human beings.

This is the great challenge.

There are some people who will say that automation is just a little more of the old mechanization, when actually automation represents a very sharp departure from the normal technological progress we have made and which grew out of the very primitive beginning of the Industrial Revolution in the textile industry in England, many years back. When James Watt developed his very primitive steam engine, it was the first effort to substitute mechanical muscle for human muscle. We built upon that. We extended that idea in the very complicated modern machinery and higher levels of technology.

Automation, however, now brings into our technology a whole new element: the machine not only substitutes mechanical muscle for human muscle, it now thinks, and it substitutes mechanical judgment for human judgment. The automated machine has a memory which can store complicated instructions, which, with the right electrical impulse, can bring those instructions out of its memory to execute very complicated mechanical operations.

This is where we are. And this problem will get more and more difficult unless, somehow, we can begin to square our scientific, technical, and production know-how by developing comparable human, social, and moral know-how.

Why do we have these machines? Is economic effort an end, or is it a means to an end? Obviously it must be a means to an end. And the end must be the enrichment of human life, and the expansion of frontiers for human growth, not for just the few, but for the many. Only as we begin to demonstrate that sense of social know-how and know-why will we be able to meet these complex problems.

I went through this Ford engine plant about three years ago, when they first opened it. There are acres and acres of machines, and here and there you will find a worker standing at a master switchboard, just watching, green and yellow lights blinking off and on, which tell the worker what is happening in the machine. One of the management people, with a slightly gleeful tone in his voice said to me, "How are you going to collect union dues from all these machines?" And I replied, "You know, that is not what's bothering me. I'm troubled by the problem of how to sell automobiles to these machines."

This is the very difficult, very delicate challenge. How do we achieve balance between greater productive power and greater purchasing power, a balance which we need to raise the living standards of all people by sharing the economic abundance?

Thus I look at American education which, I believe, faces two essential challenges. First, there's the task of extending the frontiers of human knowledge in the physical sciences and in the art of working with materials and machines. Secondly, and at the same time, greater attention must be given to the expansion and the extension of human knowledge in the social sciences and in the art of working with people. Only as we do both, I think, can we achieve this essential balance between technical and scientific know-how and social and moral know-why.

While we are dealing with these problems in America, we also face a challenge in the world, a challenge quite unlike any a free people have ever faced in any other comparable period of world history. We face the challenge of world Communism. This is a challenge more difficult to deal with than any we have ever met before, because essentially it is a challenge of an idea, implemented by naked military power.

Somehow, people arrived at the idea that you can stop Communism with guns. Nothing could be more tragic than for America to believe that or for America to fashion its policies in the image of that concept. We need to be strong in terms of military power, as does the whole free world—strong enough to stop aggression wherever it may raise its ugly head. But we always need to understand that military power is but the negative aspect of a dynamic foreign policy. It is only a holding action which gives you time and opportunity to carry on the positive struggle against the forces of Communist tyranny and immorality.

I have been trying to get people to realize that the struggle between freedom and tyranny, between democracy and Communism, is essentially a struggle for the hearts and minds and loyalties of people.

There are hundreds of millions of uncommitted people in the world who have not made up their minds where they belong in this struggle. I was in India last April. I was in the Middle East and in North Africa, and I could sense the social dynamics that are sweeping these portions of the world. They are in revolution. I came away believing more than ever that we really cannot win this struggle unless we wage it in terms of the ideals, the ideas and the values that we as a free people believe in.

We cannot go on trying to fight only against the things we are opposed to. We need also to fight with equal courage and dedication for the things we believe in.

Last summer I spoke in Tunisia at a mass meeting in the public square in the center of their ancient city of Tunis. At the end of the meeting on this very hot and sultry day, the chairman of the meeting, who was the Secretary-General of the Tunisian Labor Federation which we are trying to help build there to stave off the forces of Communism, said to me, "Would you like a cold drink?" That was precisely what I needed, so we went around the corner in this main square in the center of Tunis in North Africa and there was a Coca-Cola vending machine. Put in your nickel and get your ice-cold bottle of Coca-Cola; and on the billboards and in the shop windows there were ads advertising American cars and the American cosmetics.

I came home believing we in America know how to sell our cars, our cokes, and our cosmetics, but we have not yet learned to sell our ideals and our ideas. That's why we are getting in trouble in the world. Only as we can sell the basic values that we as a free people believe in and cherish, can we sucessfully compete with Communism. We can't just talk about having more bathtubs, because the contest cannot be in terms of purely material values.

We have values the Communists cannot match: freedom, spiritual growth, the right to live your life as a free human being.

The Soviet Union still represents the most challenging adversary we have ever faced. Those few people in America who were under the impression that the spirit of Geneva brought about a fundamental change in the Communists have now been disillusioned. The tragic lesson of Hungary has certainly dispelled any concepts that the Russians have changed. The new look was not a change. It was a tactical shift in their struggle for world domination. It means that the Communists have now recognized that they must perfect new techniques for military and economic penetration to create the climate that will enable them to push successfully programs of political subversion.

The Russians are not going about this in an unorganized fashion. They are planning their program for world conquest with great care. When you look at their educational system, you can see how they are working it out in great detail. They are, for example, training technicians in the Soviet Union who are not only being taught to be competent technicians, but who are also trained to speak a dialect spoken in a certain section of North Africa, or Central Asia or India, so that when that technician is sent there he doesn't need an interpreter who might only interpret half of what the technician is trying to put across. He goes there knowing the native language and the whole cultural background, so that he can be not only a competent technician, but an effective shock trooper in the program of economic penetration and political subversion.

Because the Russians have recognized this as they expand their trained manpower base, they grow stronger, industrially and economically, and that gives them greater economic and military power. It gives them the economic base to extend their new techniques of penetration in order to subvert politically. I think it's a frightening thing when you look at what the Russians are doing and you compare that to what we are doing in terms of our educational efforts as the strongest of the free nations in the world.

Let me give you just a few figures which I think puts this problem in sharp focus. In 1920, there were in the whole of Russia 41,000 graduate engineers, while the United States had 215,000 graduate engineers. In 1954, the Soviet Union had 541,-000 graduate engineers, and the U.S. had 500,000. But that's not the whole picture. In 1950, the Soviet Union graduated 28,000 engineers. We graduated 52,000 because the G.I. Bill of Rights greatly expanded our educational effort. But in 1956, based upon the enrollments in the universities and the higher schools of learning in the United States and the Soviet Union, we will graduate roughly 70,000 people in the engineering fields and they will graduate 120,000.

I served on the special panel created by the Joint Congressional Committee on Atomic Energy and with eight other prominent Americans, I spent a whole year working on this question of the peacetime application of the atom. We went into this question of our educational needs and every phase of the peaceful use of the atom. Our progress is currently being limited and retarded by the fact that there is not sufficiently trained manpower available —whether it be in medicine, in the atomic development of power reactors, or in experimental work in agriculture. In every phase there is a shortage of manpower.

One of the people on this panel was the dean of one of the leading engineering schools. I asked him whether, in terms of these figures, the Russians were just doing a kind of a mass educational job or whether they were doing a better job qualitatively. He said, "They're doing a better job qualitatively." The average graduate of a four-year engineering course in the

Soviet Union knows as much as the average U.S. graduate with a master's degree in a comparable field of engineering. The Russians are giving their students more science and more mathematics in the lower grades and are concentrating in this field.

This is the challenge. We must work on two fronts, extending human knowledge in the physical sciences and in the social sciences as well, but we in America are not even trying. We are in trouble in America, as any society would be in trouble if it were more concerned, as we seem to be, with the condition of its plumbing than with the adequacy of its educational system.

Look at the fact that last year we spent more money on comic books than we did on textbooks. Look at our school buildings; many are antiquated fire traps. During the war, we had the factories on swing shifts and when the war was over, we took the factories off the swing shifts and we put the schools on swing shifts. Tens of thousands of American children are being robbed of their rightful educational opportunities because they are going to school half-time in antiquated buildings, in overcrowded classrooms where teachers spend, because of the overcrowding, more time teaching discipline than educational work.

Then look at teachers' wages. The average sweeper in the automobile factory under contract with my union—the man on the lowest rung of the wage ladder—last year made more money than 50 per cent of the elementary school teachers in America. It doesn't mean that the sweeper is getting too much. It means that the teachers are getting too little.

These are the basic facts of life. This is not just a matter of denying children the opportunity to grow. We, as a free people, cannot survive unless we begin to do, and quickly, an effective, adequate, and realistic job of bringing our school system up to its basic needs and requirements. I've been making a lot of noise about this and I'm going to go on making a lot of noise because I believe that there is no other problem in America which should have as high a priority.

I believe we need to raise our sights and we need to sharpen our vision and find a way to raise our school problem above the level of political controversy, so that all people in public life can stand together to find a common answer to this basic challenge.

I ask this simple question. I ask it of you and I ask it of my fellow Americans everywhere. Why is it that we have the courage to mobilize the power of America to meet the challenge of war, but we fail to have the same courage to mobilize America to meet the challenge of peace?

I served in Washington in the last war on many boards— the War Production Board, the Manpower Commission, and several others. I had an opportunity to watch Congress, and when the admiral said, "Give us billions for battleships," and the Air Force general said, "Give us billions for bombers," nobody said that we can't afford battleships and bombers. Yet when you talk about schools, about the chance and the opportunity for children to grow, they somehow don't get around to appropriate for them.

I have told Auto Workers many times that they had a big 24-inch pipe line down there during the war, that went from the Committee on Appropriations to the Congress, and when the generals and the admirals asked for funds, they opened up this big pipe line and they appropriated billions and billions and billions. But when you talk about schools, or about decent housing to clean out the cesspools in the cities and to create healthy, wholesome communities for kids to grow up in, do they ever open up the pipe line? Oh no! They'll give you a patriotic speech and then go to the Congressional medicine cabinet, get out an eye dropper and give you a couple of drops.

There is something basically wrong with the moral fiber of a free people who have the courage to spend billions in war and haven't the courage to make an effort in peace to provide educational opportunities for their children. Look at the money we spend. Do you know what it costs to train a jet pilot? Two years ago I was told it cost over two hundred thousand dollars to train one jet pilot. Does anybody say we can't afford to train jet pilots at two hundred thousand dollars per head? We can spend billions to train people to die in war, but we haven't got the good sense to spend money to equip people to live in peace.

These are some of the values that get out of focus in our kind
of a world, and we need to bring them back into focus.

We all know that the tax structure of our state and local communities is inadequate to meet the present-day needs. We know
that while the local community and the state must carry their
share, they cannot carry the whole load, and that the federal
government, of necessity, must move in, and must provide an
important share of the educational budget if we are to overcome
these tragic deficits.

What do we get, however? We get a flood of noble talk about
our children as our most priceless national asset. How many
times I've heard people make that speech! Unfortunately, these
people are long on pious platitudes and extremely short on practical performance, and you cannot educate children with pious
platitudes. You need schools, teachers, and facilities, and you
need all the other things that make up a balanced program. We
haven't got these things.

I'm proud of the role the American labor movement has
played historically in fighting to make education possible for
everyone's child. We share the belief that every child is made
in the image of God and that every child ought to have the right
to an educational opportunity that will enable that child to grow
intellectually and spiritually and culturally—not limited by antiquated classrooms, overcrowded classes, or underpaid teachers,
but limited only by the capacity which God gave that child to
grow, and by none other.

Yet, because of our shortcomings as a society we have imposed
harsh restrictions upon the right of every child to grow and to
expand into a better human being. We need to look at this harm.
I read in the papers, as you do, about juvenile delinquency. I've
always had the feeling that the problem in America is not
juvenile delinquency, but adult delinquency. Our children are
not failing us—it is we who are failing our children. It seems to
me that we'd better look within ourselves first before we try to
probe what's within our children.

I'd like to suggest what I believe to represent a realistic approach to the question of overcoming our educational deficits.

First, I think we need to approach this problem in other than the terms of the standards of yesterday, because the tools of yesterday will not meet the challenge of tomorrow. What was appropriate and adequate yesterday is not appropriate and adequate today and tomorrow.

I propose that we look at the educational problem within the framework of these new and challenging dimensions of war and peace, of freedom and Communism in the atomic age, because this is the historic background against which the play in which we are actors will be carried on. I propose a five-year federal aid to education program in which the federal government would make available a sum equal to from 1½ to 2 per cent of our gross national product. I propose further that that amount of money would be used first to launch a comprehensive school construction program, to overcome at the earliest possible date the shortage of classrooms, to retire antiquated firetraps from use, and to take our children off the swing shifts.

Secondly, we ought to provide substantial salary increases for schoolteachers, to give them a salary structure commensurate with the training they have and the responsibilities they carry.

It seems to me that the teachers of America ought to be just about fed up with being second-class economic citizens. If you went into an automobile showroom and you said to the dealer, "Well, I'd like to buy this particular model, but I'm a schoolteacher," I will guarantee you that he will not say, "Oh, you're a second-class economic citizen, we'll sell this to you for five hundred dollars under the list price." You are second-class economic citizens, but you always pay first-class prices for the things you have to buy. It is about time that we made the teachers of America first-class economic citizens.

Thirdly, I believe we need a federal scholarship program on a competitive basis, so that we will not continue to lose almost 60 per cent of our top high school students, who cannot go to college. This is a tremendous waste of human resources. The only way we can stop it is by a federal program of scholarships. I propose that if a young person is willing to sign up in one of these federal scholarship programs, that, after graduation, they

would have the choice of enlisting in the teaching profession—
or in some other fields where they are needed—for a period of
one year longer than and in lieu of their military service.

I think it is nothing short of insanity to train people and then
to have tremendous shortages in the field of their specialized
training because we dumped them in the army for two years of
boot training. The Russians are not doing it, but we are. Perhaps
we could enlist these young people as technical missionaries
whom we ought to be sending around the world to fight poverty,
hunger, ignorance, and disease, which is the positive aspect of
the struggle against tyranny. We could send them over there in
lieu of their military training.

I happen to believe—and my belief is based upon the fact
that I have been around the world studying these problems,
finding out why it is the Communists are able to forge poverty
into power—that the more young Americans we send throughout the world as technical missionaries with slide rules, with
medical kits, with textbooks, to fight Communism on a positive
basis, the fewer young Americans we will need to send with guns
and flame-throwers to fight Communism on the battlefields of the
world. The kind of educational program I am thinking about
would make it possible to enlist thousands of young Americans
in the rewarding struggle to win the peace.

Finally, we need to do more about the gifted child. We do
more for the child who doesn't make the grade, and we do less
for the gifted child. These are the students whom God has given
that special little extra spark of genius, the capacity to grow, the
capacity to comprehend things beyond the reach of the average
man. But what do we do in the average school? The gifted child
gets no special attention. We need to develop a new kind of
program to meet this problem and to enable these gifted children
to grow to their maximum capacity. How many of these children
do we have in America whose genius never had a chance to
bloom? No one can know, but there must be many. How many
Jonas Salks did we lose? How many Thomas Edisons? How many
other people who have this special gift of genius? We never shall
know.

So these are the problems. When you talk realistically about federal aid to education, you always get the men of little faith and little vision saying, "Oh, you can't do these things," because they are always trying to measure what we do tomorrow by what they did yesterday. They'll always say we can't do it. I like to think that they have no faith in the greatness of America, and that we have truly fashioned America's greatness by doing what the men of little faith said was impossible. We have literally fashioned our greatness out of doing the impossible.

When you look at the figures I am proposing—1½ to 2 per cent of the gross national product for a period of five years—you may ask how much money is that. Well, it's between six and eight billion dollars. But how much really? You don't know, and neither do I. It represents one week of the cost to the American taxpayers of World War II.

I ask you, do we not have a right to expect that America, with all its greatness, all its productive power and material resources, be able to make available at the federal level, through federal aid to education programs, an amount for the whole year equivalent to what we spent in one week in waging war upon the enemy?

Look at it another way. Over a five-year period, we're talking about forty billion dollars. Consider now what the American economy did—and you can get the basic information from the government—and you find out what the gross national product was in 1950, in 1951, and in 1952. You will find a certain measurement of economic growth and expansion. If we had sustained that same rate of economic growth and expansion through the years of 1953, 1954, and 1955, we would have had eighty-six billion dollars more in our gross national product.

We did not sustain that rate of growth, however, and because we failed to sustain it, we lost eighty-six billion dollars. In three years, we lost more than twice the cost of the educational program that I suggest represents a realistic approach to the basic educational needs of America.

These are the sober facts. This is where we are. We stand there in that delicate, precarious balance on the rim of hell, and on the other side is this brave new world that lies there ready to be realized. This is one of the great tragedies of the world— and you history teachers perhaps know it better than I—that we find chapter after chapter of the history books filled with the stories of man's inhumanity to man and of the great wars. In those great wars of the world's history, many nations achieved their highest expression of collective action—they worked, they marched, they sacrificed, and they died because they were driven forward by the negative motivations of war and because of their common fears and common hatreds.

I believe that the great challenge of the leadership of the world is to find a way to tap the great spiritual reservoir, the great spiritual power that lies deep within the human breast, and find a way to get people working, marching, building, and sacrificing because of positive peacetime motivations and because they have common hopes, common aspirations, and a common faith.

This is a great challenge. Whether this challenge will be met, or whether we shall fail, depends upon what we do on the educational front and on how well we equip ourselves as a free people to take on these problems. I for one have unlimited faith in the capacity of free men. I believe that, somehow, we can get our bearing, that, somehow, we can get our values in their proper relationship, one to the other; that, somehow, we can raise the banner high and go forward; that freedom can win out over the tyrannies, the immorality of Communism; and that, somehow, we in America can provide that measure of moral leadership necessary to mobilize the free people of the world, so that together we can march forward and build that better tomorrow that we dream about.

This is what the philosophers have talked about throughout the centuries. We can fashion that better tomorrow in the image of freedom, in the image of peace, in the image of social justice, and in the image of human brotherhood.

Racketeering and Corruption in the Labor Movement

Section of the opening address of the sixteenth constitutional convention of the United Automobile, Aircraft and Agricultural Implement Workers of America

Atlantic City, New Jersey
April 7, 1957

During the last few weeks you and I and millions of decent, honest trade unionists all over America have been shocked and have been saddened by the headlines that we have been reading—headlines exposing corruption and racketeering in the leadership of certain unions.

I think that we can all agree that the overwhelming majority of the leadership of the American movement is composed of decent, honest, dedicated people who have made a great contribution involving great personal sacrifice, helping to build a decent American labor movement. But, unfortunately, in certain unions the gangsters and the crooks and the racketeers have moved into positions of power.

We happen to believe that leadership in the American labor movement is a sacred trust. We happen to believe that this is no place for people who want to use the labor movement to make a fast buck. We say to these people, "If you want to make a fast buck, that may be your business, but you better make it outside of the American labor movement, because we are not going to tolerate gangsters and racketeers inside the American labor movement."

We happen to believe that the American labor movement is a movement dedicated to human service, and if people want to apply the ethics and the morality of the market place, then those people ought to be kicked out of the American labor movement. We say there should be no room for either crooks or Communists in the leadership of our kind of free labor movement.

I believe that I can say with complete confidence that the action of the AFL-CIO Executive Council in dealing forthrightly with Mr. Beck, when we suspended him last Friday, indicates that we are not going to compromise with corruption in the American labor movement.

American labor had better roll up its sleeves, it had better get the stiffest broom and brush it can find, and the strongest soap and disinfectant, and it had better take on the job of cleaning its own house from top to bottom and drive out every crook and gangster and racketeer we find, because if we don't clean our own house, then the reactionaries will clean it for us. But they won't use a broom, they'll use an ax, and they'll try to destroy the labor movement in the process.

Now, when the AFL-CIO came into being we knew that this problem was there, and we said, "We have to have both a set of moral principles and we have to have effective machinery for the implementation of those ethical and moral standards." So we created in the constitution of the merged labor movement practical machinery that we call the Ethical Practices Committee. That committee is chaired by Brother Al Hayes, the President of the Machinists Union. The other members are Dave Dubinsky of the Garment Workers; Joe Curran of the Maritime Workers; George Harrison of the Railway Clerks; Jack Potofsky of the Amalgamated Clothing Workers. These five men, along with President Meany, are all men of great personal integrity, and I can say to you and I can say to them, that in doing this job of cleaning out the racketeers and the crooks they can count upon 100 per cent support of the UAW until that job is completed 100 per cent.

We urge the McClellan Committee to expose every crook and every racketeer that they can find in the American labor movement, but we also insist that they expose with equal vigor, cor-

rupt and crooked employers in America. All the corruption is
not on labor's side.

Here is *The New York Times* of yesterday in which Mr. Rob-
ert Kennedy, who is the chief staff person for the McClellan
Committee, said: "It is striking to us how little help business
has been giving to the Committee. Often management would
rather have the *status quo* and make their payoffs."

These reactionary, corrupt managements would rather pay a
bribe to a crooked labor leader than to pay a living wage to the
workers represented by that crooked labor leader.

I say to the McClellan Committee, we will give you full
support and cooperation. Go after the crooks in the labor movement, but go after the crooks in management's side of the problem, and when you find a crooked labor leader who took a bribe
from a crooked employer, put them both in jail for about fifteen
years and give them plenty of time to talk it over between themselves.

I say that an employer who bribes a labor leader is as morally
guilty as the crook who took the bribe. You see, we have had a
double set of standards. Until we have a single set of moral standards where you put both the taker of the bribe and the giver
of the bribe in jail, you will not put an end to this corruption.
You put a few of these people in jail for about fifteen years.
Give them plenty of reading material about ethics and morals,
and see how fast they will slow down these crooked employers
trying to buy off labor leaders rather than paying decent living
wages.

The UAW is not perfect, but I can say without fear of challenge that we are clean and we are democratic, and we are going
to work and fight to keep our union clean and democratic.

At this convention we are going to recommend for your consideration the creation of a public review board composed of
seven outstanding public citizens whose integrity is beyond question, and have them participate in the affairs of our union as
they relate to our trial procedure, so that we do everything possible to protect the democratic rights of each member of our
union, and secondly, to act as a public watchdog committee to

help us maintain the high ethical and moral standards for which our union has stood.

We in the leadership of our union are prepared to have a public committee judge and measure our conduct.

We hope that before this convention is over you will not only enact this provision in the constitution but that we can present for your approval a list of names of the seven people who will serve in this capacity.

Address before the annual convention of the National Association for the Advancement of Colored People

Detroit, Michigan
June 26, 1957

Mr. Chairman, friends, it's difficult for me to tell you how happy and proud I am to be here, because when I come to an NAACP meeting, I have a feeling that I belong here. I'm home here. And I can never escape the same reaction every time I hear that wonderful song, "Lift Up Our Voices and Sing." It always gives me a sense of renewed faith and dedication, because I feel that a people who can sing that song cannot lose.

I'm proud to belong to the NAACP, because it is made up of people who are dedicated in a great crusade to make America true to itself. This is what this is about. Make America live up to its highest hopes and aspirations and translate those hopes and aspirations into practical, tangible reality in the lives of all people, whether they are white or black, whether they live in the North or in the South. I say that each of us is blessed that we can be engaged in this crusade, in this struggle for justice for human dignity—in this struggle to wipe out in every phase of our national life, every ugly and immoral kind of discrimination.

A couple of years ago I had the privilege of attending an ADA meeting in Washington and Roy Wilkins was the principal speaker. And I want to say that Roy did himself proud that night. He was reporting on some of the struggles in the South. He had just returned from a speaking tour in a number of the Southern states, and he said there are three organizations that are being held responsible for the drive for civil rights and human dignity in the South. He said there is the NAACP. There is the ADA, and there is the CIO. Mrs. Roosevelt was my dinner partner and I said to her, "No wonder I'm having trouble. I'm an officer of all three of those organizations."

Now why did they come together? Well, because they shared the same values, the same respect for human dignity. They shared the same hopes and the same aspirations. And they dreamed the same dreams about that bright new tomorrow that we're working and fighting to build. A tomorrow where discrimination will be no more. Where Jim Crow will be buried for keeps in every phase of our national life. A bright tomorrow where every child, regardless of race, creed, or color, all created in the image of God, will have equal educational opportunities so that every child can grow, intellectually, spiritually, and culturally, limited not by a segregated schoolroom, but limited only by the capacity that God gave each child to grow.

But the NAACP and the American labor movement do more than just dream about that better tomorrow. And that's why you can preach about the brotherhood of man from morn til night, and the Eastlands and the Talmadges and the bigots will never raise their voices in protest. But when you begin to work to translate the brotherhood of man into practical fulfillment, that's when they begin to fight back. They are fighting us because we are working, trying to give practical substance and meaning and purpose to the noble concept of the brotherhood of man.

We had a distinguished churchman, Bishop Oxnam, who addressed the UAW convention some months ago. He said, you know there is a lot of noble talk about the brotherhood of man, but there are some people who keep the hood and drop the brother. And those are the people who are fighting us. And because they are fighting us, we meet at a time of great crisis. The challenge is compelling, but when the burden is heavy, always remember that the reward is so great and wonderful in terms of basic human values that it's more than worth the struggle and the sacrifice that go into winning the reward. Since you meet in the city in which the headquarters of the UAW is located, I am sure you will permit me to bring to you the fraternal greetings and the best wishes from the one and a half million members of the UAW, and I would like to say for them that we are with you all the way until victory is ours in this fight for civil rights.

You have come back. You were here in 1943. Detroit was the great arsenal of democracy. We were turning out more weapons of war with which to fight Hitlerism, totalitarianism, than was any other city in the world. But unfortunately, this city went wrong and we had tragic, ugly race riots back in that period. But one of the things that we have always been proud of about the UAW is that when the people of Detroit were rioting and destroying and killing each other on the streets, white and Negro workers worked side by side in brotherhood in the plants under our contracts. Because they had learned to know the meaning of human solidarity, of brotherhood, because they had learned through the hard experience of struggle that when the employer can divide you and pit white against black, American-born against foreign-born, he can divide and rule and exploit everyone. And we learned a lesson that only in the solidarity of human brotherhood, only as you stand together with your fellow man can you solve your basic problems.

That's the lesson the whole of America needs to learn. I've often thought—why is it that you can get a great nation like America marching, fighting, sacrificing, and dying in the struggle to destroy the master race theory in Berlin, and people haven't got an ounce of courage to fight against the master race theory in America? We need the same sense of dedication, the same courage and the same determination to fight the immorality of segregation and racial bigotry in America as we did in the battlefields against Hitlerism.

We've made progress in Detroit since you were here in 1943. We haven't made enough progress, but we have made great progress, and I think that we can take great satisfaction and encouragement from the progress that we have made. The delegates to this convention in 1943 were treated as second-class citizens, and you were put in second-class hotels. This time you are in the best hotels where you ought to be.

We made progress on the FEPC front. The NAACP, the trade union forces, the church groups, civic groups worked together, and despite the overwhelming opposition of the Republicans in our State Legislature, we finally got an FEPC law on the books in the State of Michigan. Negro workers have made progress, but we still have not broken down the barriers to equal job opportunities in every phase of our economic life. They are in the factories, but they are not in the offices, where they have a right also to equal job opportunities.

And just as the Negro workers have proven themselves in the factories and on the assembly lines, Negroes have proven themselves in the field of public service. Since 1943, we have elected four Negroes to important political positions in the City of Detroit. They were elected by tremendous majorities, and they have demonstrated the good judgment of the people who put them there, by dedication and by a high sense of public trust and service. We're proud of the fact that the Honorable Judge Wade McCree sits in the highest court in the City of Detroit. And we are proud that another Negro, the Honorable Judge Davenport sits in another court of Detroit. And we are equally proud that in the City of Washington from the Thirteenth Congressional District, a Negro, the Honorable Charles Diggs, is in that position. And we are proud that a distinguished Negro doctor, Dr. Remus Robinson, sits on the Detroit Board of Education. Because of the outstanding public service and the sense of dedication that these four outstanding Negro citizens have demonstrated in the public positions to which they have been elected, I would like to predict that in the fall election in 1957 in Detroit, we will elect a prominent Negro to the Common Council where we need one.

I think we all realize that the world is troubled—that we live with crisis in America and the people of every nation are living with crisis in the world. I have been saying for a long time that the crisis in the world is not economic or political or military.

Essentially, the crisis in the world is a moral crisis. It's a reflection of man's growing immorality to himself. Of man's growing inhumanity to man. The H-bomb is the highest and most terrible destructive expression of that growing inhumanity.

And in a sense our crisis in America, the crisis in education, the crisis in civil rights is not political, it is moral. We've got all that it takes to solve these problems. But we haven't demonstrated the moral courage to step up to solving these problems, and this is our basic problem. America is in crisis, not because it lacks economic resources, not because it lacks the political know-how, not because we don't know how to do the job of squaring democracy's practices with its noble promises. We just haven't demonstrated the moral courage. And until we do, we will not meet this basic crisis in civil rights and in education.

And I believe that the civil rights issue—and I don't say this because this is an NAACP convention, I have been saying this wherever I go, because I believe it—I believe that the question of civil rights must be made the top priority item on American democracy's unfinished business in the twentieth century. Civil rights is not a political issue, because when a matter or issue is essentially a moral matter, it must transcend partisan politics. This is exactly the approach that we have been making together. We have been trying not to play politics with civil rights, but to put the civil rights question in its proper focus and mobilize people from all political parties to try to adopt legislation and to take necessary steps to implement an effective civil rights program.

We have been saying that there are three basic reasons why we support civil rights. First, we support it as a matter of simple justice. As a matter of human decency. As a matter of dignity and as a matter of basic morality. Secondly, we fight for civil rights to make them universal, because as Joe Rauh said in his speech, civil rights and human freedom are indivisible. You cannot have those things unto yourself. You can be free only as your neighbor is free. You can be free only as you share freedom with the people you live with. Hitler taught us that when he jeopardized the freedom of the smallest country in the world, he jeopardized our freedom. And when Mr. Eastland and the Dixiecrats and the bigots in the South jeopardize the Constitution and deny Negroes their freedom, they are putting my freedom in jeopardy, even though I live in the City of Detroit.

Those people who can't understand the first two basic reasons that ought to put America on the highroad in the struggle for civil rights at least ought to understand the third reason: that civil rights is no longer a domestic question confined to the geography of the United States. The question of civil rights in the United States is an international issue. As a matter of fact, there are more people thinking about it abroad than there seem to be in America thinking about this problem. Because more than one-half of the people of the world are dark of skin, and they look at America, and they brush aside our noble slogans about the virtues of American democracy. They brush aside our economic indexes which say that we are the richest country in the world. And they say, yes, but how do you square your noble professions with your ugly practices in the civil rights field?

Mr. Eastland sits there in his Committee, and you would think that he is really trying to fight the Communists. He doesn't know anything about what makes a Communist. What he does not understand are the great social, dynamic forces sweeping the world. This struggle between freedom and tyranny is not an old-fashioned struggle for geography. This is a struggle for the hearts and minds of people. And you can't win it with an H-bomb, even though you need one to defend yourself. You can't win the struggle of ideas and ideals with guns, although we as a part of the free world must of necessity be strong on the military front, in order to meet the challenge of aggression no matter where it may raise its ugly head. But what we need to understand in the world is that military power is the negative aspect of a dynamic foreign policy, and that if you want to win the struggle of ideas and ideals for the hearts and minds of men, you have got to wage the struggle on the positive basis, and civil rights is the key issue in the world. Mr. Eastland and his associates and the association of bigots don't understand this. We need somehow to get through to the dark corners of their small mentalities on these kinds of things.

My feelings on this are not based upon reading a book. I have been in Asia, India, and North Africa. I have talked to people—workers in the big cities, intellectuals, businessmen, government officials. I have gone into the mountain villages. I am here to tell you that they know what's going on in America. I went up into the foothills of the Himalaya Mountains in Northern India, in a little village of three hundred people, and we had a meeting, and I talked about America—what we were doing trying to bring to fulfillment the great promise of America. They didn't want to know about how many Chevrolets General Motors made last year, or whether the Chrysler fins had a bigger sweep than the Cadillac fins. They asked me about Montgomery, Alabama. Just sit down on a doorstep with a peasant in a village of Northern India and take on the task of trying to explain to him why America, conceived in freedom and dedicated to the proposition that all men are created equal, a nation that can split the atom, that can make a pursuit ship go three times as fast as sound and yet, in this twentieth century, we can't live together in brotherhood and we continue to discriminate against Negroes. It will tax your ingenuity, and you will give them no answers. You can only give them excuses. And excuses are not good enough, if we are going to win the struggle of freedom in the world.

I came back more convinced than ever, after talking to people in North Africa and India and Asia, that America's immorality in the field of civil rights could be the Achilles' heel of American democracy in the struggle against Communist tyranny. Because when you have to put footnotes to try to explain in a feeble way why American democracy fails to meet the challenge on the civil rights front, when you have to make excuses, you are in serious trouble, and we are in serious trouble, because the people of the world are not going to judge America by the number of tons of steel that the U.S. Steel Corporation can roll in a year, by the number of shiny new automobiles with more chrome that we turn out every year. They are not going to judge us by these things. They are going to judge us by what we do about basic human problems. Not how modern is our plumbing, but how modern is our civil rights program as it affects people. These are the things they will judge us by, and if this Congress would step up to its responsibilities and pass a civil rights bill with teeth in it, with effective enforcement machinery, that civil rights bill would give America a moral force in the world more powerful than all the H-bombs that we will ever make in the fight against Communism.

And yet we have enemies. I get a lot of literature, you know. I don't read it all, but I read a couple that came over my desk the other day. Here's one: "Behind the Plot to Sovietize the South." And on the back it tells you in summary what this pamphlet is about, and I'll quote it to you: "This booklet tells about the activities of Walter Reuther and his collaborating white and Negro Communist, Socialist and Marxist kind of labor agitators who are mobilizing a massive offensive to impose an insidious civil rights program on the South." I want to say to the people who put out this kind of literary trash that the NAACP, the AFL-CIO, and all of the good people who are joined together in the fight for civil rights, we do more to fight the Communists in one week, than all these people would do in their whole lives put together.

We need to understand that this fight between freedom and tyranny is for keeps. It's the only world series in which there is only one game. No play-offs, no return matches, no next year's season. You either win the first game, or you lose for keeps. That's what we are in. Now you would think that in that kind of a game you would put your best team in, and Mr. Eastland and Mr. Talmadge and those fellows shouldn't even be on the scrub team. We've got to put our best team in, because we've got to demonstrate not only that we have great economic muscle, but we have the sense of moral responsibility to find a practical way to equate economic muscle with social and political morality in terms of the lives of everyone, because, you know if we were just a little country, no bigger than Luxembourg, it really wouldn't be tragic if we were doing so badly. But in truth, America is the last best hope of freedom. If we can't make freedom and democracy work in America, then it can't be made to work any place in the world. And I say we are going to make it work in America, because it must be made to work.

Now the task ahead is a difficult one. We will need to mobilize all of our forces. We will need to pull together men and women of good will and good faith—people in the NAACP, our good friends in the churches, the labor movement, the liberal people who are willing to stand on the side of morality in this struggle. We need to broaden our efforts to get more allies in the leadership conference that has been working so effectively in the past. And we need to have the courage to tell both political parties that they both should be ashamed of the shoddy record that they have registered on the field of civil rights.

The Supreme Court is living in the twentieth century and the Congress is still somewhere back in the dark nineteenth century. It's about time they catch up. You know, these fellows are the same fellows who passed the Taft-Hartley Act. The same people who fight against civil rights are the same people who fight against raising minimum wages, the same people who fight against social progress. Well, I want to say to these people in Congress that they have been on the longest sit-down strike in the history of America—eighty long years. And we think it's about time that they terminate that sit-down strike on civil rights and begin to turn out some legislation. Now the bill has passed the House, but that's nothing new. That's happened many times, but now it's over in the Senate, the graveyard of civil rights legislation. I think that we've got a job to do. It can be done. We must mobilize the American people, and we must translate their moral will into practical political pressure and say to that Senate, "Stay in there. Outlast the filibuster, if it takes all summer and all fall, until the next Congress meets in January." And if these evil men who use the right of unlimited debate to block the will of the majority, if they know that the majority is going to stay put through the hot summer into fall, and into the winter months, maybe they won't try so hard, because they know it will not succeed. And the only people in America who can see to it that the filibuster does not succeed are the American people, and our job is to mobilize the American people, so that their will and their moral pressure will exert itself upon the Congress.

We also must make it clear there can be no compromise on the jury trial provision. We don't want a civil rights bill in name without any substance. We don't want a civil rights bill that looks good on paper, that has no enforcement machinery, and these people who talk about the jury trial, they are using that only to try to destroy a civil rights bill that can be enforced through the federal government and the federal courts.

Then we have got the long-range fight on Rule 22. Because even though the present limited civil rights bill is adopted, this is only the beginning, because there are many other areas in which the ugly forms of discrimination are working every day in the lives of millions of Americans and Rule 22 is the key that will open the door in the Senate so that majority rule can prevail and the filibuster can be ended. We have been saying a long time that the right of debate does not mean the right to prevent the majority from acting. Debate is not an end. It is the means to an end, and the end must be legislative action.

We are very happy that the UAW was able to join forces with the NAACP in originating the original approach to changing Rule 22. We helped finance some of the constitutional lawyers who went back to the Hamilton papers and the early constitutional papers and developed the whole case to prove that the Senate was not a continuing body. Therefore, every new Senate on the day of its organization can adopt its own rules and, any new Senate can abolish Rule 22 and substitute in its place a rule providing for majority rule. And because we participated in that historic effort, with the NAACP, we have received many brickbats from the people in the Senate who believe that filibuster is their best line of defense.

Now we made progress on Rule 22. In 1953, we only got twenty-one votes. We had fifteen liberal Democrats with us. We had five liberal Republicans, and we had Wayne Morse, the Independent. In 1957, we got forty-one votes, seven votes short of what we needed. I say we need to intensify our efforts between now and the January date in which the new Congress in 1959 is organized to get those other seven votes, so that we can abolish the filibuster in the United States Senate for all time.

We are continuing to work on this matter. As a matter of fact, hearings are being held now. Friday morning, June 28, 1957, I'm going to testify on Rule 22 before a Subcommittee of the United States Senate dealing with rules of procedure. But Rule 22, let us always remember, has been the shovel with which the Dixiecrats and reactionary Republicans have always dug the grave for our civil rights legislation. And until we abolish Rule 22, we will never be able to translate our civil rights program into practical legislation and implementation.

We have the question of FEPC. Yes, thirty-eight major cities have adopted local FEPC ordinances. Fifteen states have state FEPC laws. We have made progress, but no one should kid us into believing the answer to FEPC can be found either locally or at the state level. Tell me how you'll get relief in Mississippi, at the state level, where you need it most. The only way that we can get a comprehensive FEPC law on the books is to do it in Washington, D.C., and to bind the forty-eight states in the process.

Well, there are some mighty fine people in America who tell you, yes, they are against discrimination in every phase. They are opposed to it in terms of job opportunities. They are opposed to it in terms of education. They are opposed to it in terms of transportation. But, they say, legislation is not the way to do it. Education. You've got to educate people. You've got to get hatred out of men's hearts. Well, we agree. Education is important. But you can't educate this problem out of existence by education alone. You've got to work both on the educational front and the legislative front. And you've got to parallel those two activities right down the line.

I have told a story on other occasions which I think bears repetition because it's the simplest way to illustrate what I think to be a very fundamental point. These people who talk about education as the answer to FEPC, and these other problems, I ask them to look to see what happens in America in about ten days from now. We're going to have a Fourth of July weekend. There are going to be millions and millions of Americans in their automobiles driving all over America. And on the Friday before the weekend, the National Safety Council will launch its comprehensive, intensive educational program. They'll be on the radio networks, the TV networks, and the newspapers. Everybody is going to be told and warned to drive carefully, don't exceed the speed limit. Don't go through a red light. Observe all the traffic regulations. We're going to just saturate America with education on traffic safety, but no one would propose that that's where we end. In addition to this educational program, we have thousands of fellows on motorcycles in blue uniforms. And when you go through a red light or exceed the speed limit or violate some other traffic law, the motorcycle officer pulls you over to the curb. He gets a book out, and he gives you a ticket. It costs you ten bucks, and that speeds up the educational process like nobody's business.

So we say let's educate and educate and educate. But let's expedite the educational process by some effective legislation. And if an employer will not give a qualified Negro, or a qualified Jew a job, because of prejudice, let's take that employer into court the way you go into court when a cop catches you going through a red light. And you will see how fast the educational process picks up. Now these good people who are all for education and opposed to legislation don't think it's wrong to have this fellow on the motorcycle. They think that's perfectly proper, perfectly fine, and yet, when you're dealing in a field of basic human values of human rights of basic morality, they just want the educational process to take its own course. We've got to keep pressing and pressing and pressing until we get a federal FEPC law.

We're proud in the Auto Workers Union of the progress we've made. Other unions have made great progress in breaking down discrimination in the factories. But we haven't got one single major contract, although we've got one and a half million workers under contract, and although we try and try and try at the bargaining table in which the employer has agreed to a clause prohibiting discrimination because of race or creed or color at the hiring gate. They say to us, "Oh, you don't represent the workers until we employ them. We aren't going to let you say anything about whom we hire. After we hire them, then you can talk about their work, their conditions of employment, their wages." Well, we believe that the question of the policy at the hiring gate is important, and if we can't do it at the bargaining table, then we have to do it in the halls of Congress.

Now there are many other things we need to be thinking about. I want to say to this convention of the NAACP, the American labor movement is not a fair-weather friend of yours in the fight for civil rights. I want to say for the AFL-CIO, its leadership, George Meany, and the people involved in directing that organization: "We are with you all the way, and we are going to stay with you all the way until we get on the statute books of America effective civil rights legislation in all of these fields, not only in FEPC, but in every other aspect of our national life."

We want an America in which every citizen is equal when he walks into the polling place to cast his ballot. We want an America in which every child has educational opportunity, an America in which every citizen has equal job opportunity, equal rights to the use of all public facilities, the right to live in a decent neighborhood, in a decent house.

It's about time we look at this problem of clearing the slums in our major cities. We're not clearing the slums. We're just modernizing them. We're just creating new ghettoes. I say it's about time we had some courage to build decent communities in which all Americans can live on an integrated basis as decent citizens living together in a wholesome community.

Now these are not matters of special privileges. These are basic rights to which every American is entitled. And no American should be satisfied with less.

The task is difficult. The struggle will be hard, but let us always remember that human progress has never been served to mankind on a silver platter. The history of the world shows chapter after chapter that men of faith and courage have had to fight to bring to fulfillment their dreams and their hopes and their aspirations. What we need to do is to keep the faith. Keep the faith in ourselves. And when the going is rough, as it will be, let us remember that the test of one's convictions is not how did you behave, how did you stand up when it was convenient and comfortable. The test of one's convictions is: do you stand up for the things that you believe when it takes courage? Do you stand up in the face of adversity, in the face of great controversy? This is the kind of fight we are engaged in. That's why when the going is rough, always remember that there are millions of us, and that together we can move mountains, and that together we can solve this problem and make America in the image of what it really stands for.

So I say to you, we pledge our hands and our hearts, we pledge our all to you in this struggle, because we believe that this is the most important struggle that America must win, if it is going to be true to itself and provide leadership to the free world. And if we mobilize our multitudes, if we mobilize all the people of good will and good faith in America, I say that we can do the job, and together we can build that brave new tomorrow that we dream about and fashion it in the image of peace, freedom and justice, and human brotherhood.

Profit-Sharing and Other Goals

Address before the special constitutional convention of the United Automobile, Aircraft and Agricultural Implement Workers of America

Detroit, Michigan
January 22, 1958

I would like your undivided attention for just a couple of minutes because I think that I am obligated to say something to you and to the people that we represent and to the people of our great countries, both the people in the United States and in Canada, so that they will know why we have adopted this strike relief program and so that the editorial writers will have a little more difficult time of distorting our purposes.

We have adopted a collective bargaining program which we insist is sound and just. We have now adopted a strike relief program to implement at the bargaining table our 1958 demands, and I think we ought to get people to understand that we have adopted this strike relief program not because we are strike-happy, not because we want a strike in any company, large or small, in 1958. We are in the same position at the bargaining table that the free world is in terms of the world situation.

Every person in the free world prays for peace, but we don't let our peace and security rest just upon our prayers. We have to mobilize the economic power of the free world to put the free world in a strong defense posture because we know that while we hope and pray for universal peace in the world, that the prospects of having peace are improved if the free world is strong enough to meet the threat of war. And the same thing is true at the bargaining table.

We pray that when we approach the bargaining table in 1958, labor and management can sit there in a spirit of good will and conduct their collective bargaining responsibilities in good faith, always in the knowledge that free labor and free management have responsibilities to the whole community which we have said before transcend their separate responsibilities.

We want to bargain based upon the economic facts, based upon the interpretation of those facts as they bear upon the needs of all the people of these two great countries. Therefore, we vote for a strike assistance program not because we want strikes any more than the free world votes for a strong military program because the free world wants war.

We vote to put ourselves in the strongest position, because we believe only if we are strong in the free world can we ensure the prospects of peace. Only as we are strong at the bargaining table, can we improve the possibilities of avoiding a strike.

I think our people need to understand that we are going there in good faith. We will do everything humanly possible to resolve the problems at the bargaining table in 1958 on the basis of reason, on the basis of justice, on the basis of economic facts, on the basis of simple human decency and morality.

But, unfortunately, while we attempt to get these big corporations to approach the bargaining table in that spirit, they are heating up the cold war. Instead of sitting down and trying to create the kind of climate in which a rational, sensible, constructive approach could be made, they have already launched the cold war.

I said the other day, I believe that Mr. Curtice rejected our proposal before he read it—certainly before he studied it. Mr. Breech followed and Mr. Colbert followed. Then the Goldwater episode followed, and then last night another part of that offensive was made—not an effort to create that kind of rational, constructive climate of good will, but an attempt to try to create the kind of tension in which constructive and sensible collective bargaining is difficult.

Here is the headline on Mr. Breech's speech. Here is another page, the full text. I wonder if the *Detroit Times* will permit our union to state its case and give us equal space in their pages setting forth our arguments. I wonder if the *Free Press* can claim it is free if it continues to slant news and only represents one side of a broad public issue.

But this is what we are up against. Mr. Breech went to Tennessee, spoke to a Chamber of Commerce dinner last night. Now, he has a perfect right to do that. He has a perfect right to make any kind of speech he wants. But he has a responsibility. Ultimately he will be at the bargaining table, and if he makes more difficult the solution of bargaining problems because he corrupts the climate, then he is responsible for sowing the seeds that can cause difficulties, and he is not meeting his broad public responsibility, to say nothing of his responsibility to the stockholders and the workers of the Ford Motor Company.

He made a very inflammatory speech last night, and I want to say to him that his economics were erroneous and they will not stand careful examination.

What he said last night was a concoction of erroneous economics and just plain propaganda. Maybe his audience liked it and maybe they cheered him, but unfortunately at the bargaining table you have got to deal with facts, with problems, with moods of people, and the applause at a Chamber of Commerce dinner is not a substitute for the kind of positive approach that these human problems require in this period of economic difficulty at home and difficulties in the world.

Mr. Breech didn't say one word in his speech—it is all in this text here—not one word about the profits of the Ford Motor Company. That's what we are talking about. We are not talking about the profits of somebody that we don't bargain with. Why doesn't he stick to the economic facts? He doesn't care to because they prove our points and they disprove his conclusions.

But he said some interesting things. The headline here is "Breech Rejects UAW Fishhooks."

You know, if I were Mr. Breech, or if I were Mr. Curtice, or if I were Mr. Colbert, I would never use a word that has "hooks" in it, because the problem is not that we have put fishhooks into our demands. The problem is they have their hooks into these profits and they don't want to give us our share. That's the basic problem.

Now, Mr. Breech didn't talk about how much he got out of the bonus plan. In 1955 he did pretty well. He got in salary and bonus, $565,000 in one year. The Ford Motor Company executives, some of them who only a few years ago didn't have probably more than $25,000 to their names, are now millionaires many times over.

Where did all of that money come from in this very short time? It came out of the profits of the Ford Motor Company.

What we are saying is that the workers who build Ford cars and Lincolns and Mercurys and trucks, maybe they don't make, each individual worker, the same contribution that Mr. Breech makes, and we don't claim that they do. But we do claim that they make a contribution; and if Mr. Breech is entitled to a share of those profits because he makes a contribution, then I say the Ford workers are entitled to their share because they, too, make a contribution.

Mr. Breech says, and I quote, "The UAW proposal was like blaming a cow for giving too much milk."

We are not blaming the cow because it gives too much milk. We are blaming the companies because they take all the cream and give us the skim milk. That's what we are claiming.

We would like to increase the production. We would like to raise the production of milk by putting the unemployed back to work, by getting the American economy in high gear. Then we would like to say, well, let's share that increased milk supply so that the kids of every unemployed worker can have enough milk to drink every day and not just the people who are now having a problem of running over to France to build their fourth estate. These are the simple facts of life. (This reference was to Mr. Ernest Kanzler of the Ford Motor Company.)

Mr. Breech can use the press all he wants. They have done it all these years. But they will not stop us in our struggle to get justice for the people we represent in these great countries of ours. I hope and I pray that these fellows will not be overcome by their own propaganda.

I worked in Ford. I didn't just fall off a tree and get into this movement. I worked in Ford when I saw Harry Bennett and his gangsters running that company. I worked in the B Building back before the depression when they were driving fellows in the skilled trades departments, not only on the production lines. When a die broke down on the day shift, in order to get that die back into production they drove the men. Two fellows wouldn't put a section of a die in a hydraulic press in the craneway of the B Building and they protested to the foreman on the second shift that it was too dangerous because they had a chunk of steel a little larger than this book and they were putting a piece of tempered steel on the corner. They were supposed to come down with a press that can exert millions of pounds of pressure to force out the cutting edge of this die so that there would be enough material to rework it and get it back in production.

When the workers said, "If you put that much pressure on that piece of die section it will tilt and will fly out like a bullet and kill somebody," they said, "You do it or you are through." The two fellows said, "We won't do it." Five minutes later, four big plug uglies from the Service Department dragged them out in the plant and threw them out in Miller Road. They intimidated some guy with a lot of kids and he went over to do it and he was killed. I don't forget these things.

These fellows were sitting on their moneybags and the papers were making them the salt of the earth. These men were fighting us and they were using the politicians of the city who were in league with the underworld. We know where we came from. We know that the world is a little better place to live in not because they wanted it that way, but because, thank God, there were enough people in the world willing to fight to make it a better place to live through great organizations like ours.

Have they ever been hungry? You know, they may have been because they got home late for supper, but that is not what I mean. Did they ever go home to their wives and their kids knowing there was nothing in the icebox and there was nothing in the bank and the rent wasn't paid and the landlord was breathing down their necks and the sheriff was ready with the eviction papers, and they couldn't find a job? They have never felt that kind of human emotion. We have.

I say about these fellows, I don't begrudge one penny they

get, not one penny. My difference with them is that they begrudge the workers having their share. So I say to these gentlemen in the high places of American industry, in the high councils of the companies with which we bargain: What good will all of your millions do you if the free world cannot meet the challenge of Communist tyranny?

I came out of a hotel some time back when the first news of the fall-out came out. We had these headlines about the atomic fall-outs. The doorman was chuckling. He was having a good time. I said, "You seem very happy. Why are you enjoying yourself so immensely?" He said to me, "You know, I have been seeing these millionaires come and go. They have all been moving out farther into the suburbs, getting away, because they figure that maybe if the atomic bomb dropped in Detroit they would be far enough out that they wouldn't be bothered. Now the fall-out covers the whole area and these guys have moved for nothing."

But the idea behind what he said was really important. We live in a world in which the common denominator that binds the human family together has been reduced to its simplest fundamental term—human survival. If we have an atomic war, the poorest sharecropper and the multimillionaire will both wind up in the same kind of radiated ashes. What we need to get people to understand is that they somehow have to exercise their great powers by meeting their responsibilities in a world in crisis in which they can't hang on and cling to the stubborn, selfish patterns of the past without putting in jeopardy the future of human freedom and human security and perhaps human survival. This is what is at stake.

What good are a couple of million dollars more or less to corporation officials who have so much money now they don't know what to do with it? It won't make them happier. But if they will share these things with the people who need more purchasing power, then the whole economy will get stronger. The position of the whole free world will be improved. Their chance, along with our chance of surviving, is that much better.

I don't know how you reach the dark places in people's mentalities, but we are going to keep trying. We are going to keep preaching the gospel that freedom and democracy in peace are indivisible values in the world and that no one can have them unless they are universal and all people may share them. We are going to the bargaining table. We are not going there flexing our muscles. We are not going there with a chip on our shoulders. We are not going there saying, "Let's get it over with and get on the bricks." We are going there in the cause of humanity, in the cause of freedom, because we believe that only as freedom meets these basic economic and social problems will it have the moral strength essential to survival in this critical period in man's history.

I felt obligated to say these things because we—you and I together—represent a lot of people, a lot of men and women and behind them a lot of kids. We are an important segment of the American labor movement. What we do will have a broad impact upon what other workers will do. We want our membership and the people of America and the people of Canada to know that we are going to discharge our responsibilities with a high sense of understanding that what we do affects the well-being of many people outside our ranks. We pray that management will come to the bargaining table in the same spirit, the spirit that reflects an understanding that the free world is in crisis and that free labor and free management must work together in trying to contribute to the ability of the free world to meet and surmount this crisis so that human freedom and peace can be made secure.

Administered Prices in the Automobile Industry

Statement to the Antitrust and Monopoly Subcommittee of the Senate Committee on the Judiciary

Washington, D.C.
January 28, 1958

Mr. Chairman, and members of the Senate Antitrust and Monopoly Subcommittee: These hearings represent for us the culmination of more than two years of effort to get some attention directed to what we believe to be unjustified, extortionate and dangerously unwise automobile price increases imposed upon the American people by the "Big Three" producers behaving in essentially the same way as the steel producers who have already appeared before your Subcommittee.

For myself and for the members and officers of the UAW on whose behalf I am here, I offer you and the members of your Subcommittee our heartfelt appreciation for undertaking this investigation and for the opportunity to appear before your Subcommittee.

We welcomed and immediately accepted your initial invitation to appear together with the presidents of General Motors, Ford and Chrysler for the purpose of examining the price-profit-wage picture in this industry.

We regret, and in a very profound sense we resent, the fact that these three gentlemen, Messrs. Curtice, Ford, and Colbert, acting with remarkable unanimity, have failed to comply with your original request to appear here for testimony and questioning at the same time that we make our contribution to your investigation.

Instead, as we understand it, they will appear later, one at a time, presumably to recite prepared statements, to promise to get answers later to some of the most important questions put to them by your Subcommittee, to duck others and, in short, to avoid getting down to brass tacks on the issue of administered prices, vital as that issue is to the health of our economy and the strength of our nation in this time of unparalleled peril.

We were willing, we are willing now, to take part in a joint appearance.

I understand the excuse has also been made that to appear with me before the Subcommittee would have involved the corporations in public collective bargaining with the union. I want to repudiate that suggestion completely. When I accepted the Subcommittee's invitation to a joint meeting, there was no thought in my mind of raising any issue which should rather be dealt with in negotiations around the collective bargaining table. The issue in which this Subcommittee is interested is that of prices, and under the law of the United States that is not a collective bargaining issue upon which management is required to bargain. We have indicated that we have no intention of trying to bargain on prices, although we have called on the industry to live up to its responsibilities to the public when setting its prices.

We in the UAW maintain that instead of raising prices on their 1958 models, as they did, the automobile companies could have struck a major blow against inflation by cutting prices an average of one hundred dollars per car at wholesale. This is not a collective bargaining issue with us, but a public matter which we have raised as a group of 1½ million Americans who are particularly concerned with the role of the automobile industry in our economy. The companies, on the other hand, maintain that this year's price increases, and those of prior years, were necessary, and some management representatives at least have gone further and have claimed that the price increases were a necessary result of increased labor costs. These matters have not been raised on either side as collective bargaining issues, but as matters of general public concern. This committee is also considering the whole field of price increases as a matter of general public concern, and I believe it would have been wholly right and proper for us to have thrashed the matter out face to face before this Subcommittee.

We believe that the traditions of cross-examination and direct confrontation as developed in our courts are sound also for investigations of this kind, and that they represent a most effective method of eliciting the truth from conflicting claims.

A still more desperate excuse for the refusal of the auto corporation heads to appear with me before you has been the suggestion that it would be improper under the antitrust laws for the presidents of competing companies to discuss prices together. I would just point out that they already have ample opportunity to discuss prices in meetings of the Automobile Manufacturers Association. The antitrust laws do not provide, and I am sure that Congress never intended, that it should be considered a violation or an offense for manufacturers to appear jointly with a union, before a Congressional committee in public hearings, in order to give testimony and answer questions as to their pricing policies, particularly when the purpose of the inquiry is to promote free competition and lower prices.

The bald fact is that the corporation managements have consistently evaded any discussion, and in particular any public discussion, of their price and profit policies with any representative of the union, because they know that there are too many embarrassing questions we could and would ask them. A number of the questions we would like to have asked the corporations are embodied in this statement. I hope that when the corporations do appear before this committee, you will make sure that they are not permitted to get away with issuing meaningless statements drafted in their public relations offices, but will put to them searching questions about the operation of their policies, including those questions which I shall be suggesting here.

So that we may have the background for this appearance in the record may I state that since the summer of 1955 we have been asking that Congress do something about the needless price increases that have been sapping the strength of our economy, fix responsibility for those price increases, and take action to inhibit such picking of consumers' pockets in the future.

On July 7, 1955, the UAW International Executive Board

adopted and published a resolution calling for a Congressional investigation of price increases which were then threatening in the steel and automobile industries. In that resolution, ratified by our April, 1957 convention, we said:

Full employment and full production are possible within our free economy only as we maintain a dynamic balance between our growing productive power and expanding purchasing power. Workers, farmers, professional and white-collar groups, and small business men all must enjoy greater purchasing power to provide an expanded market for America's growing abundance.

Purchasing power can be expanded by increasing incomes through higher wages and salaries, by reductions in prices, or a combination of both. Since management has always maintained that prices are their sole prerogative and not a proper subject for collective bargaining, unions have had to make their contribution toward increased purchasing power by securing higher wages and salaries. Nevertheless, workers, as consumers, are vitally concerned with the relationship between wages and prices because price increases decrease purchasing power and cancel the positive economic contribution that higher wages and salaries are intended to achieve.

The past two years have proved the accuracy of those words. Long lines of jobless men and women waiting to register for unemployment compensation now underline their tragic meaning.

Today, when the strength of our economy is more important than our military strength because, as former Secretary of the Treasury Humphrey told you November 4, our military strength must depend upon our economic strength, when we need both military and economic strength to meet the challenge of the Sputniks and expanding Communist imperialism, the United States is already dangerously far gone into recession.

It is a recession that was foreseen and predicted and warned against. It was avoidable. Many, including ourselves, warned against it and said how it could be avoided, how by private and public policies to maintain and expand mass purchasing power to keep pace with improving technology and productivity, the American people and the American economy could avoid a repe-

tition of the boom-and-bust cycle which Mr. Humphrey seems
to think is divinely ordained and inevitable. We urged management to exercise some girth control, to curb its appetite for short-
run profits at the long-run expense of the entire economy, themselves included. We might as well have been talking to the
blind and deaf.

Today, partly because of tight money policies that Mr. Humphrey supported while Secretary of the Treasury, partly because
of a series of unjustified price increases which Mr. Humphrey
as Chairman of the National Steel Corporation defended for two
days before this Subcommittee, the purchasing power of the
American people, most of them wage and salary earners or
farmers, has been eroded far past the danger point. Americans
cannot buy back as consumers fair and healthy shares of the increasing volume of manufactured and farm goods, foods, fibers,
and services that as producers they can turn out in increasing
quantities each year, thanks to automation and steadily advancing technology in industry, in business, and on the farm. Already billions of dollars' worth of plant and equipment lie idle
and unproductive because at today's inflated prices too many
people lack the purchasing power to buy the goods we could be
producing. A growing army of workers faces the bleak prospect
of unemployment this winter, denied by forces beyond their control the means of providing for themselves and their families, and
the opportunity of contributing to the wealth of their country.

By push-button control exercised through administered prices,
Mr. Humphrey, Mr. Blough of U.S. Steel, Mr. Homer of Beth-
lehem Steel, all of whom have testified before your Subcommittee,
and Messrs. Curtice, Ford, and Colbert who will shortly come
before your Subcommittee, have priced millions of consumers out
of the market and workers out of jobs.

Needless price increases have not been the sole cause of today's
recession, but they have been a major contributing cause. And
among those who must bear a major share of responsibility for
such price increases are the giant corporations which dominate
key industries, including the automobile industry. The automobile industry, in fact, is in a particularly vital position. At the

beginning of each new model year, business analysts and business-men generally watch eagerly to see how automobile sales are shaping up, because the difference between a good year and a bad year in the automobile industry can very well mean the difference between a good year and a bad year for the many industries which supply it, and eventually for the entire economy. The major automobile manufacturers, whose pricing policies can determine each year whether millions of American families will be able to afford a new car, have the responsibility of making de-cisions whose economic impact is felt far beyond the confines of the automobile industry alone.

It is the contention of the UAW that for many years past the leading automobile corporations, and in particular the biggest of them all, General Motors, which sets the pace for the rest, have insulated themselves from the play of competitive market forces which are supposed to determine price levels in a free enterprise economy, and have been able instead, in large measure, to set the prices of their products in accordance with predetermined policies established by the corporations.

The term "administered price" is often loosely used without any very clear recognition of exactly what it implies. But in the price policy which was developed at General Motors in the 1920's and has been followed by the corporation with very little change for almost thirty-five years, it is possible to see price ad-ministration in action. As practiced by General Motors, it in-volves, first, a recognition that the corporation is a law unto itself, that prices are set according to "company price policy" and not through the play of market forces. It involves, second, a deliberate policy of attempting to make the corporation depres-sion-proof, of setting prices at a level which assured the corpora-tion some profit even in the worst years of the depression, and in boom years boosted return on investment to such fantastic levels as 76 and 86 per cent before taxes. It involves a policy of setting prices at a level theoretically designed to assure the corporation of profits after taxes which through good years and bad will average about double those enjoyed by other manufacturing companies, and which in practice have been even higher.

Needless to say, this form of price administration, as practiced by General Motors, has not been in the best interests of the American people, nor has it been in the tradition of American free enterprise. It has cast aside the principle of keeping prices down to maintain high volume and low unit costs, with over-all profits arising out of a high volume of production. Instead, prices have been established at artificially high levels, achieved by gouging the buying public through round after round of needless price increases. The consequence of these policies has been to limit the size of the automobile market, to reduce job opportunities in the automobile industry and thus to inflict needless unemployment and loss upon the workers in the auto plants.

Elsewhere in this statement we shall analyze in greater detail the methods and consequences of General Motors pricing policies as they have been revealed from time to time by top GM executives.

It is because we appreciate so very much the great responsibilities which lie on both management and labor that we in the UAW for the past twelve years have consistently and earnestly concerned ourselves with the problem of inflation. The size and strength of America's great economic institutions, be they corporations or unions, make it incumbent upon them to recognize their responsibilities for maintaining the economic health of the nation at full production and full employment levels. This requires the steady expansion, side by side, of productive capacity and purchasing power. The role of major corporations and unions in the setting of prices or negotiating on wages vitally affects this expansion and has repercussions on virtually all sections of the community.

The very nature of our free society makes it mandatory for its parts to function within a framework bounded by something more than a philosophy of "this is my own private business and my wages, prices, and profits are of no concern to the public." It is precisely because we in the United States have chosen not to subject the entire economy to government regulation that we must conduct our affairs with a sense of responsibility and restraint. To do otherwise is to risk either (1) spreading inflation to be followed eventually by a recession or depression, or (2) steadily increasing government intervention, direction, and control.

It should, therefore, be no surprise that the UAW has consistently sought ways and means to combat the inflation which has been insidiously sapping our economic strength during most of the postwar period. In the past few years we have redoubled our efforts in this respect. We have done so despite the fact that the day-to-day earnings of the great majority of UAW members are protected to some degree through the so-called "escalator clauses" in our wage agreements. These clauses provide for automatic adjustment of wage rates at regular intervals in accordance with changes in the official Consumer Price Index. Even with this protection, however, when prices go up, the value of workers' hard-earned savings goes down, their insurance protection is eaten away, and the buying power of pensions paid to retired workers is forced downward.

While UAW members have some protection against inflation, we are deeply concerned about the millions of American families who lack any real defense against the eroding effects of rising prices. I am thinking especially of those on fixed incomes, including schoolteachers, government workers, pensioners, and others who suffer the heaviest blows during an inflation. Virtually every month brings them a lowered living standard. The value of savings counted on to provide security and dignity in old age melts away as prices continue to rise.

Moreover, we know that if other groups in the community find their purchasing power reduced by inflated prices, so that many people have to postpone the purchase of new cars they would otherwise have bought, the jobs of auto workers are immediately threatened. The members of our union understand that we can enjoy full employment and prosperity only so long as our whole economy is healthy and growing. To achieve that end, all the people must share in the broad base of purchasing power, expanded and continually expanding to match our growing productivity. This purchasing power should neither be held down by economic stagnation nor eaten away by man-made inflation.

The UAW has constantly battled unjustified price increases, both in the industries in which our members work and in the economy as a whole. In World War II we supported price controls, and our union maintained in Washington a full-time consumer counsel whose job it was to help protect the price front against the inroads of profiteers who endeavored, with considerable success, to infiltrate and weaken government agencies which had been established to prevent price gouging.

At the end of the war, from November 21, 1945, to March 13, 1946, UAW members employed by the General Motors Corporation engaged in a costly 113-day strike in which the major issue involved the union's concern about preventing automobile price increases. Before entering into negotiations, we had made a careful analysis of the corporation's financial position, and the economic demands which we placed before the corporation were those which we had assured ourselves could be granted without a price increase. But we did not rest our case upon our own judgment alone. We made this offer: if the company claimed it could not meet our demands and still enjoy a reasonable profit without increasing prices, and if the company could establish that claim, we would reduce our demands by whatever amount might be necessary to avoid a price increase.

General Motors Corporation refused to accept that challenge. It walked out on the impartial fact-finding board, which had been appointed by the President to make a public investigation, rather than submit to a test in public hearings of its ability to meet our demands without raising prices. Its management adopted in 1945, as it did again in 1957, the arrogant attitude that no one has the right even to question or examine the prices charged or the profits made by the world's largest manufacturing corporation.

General Motors at that time also did its best to persuade the UAW to adopt the same arrogant, irresponsible, consumer-be-damned attitude. At the commencement of our negotiations, the union presented a brief to the corporation substantiating in detail our contention that a wage increase without a price increase was possible and desirable. In the talks that followed, the following discussion took place between Mr. Harry Coen, director of labor relations for the corporation and myself. I am quoting from the stenographic transcript of the proceedings:

MR. COEN: Is the UAW fighting the fight for the whole world?

MR. REUTHER: We have been fighting to hold prices and increase purchasing power. We are making our little contribution in that respect.

MR. COEN: Why don't you get down to your size and get down to the type of job you are supposed to be doing as a trade union leader, and talk about the money you would like to have for your people and let the labor statesmanship go . . . for a while?

Then, a few pages farther on in the record:

MR. REUTHER: The point you make is this. What you think we are doing—I am trying to get the thinking, because if we can understand each other, maybe we can move in the right direction. I understand you are critical of our position, and you think our position makes it more difficult to work out a solution because we are getting into issues here that lie outside the narrow limits of collective bargaining.

MR. COEN: I think that is very well stated.

MR. REUTHER: That is your argument?

MR. COEN: Yes.

MR. REUTHER: That if we came in here on the basis of old-fashioned labor bargaining and said, "We think we are entitled to so many cents an hour, and we are going to fight to get it," if we didn't think about prices and the OPA, that you think we would get further down the line?

MR. COEN: That is our business with the government, our business of setting prices on the cars, in a free economy, without the OPA dictating it, and the profit is something that expands and contracts along with your volume. I don't think those things—

MR. REUTHER: Don't you think it is constructive for us—

MR. COEN: No, I don't think it is constructive.

MR. REUTHER: —to be interested in the price question?

MR. COEN: You can be interested in it, but you are getting clear out of your sphere as a trade union leader.

MR. REUTHER: But don't you think it is constructive for us to try to relate our wage question to prices?

MR. COEN: Nobody else is doing that but you. . . .

There was a good deal more along the same line. But the representatives of General Motors made it clear that in their opinion our proper function was to demand from them what we wanted, what we thought we had the economic power to obtain, and that we ought not to concern ourselves with what the effect on prices would be.

We in the UAW could not then and cannot now agree with that position. We believe we have a duty to act responsibly, and we are prepared to accept proper responsibility for the consequences of what we do. By the same token when corporations such as General Motors or Ford, with their power to administer prices, put through round after round of needless price increases, whether or not they falsely attribute them to the pressure of wages, then we must make a public issue of the entire price-profit-wage relationship. As a responsible union, we can follow no other course.

The automobile companies have sometimes been heard to claim that during the late 1940's, before the backlog of demand for new cars had been satisfied, they refrained from raising prices as high as the market would have permitted. When you look at the profit figures for those years, which are presented later in this statement, it is hard to believe that any corporation would have dared to gouge the public for more. But if the companies did exercise some small measure of restraint, a substantial share of the credit should be given to the determination and self-sacrifice of General Motors' employees who, in 1945, first challenged the industry's greedy and irresponsible price and profit policies.

In the summer of 1950, when we were threatened with a serious inflationary spurt as a result of the Korean War, as president of the UAW and on behalf of UAW members and their families, I called on President Truman and Congress to impose price controls. On many occasions, when the automobile, steel, and other basic industries have planned price increases, the UAW has done its best to ensure that the American public was made aware of the strong economic positions of the corporations, positions which made price increases wholly unnecessary. In October, 1950, we prepared and distributed to the press a thorough analysis of the automobile industry, both the industry as a whole and the six leading firms individually, establishing that there was no necessity for a price increase to ensure satisfactory profits. In July, 1955, after the steel corporations had raised prices, and when it was evident that price increases were also planned by the major automobile companies, the UAW International Executive Board formally called for a thorough Congressional investigation of those inflationary moves.

That was many months before the current sharp upward trend in prices began. But there were already signs of trouble to come. There had already been a creeping rise of industrial prices, which was not being reflected in the over-all price index only because agricultural prices were falling and thus holding the general index down. In the opinion of our union, these repeated and unnecessary price increases were contributing to the continuing decline in the standards of living of our already depressed farm population. We recognized that the farm depression was masking the creeping inflation imposed by corporate administered price policies. We understood that inflation and troubled times lay ahead if public opinion were not aroused in time to induce restraint on the part of executives in big corporations who were grossly abusing their power to fix prices.

We believed, and we still believe, that a Congressional investigation, by digging out and publicizing the true facts about prices and profits, and recommending such legislation as may be deemed appropriate, can put the brakes on administered price and profit gouging by industry. Through effective use of this procedure we can avoid, or at least minimize, future repetitions of unjustifiable price increases which month after month force the cost of living upward to new record highs.

As we had predicted, the automobile companies did raise prices in the fall of 1955. As was to be expected, they tried to justify their action by attributing the price increase to economic gains made by UAW members earlier in the year. But when the facts are examined, it becomes clear that the major auto companies, on the evidence of their own financial statements, could have absorbed these relatively small added costs without a price increase. In fact, they could have absorbed the costs, cut prices substantially and still have received a far higher return on their investment than the great majority of American corporations.

During the first nine months of 1955—before prices had been raised, but after the gains of the workers had been largely in effect for four months—General Motors' profits represented an annual rate of return on investment of 78.9 per cent before taxes and a return of 36.5 per cent even after all taxes had been paid. Ford's profit was equal to a return of 57.7 per cent before taxes, and 26.1 per cent after taxes. Chrysler's profit was equal to a return of 36.9 per cent before taxes, or 16.0 per cent after taxes. By comparison, the profits of all manufacturing corporations for this period equaled an annual return of 23.5 per cent before taxes and 12.2 per cent after taxes.

In other words, for the first nine months of 1955, before any price increase, General Motors' profits after all taxes were paid were at a rate three times greater than those of all manufacturing corporations combined. Ford profits were at over twice the rate, and Chrysler profits, although its share of the market had shrunk, were nevertheless at a rate 31 per cent greater than those of all manufacturing companies.

Yet it was after chalking up such fabulous rates of return for the first nine months of 1955 that the motor corporations made the decision to raise prices still higher, to gouge still greater profits from the helpless consumer.

This policy of reckless and shortsighted profiteering by the motor companies deserves the closest attention of Congress and the administration, because its impact was felt, not only by car buyers who were forced to pay a higher price than necessary, or would-be car buyers who were priced entirely out of the new car market, but by every community in which automobile production was centered, and indirectly by the economy as a whole. It was the reckless greed of the automobile companies, combined with their headlong production race for the 1956 market, which piled up car inventories, produced the grave unemployment crisis of 1956 in the automobile centers, and contributed to the weakening of the whole economy.

The great importance of the automobile industry as well as the enormous concentrated power of its major companies inevitably makes it the pace-setter for much of the economy. Price action by the major automobile producers frequently serves as an example, good or bad, for other industries and companies. Unless major automobile, steel, and other big companies recognize and accept the full responsibilities that go with their great power, it is hard to foresee price stability and a sustained state of economic progress in our form of society.

Our union continued its efforts to put the brakes on inflation. In August, 1955, as prices moved upward another notch, I repeated our demand for a Congressional investigation. In March, 1956, when still another round of steel price increases was called for by the Chairman of the National Steel Corporation, I again called for "an exhaustive, fearless, and remedial investigation of industrial prices and profits, including a thorough examination of the relation of hourly wages and unit labor costs to this continuing wave of price increases. . . ."

In August, 1956, when the rising Consumer Price Index resulted in an increase of four cents in the cost-of-living allowance under our agreements with the motor manufacturers, I issued a statement pointing out that this represented no gain in real wages but merely partial protection against inflation, and I called upon the candidates of both parties to pledge an investigation of profits and prices.

In the fall of 1956 the auto companies again raised their prices, despite the depressed market and widespread unemployment among auto workers, and despite warnings from their own dealers that price increases could cut sales by as much as a million units. Early in September, as reported by *Automotive News* for September 10, 1956, Mr. Carl E. Fribley, then President of the National Automobile Dealers' Association, warned that dealers were unable and the public was unwilling to absorb price increases on 1957 models. The report stated in part:

Fribley said that 1956 price increases were absorbed entirely by dealers which caused a net profit reduction from 3.1 per cent before taxes for the first six months of 1955 to 1 per cent in 1956, a per-car reduction from $138 to $48.

"Customers," he added, "are more price conscious than ever.

Resistance to buying is far greater because of price than anything else."

Despite the fact that auto manufacturers will introduce many improvements and important changes in the 1957 models, Fribley believes it quite obvious that dealers will be unable to absorb a price increase and will be forced to pass these on to the public. . . .

Fribley pointed to prewar pricing methods as ideal for the industry to follow this year.

He said: "In the years before World War II when new model prices [were] held or reduced, the result was increased volume for manufacturer and dealer alike.

"I am wondering," he told his dealer audience, "if holding the price line this year, despite increased costs to manufacturers, would not produce enough additional revenue for the manufacturers so that the end result on higher volume would be more profitable than raising prices which would thereby result in lower volume.

"It is the prerogative of the manufacturer to price his cars at wholesale, but dealers throughout America have a tremendous interest and stake in the final pricing of automobiles.

"In my opinion, pricing of 1957 models could mean the difference between a 6½- to 7-million-car-year or a 5½- to 6-million-car-year for the automobile industry," Fribley concluded.

Present indications are that domestic sales of U.S.-made cars for 1957 totaled about 5.8 million passenger cars. This compares with 7.4 million in 1955 and 5.9 million in 1956. A continuation of the downward trend is anticipated, for Ward's *Automotive Reports* has forecast total production of only about 5.3 million in 1958, including one hundred thousand for export. We do not believe there has been any decline in the American people's need for new cars, but there has certainly been a decline in their willingness or ability to buy new cars at ever rising prices. There can be no doubt whatever that a substantially higher number of cars would have been sold both in 1956 and 1957 if prices had not been raised. There can be no doubt either that the gloomy prospects for 1958 could be remarkably brightened if the recent price increases were canceled and replaced with a price cut or the assurance of a rebate.

Mr. Fribley restated his position in April, 1957, when he said,

"Today, almost eight months later, I can see nothing that would change these remarks." Following the publication of our proposal for a hundred-dollar price cut on 1958 model cars, he again indicated that his position had not changed. The *Wall Street Journal* on August 19, 1957, reported:

At his home in Norwich, New York, yesterday Mr. Fribley said his views were still the same on auto pricing as those quoted in the Reuther letters. "If at all possible," he said, "the price line should be held because dealers can then reasonably expect an increase in volume."

In December, 1956, UAW members in the auto industry received a two-cent increase in their cost-of-living allowance as a result of the continued rise of the Consumer Price Index. Ironically enough, a major factor was the increase of prices on passenger cars. I wrote President Eisenhower and urged him to call for a Congressional investigation of the wage-price-profit relationship.

In reply, the assistant to the President, Mr. Sherman Adams, indicated that the President felt that such an act on his part would be an intrusion on the prerogatives of Congress.

Because we in the UAW felt that it was right and proper to call upon the representatives of the people to act when action in the people's interest was obviously necessary, I then wrote personally to each member of the House and the Senate, urging them to take the initiative in ordering an investigation of the causes of inflation.

When it became apparent that a still further round of price increases was to be expected at the end of 1957 on 1958 models, I wrote to the presidents of General Motors, Ford, and Chrysler, with a proposal which not only would have made a price increase unnecessary, but would have made a price cut possible.

What I, in the name of the UAW, proposed in brief is this:

1. That the leading automobile producers reduce prices on 1958 models to levels averaging at least one hundred dollars below the prices for comparable 1957 models.

2. That if such price reductions were put into effect, the UAW on its part would give full consideration to the effect of such reductions on the financial positions of the respective corporations in the drafting of our 1958 contract proposals and in our negotiations which will be taking place in a few months.

As I pointed out in my letters to the companies, the second part of this proposal, if accepted, would in fact have been self-enforcing. If price reductions had an adverse effect on the industry's financial position, we would have had no alternative but to take that fact into account in our negotiations.

However, we were prepared to take a further step. We were ready to set up machinery which would assure that our bargaining was conducted within the framework of the economic conditions resulting from a price reduction of one hundred dollars per car. We proposed that if, in the course of negotiations, a question should arise as to whether the granting of our demands would necessitate a restoration of part or all of the hundred-dollar per car price reduction, we would be willing to submit that question to impartial review and to be guided in further negotiations by the results of such review.

Details of the review procedure would have been worked out jointly, but we suggested as one possibility that each party name one member to a review panel, they in turn to select a third as chairman, or if they could not agree on a chairman he might be named by some clearly impartial person in public life. The panel would receive testimony from both parties, and after considering all the evidence would determine whether or not the union's demands exceeded the amount that could be paid without necessitating restoration of any part of the one-hundred dollar price cut in order to yield the corporation a reasonable rate of return on its investment, and if so, by how much.

The panel's findings would be made available not only to the parties but also to the public.

Following publication of the panel's findings, the union and the corporation would resume collective bargaining in the light of those findings.

As I pointed out, the price action we proposed would have exercised a powerful effect on the general economic climate. Corporations in other industries, which might otherwise have been tempted to raise prices, would have been under strong public pressure to exercise restraint. Similar price action, taken even now, would have a tonic effect on our now obviously sagging economy.

At this point I would like to deal with one matter which was raised by Senator Kefauver in his letter inviting me to attend these hearings. The letter described our offer to the automobile companies as "rather vague and indefinite." I would like to submit, with all respect, that it was not vague and indefinite at all. It is true that if the question of whether the employers could grant the union's demands without restoring any part of the hundred-dollar price cut were submitted to the panel we propose, the findings of that panel would not be binding.

At the same time, if the panel were to find that the union's demands could not be met without a restoration of all or part of the price cut, then I think we have committed ourselves so deeply and so publicly to the proposal for a price cut that it would be impossible for us to reject the panel's finding and refuse to reduce our demands accordingly. We would be committed to confine our bargaining within those findings. But the corporations, under our proposal, would not have been committed to yield everything possible within those findings. Thus, to the extent that the proposal was "vague and indefinite" its lack of precision favored the corporations rather than us.

If the corporations had accepted this proposal we would have been committed, and we would have been happy to be committed, because in exchange we would have helped to strike a real blow against inflation. Its consequences in expanded automobile sales and higher employment in the auto industry and all those industries which supply it would mark a major step toward ending the current recession.

Before we in the UAW made this proposal we naturally took a good look at the balance sheets of the corporations to determine its feasibility. We found that the profitability and price reduction potential of the Big Three are so enormous that the proposed hundred-dollar price reduction for consumers and significant gains for our members were perfectly compatible with reasonable returns to the corporations' stockholders.

At the time I wrote the corporations last August proposing a hundred-dollar price cut, financial reports on their 1957 operations were available only for the first six months of the year, and estimates as to the probable cost of the price cuts were made on that basis. Financial reports are now available for nine months, including the third quarter of the year when model changeovers had an adverse effect on profits.

On the basis of these latest figures, if they reduced prices on their 1958 models by one hundred dollars per car, but did not increase their sales at all above the 1957 level as a result of that reduction, Chrysler corporation would still make a profit equal, at annual rate, to a return on investment of 25.5 per cent before taxes and 12.2 per cent after taxes. General Motors' annual rate of profit would be 29.5 per cent before taxes and 14.5 per cent after taxes.*

With regard to Ford, it is necessary to take into account the fact that Ford's profit figures for 1957 were greatly reduced by the extra costs of producing the new Edsel line. A press release issued by the Ford Motor Company on October 28, 1957, summarizing their finances for the first nine months of 1957, said:

Profits before taxes for the period were reduced by unusual costs associated with the company's major product line and facility expansion program. In the first nine months of 1957, such costs totaled over $115,000,000; in the same period of 1956, they were $60,000,000.

In other words, Ford's actual profit *on its current 1957 operations* was $115 million greater than the balance sheet shows. The $115 million in extra costs have now been met. They will

* In these calculations and those which follow, no adjustment has been made for changes in executives' bonuses due to profit changes.

not recur in 1958. Therefore, all other things being equal, Ford Motor Company for the same volume of sales in the first nine months of 1958 could expect to show $115 million more profit than in the first nine months of 1957.

After making this adjustment, and on the same other assumptions as were made above for Chrysler and General Motors, the final result of the proposed price cut would be to leave the Ford Motor Company with a return of 29.8 per cent on its investment before taxes and 14.3 per cent after taxes if the price cut did not result in any additional sales.

These figures all compare very favorably with an average return on investment of 21.9 per cent before taxes and 11.8 per cent after taxes for all manufacturing corporations during the same period, when calculated on the same basis.

The above calculations were made on the assumption that a cut in price would have no effect on the number of cars sold. Realistically, we all know that, if car prices were cut, sales would certainly increase. I have already quoted Mr. Carl Fribley, past president of the National Automobile Dealers' Association, who should have a pretty clear idea of the relationship between prices and sales. He indicated that a price differential of the same general order as the price cut we proposed could mean a difference of one million in the number of cars sold in a year.

Mr. Fribley's estimate may be too high or too low—we cannot tell, since none of the automobile companies saw fit to accept his advice. For the sake of illustration we have applied Mr. Fribley's estimate, but we have qualified it with another assumption which is conservative in the extreme—namely, that the cost per car of producing those extra million cars would be exactly the same as the cost of producing the first six million. This we know is not only most conservative but untrue, because with the huge investment and the high tooling and other fixed costs involved, the average cost per car decreases steadily as volume of production goes up.

On the basis of the assumptions made, Chrysler's return on investment would be 28.0 per cent before taxes and 13.3 per cent after taxes. General Motors' return would be 31.6 per cent before taxes and 15.6 per cent after taxes. Ford's return would be 32.6 per cent before taxes and 15.6 per cent after taxes.

As I have said, we were confident on the basis of the calculations we had made that it would be entirely possible for the corporations to make the hundred-dollar price cut we proposed, and still earn a very satisfactory rate of return on investment. If our conclusions had proved wrong, we were prepared to amend our 1958 collective bargaining proposals in accordance with the economic facts resulting from the price cuts.

The automobile companies chose to brush aside our proposal. All three replied with evasions and irrelevancies.

Not one of them denied that a price cut would mean greater sales, higher production, and increased employment.

Not one denied that the increased volume would help substantially to compensate them for the reduced profit per unit.

Not one of them questioned our demonstration that in any event they could afford to reduce prices and still enjoy a very enviable return on their investments.

Not one of them showed the slightest willingness to accept the responsibility of their dominant position in American industry by giving a lead to all industry in a practical program against inflation.

Policies for Economic Growth

Statement to the Joint Congressional Economic Committee

Washington, D.C.
February 9, 1959

These hearings are being held at a time when our failure to restore the economy to health and growth is not only causing needless hardship and suffering for millions of American families, but has brought us to a critical point in the world-wide struggle between freedom and tyranny.

Our difficulties, both at home and abroad, arise out of no lack of physical or human resources. Our problems flow from a lack of vision and determination—a failure to appreciate the vast growth possibilities of the American economy, an absence of determination to translate those possibilities into reality. We are in trouble not because we lack the means to solve our problems but because we are not trying.

At home, our failure to achieve a rate of economic growth in accordance with our potential has meant long months of unemployment for millions of men and women. It has brought tragic hardship to many families, forcing the curtailment of their spending on food and other necessities, and dissipating their savings. As savings and unemployment compensation benefits were exhausted, unemployment has brought mounting welfare rolls to states and local governments. While men and women search vainly for jobs that do not exist, our nation has suffered the loss of tens of billions of dollars in goods and services that idle hands and idle machines could and should have produced.

At the same time, our position of international leadership is threatened by the same failure of our economy to match actual growth with its possibilities for growth. In recent weeks and months, we have been forced to recognize that in certain areas of scientific achievement and the military potential flowing from it, the United States no longer enjoys the commanding lead we once held over the Soviet Union. Even in terms of general economic strength, although we are still ahead, the Communists are rapidly closing the gap between us. The failure of the United States economy in recent years to grow as it can and should is one of our major sources of weakness. It has weakened us not only in terms of physical strength, but in the struggle for men's minds, and hearts, and loyalties.

It is urgently necessary that we find prompt and effective answers to our economic problems. Failure to do so means acceptance of the suffering and loss that unemployment and economic stagnation cause for our own people, an acceptance of hardships as unjustifiable as they are unnecessary. In addition, our position as a leader among the forces of freedom requires that we prove, through example, that full employment, full utilization of productive resources, and steady economic growth can be achieved at least as effectively within the framework of freedom as under a Communist dictatorship.

In the present crisis we need to understand and to act in the knowledge that halfway and halfhearted measures, and policies of too little and too late will not meet the infinitely complex challenge of peace, as we have always understood that they are equal to the challenge of war. Hundreds of thousands of unemployed workers in great industrial centers like Detroit, Pittsburgh, and Chicago, who manned the defense plants during the war, are asking the question to which America must find an answer. They ask: "Why is it that America can demonstrate the courage, the good sense, and the know-how to achieve full employment and full production making the weapons of war and destruction, but does not have the comparable will and courage and good sense to achieve full employment and full production making the good things of life for people in peacetime?"

I earnestly hope that this Committee will have the vision and the courage to face unpleasant facts boldly and to recommend to the Administration and the Congress vigorous, effective action designed to restore our economy to health and to stimulate a resumption of economic growth at the high rate of which it is potentially capable.

The facts of our relative decline cannot be denied. The total production of goods and services in the United States, for example, may still seem far ahead of that of the Soviet Union; we are probably still producing a little more than twice as much as they are. But economic growth in the Soviet Union is advancing four or five times as fast as our lagging economy has grown in recent years. If both economies continue simply to grow at the same pace as they have done respectively since 1950, it will be a mere seventeen or eighteen years until Soviet production can match and surpass ours in volume, and from that point forward it is they who will threaten to take a commanding lead.

If we should lose this race, it will not be primarily because Russia has surged ahead so fast, but because we have lagged so far behind. Our failure has been essentially the result of faulty economic policies. We have the physical means and the technical skill to achieve continued expansion at three or four times the pace of actual growth since 1953. As I shall show, there is persuasive evidence that productivity over the long run tends to increase at an accelerating rate. Given favorable economic conditions, our productivity at the present time should be increasing at a rate in the neighborhood of 4 per cent per year. Add to this the effects of population growth, and our economy should be expanding, at the very least, at a rate of 5 per cent per year. A rate close to that was achieved during the period from 1947 to 1953, but from 1953 through 1958 the annual rate of growth has averaged closer to 1½ per cent.

The realities of the world situation necessitate that America and the free world build adequate military strength. However, we must clearly recognize that in the face of the developing technology of nuclear and missile warfare, the Soviet Union is shifting its offensive to the economic front and will continue to place increasing emphasis on programs of economic penetration and political subversion.

According to a report in *The New York Times* of January 30

last, Premier Khrushchev in his report to the 21st Communist Party Congress specifically related increases in Soviet production to increased aid to other Communist countries. In addition, however, the Soviets have also been increasing their economic assistance to uncommitted nations with underdeveloped economies. A significant example is Egypt's Aswan Dam, a project of enormous importance to that country's economic development, which is now in the preliminary phase of construction, financed by a Soviet loan. Every ruble's worth of such aid carries with it a propaganda message of growing Soviet strength. Yet when it is suggested that American aid programs should also be increased, men of little faith have repeatedly told us, "We can't afford it." This is the voice of the defeatism that would measure America's power to act only within the limitations of our present depressed economy and the boundaries of narrow vision. We must realize that only by following policies based on confidence in America's potential economic strength can we transform economic promise into practical economic fulfillment. Only by adopting programs, at home and abroad, which will expand our power to consume and make new demands on our power to produce can we stimulate the economy to respond to those demands and achieve the full utilization of our productive capacity.

The need for such a stimulus is painfully evident. While the forces that threaten our freedom have been building up their economic strength, our economy has been allowed to lag, to stagnate, and even to slip backward. Employment in the United States today is less than it was three years ago. There are 1.7 million fewer nonfarm jobs than when the recession started. Even after some industrial recovery, approximately 22 per cent of the nation's productive capacity still stands idle.

Tens of billions of dollars of goods and services that could and should have been produced have been lost in the past year alone. Over the past five years, the difference between what our halting economy has actually produced and what we could have had with full production, full employment, and full realization of our potentialities for growth, would come to more than $200 billion. This production that we have now forever lost could well have spelled the difference between an unchallenged continuation of United States world leadership and the threatened, uneasy position in which we find ourselves today.

The unrealized economic growth and the economic abundance that it would have made possible are not only the margin of economic prosperity and higher living standards. In this period of world challenge they are the margin of survival.

Economic distress has been enveloping an increasing number of industrial centers. Hundreds of thousands of people in these distressed communities have lost their jobs and are without hope of finding useful employment unless the federal government provides effective and adequate leadership to get the American economy into high gear and to achieve full employment and full production. State and local government revenues have been affected, while welfare needs have risen, threatening many states and local governments with an inability to meet operating expenses.

According to the Labor Department's report of a few days ago, 76 of the nation's 149 major labor markets and 183 smaller industrial centers report substantial unemployment. This compares with substantial unemployment in 24 major and 61 smaller labor market areas in July, 1957, just before the recession started. The 1959 outlook for most of the present distressed areas is bleak, unless there is decisive action to adopt national policies which will quickly stimulate economic growth and restore full employment.

While the economy has been drifting without direction and so much of our productive capacity has been idle, vast private and public needs of our people, as well as a large part of our responsibilities as a leader among nations, have been left unmet.

According to the Bureau of the Census, in 1957 there were still almost 25 per cent of American families, not counting single persons living alone, with incomes below three thousand dollars. One need not have a Ph.D. in economics to know that in these more than ten million families there exists a vast reservoir of needs which simply cannot be satisfied on an income of less than three thousand dollars—needs which, if they were to be met, would keep our factories operating at full capacity for years to come.

In fact, the picture of poverty in America is even darker. There are 6.5 million families, over 15 per cent of the total, with incomes under two thousand dollars, including 2.8 million with incomes below one thousand dollars. The elimination of such poverty still presents a tremendous and pressing challenge to America.

As a nation, we have hardly begun to meet the public needs of our growing population—as witness the critical shortage of educational facilities in most communities, the vital need for more hospital beds, the continued existence of slums and substandard housing, both urban and rural, the inadequacy of our highways, and the continuing deterioration of industrial and commercial properties to be found at the core of many of our cities. In many important areas of our country, we are tragically neglecting the development of our resources, upon which both the security and the prosperity of our country depend.

In informed quarters, serious doubts have also been expressed as to whether our vital defense requirements are not being subordinated to the demand for a balanced budget.

I have already referred to the expansion of Soviet aid to underdeveloped countries—a challenge which so far we have failed to comprehend fully, but which we must face if we are to avoid the tragic result of hundreds of millions of uncommitted people coming under the domination of the Soviets. We are losing ground dangerously in the contest for the hearts and minds of the peoples of the economically underdeveloped countries, who, in the long run, will tip the balance in favor of freedom or tyranny. America is losing this struggle today, not because our system of freedom is unequal to the challenge. We are losing, unfortunately, because we are not trying.

One of the imperatives of world leadership today is that we recognize the rapidity with which people around the world are emerging from colonialism, political or economic, into full-fledged nationhood. As they find their way upward, they seek not only political independence, but a rapid improvement in standards of living which can be achieved only if they can obtain from more advanced countries substantial assistance in economic and industrial development.

We in America will be guilty of criminal shortsightedness if our reply to their appeal is, "We can't afford it." We will be creating ideal conditions for the Soviet propagandists who will move boldly to fill the vacuum created by our failures.

The most optimistic spokesmen of the steel industry estimate that a substantial proportion of its productive capacity will be idle during 1959. Continuing idle capacity will be found in our machine tool and machinery industries, in our farm implement industry, in our truck manufacturing industry—in all the plants whose products the underdeveloped countries so badly need. Are we to say that we cannot afford to get those industries back into operation? Are we to say that as a free people we lack the will and the know-how to put the unemployed Americans back at work to meet those compelling needs? If we have any intention at all to demonstrate the superiority of a free society over a Communist dictatorship, we must insist that we cannot afford not to. We cannot afford to give the Soviet propagandists an opportunity to say to the peoples of these new nations, "America has idle plants and unemployed workers enough to meet all your needs—but their economy is so faulty that these resources must lie unused." What answer to such attacks can we find, except to make them untrue by demonstrating the power of democratic performance.

These issues, upon which the destiny of the world may be decided in this half of the twentieth century, are not discussed in the President's Economic Report. They were ignored in the Administration's budget presentation to Congress, which proposed curbs and cuts in essential national programs.

The Administration's obsession with balancing the budget at low levels of receipts and expenditures, which is to say at low levels of national output, is an invitation to continuing economic stagnation at home and to loss of prestige and leadership abroad.

The slow rate of growth with which the Administration seems content contrasts sharply with the concept of a dynamic, expanding economy, and also with the vast potentialities for growth which are inherent in our advancing technology. The President's obsession with balancing the budget has blinded him to the economic truth that a balanced budget is possible only as a by-product of an economy balanced at full employment and full production.

The effects of the recession are still present. The pickup that started last May has not solved the problem of unemployment and idle productive capacity, by any means. A relatively slow improvement in 1959—such as most observers expect—will leave a persistent and serious problem at the close of the year.

The recession came after several years of relative stagnation. From the middle of 1953 to mid-1957, the nation's real total output, including services, rose at an annual rate of 2.2 per cent. The population increased at a faster rate than the 1.6 per cent yearly advance of the output of factories and mines.

The economy was operating considerably below capacity during most of those four years. This can be seen in the large amounts of idle industrial capacity during most of this period—only for a few months at the end of 1955 and in early 1956 was industrial output at high-level capacity operation. It can be seen, too, in unemployment—the number of jobless was 5.6 per cent of the labor force in 1954, 4.4 per cent in 1955, 4.2 per cent in 1956, and 4.1 per cent in the first half of 1957.

The sharp economic decline between the summer of 1957 and April, 1958, wiped out some three years of snail's pace advance. At the recession low point, the volume of national output, which had dropped almost 6 per cent, was back at the level it had reached in the first half of 1955. Industrial production had fallen over 13 per cent and was back to where it had been in the fall of 1954. Nonfarm jobs were cut 2.4 million—almost 4.6 per cent—and were at the level of the late spring of 1955. Working hours were cut back drastically, lower than any level since the end of the war. Industry, generally, was utilizing merely 65 per cent of its capacity to produce; 35 per cent of the capacity was idle. The number of jobless rose to 5.2 million, or 7½ per cent of the labor force, seasonally adjusted.

By the end of 1958, after eight months of pickup, production was almost back to the prerecession levels of mid-1957, but employment lagged far behind. Real national product had almost returned to where it had been when the recession started. Industrial production had recovered 85 per cent of the recession's decline. Corporate profits were almost back to prerecession peaks. But nonfarm wage and salary jobs recovered merely 30 per cent of the recession loss, between April and September, and then remained the same through December, except for seasonal changes. The number of nonfarm wage and salary jobs recovered only to where it had been in the fall of 1955. In December, 1958, there were 1.7 million fewer nonfarm wage and salary jobs than in July and August, 1957. About 22 per cent of industrial capacity was idle. The number of jobless was over 6 per cent of the labor force.

If we look at the record of manufacturing industries alone, since the recession low point, we find a somewhat slower rate of recovery of the production decline than in upturns from previous recessions and a much slower recovery of the job loss. From the April, 1958, low point to December, 1958, 84 per cent of the recession manufacturing production loss was regained, compared to a 26 per cent recovery of the manufacturing job loss. It required a recovery of 3.23 per cent of the production loss to regain 1 per cent recovery of the job loss. In the similar period of upturn from the 1954 recession, recovery of 2.33 per cent of the production loss was enough to restore 1 per cent of the employment loss; and in the pickup from the 1949 recession, a 1.78 per cent recovery of the production decline was sufficient to wipe out 1 per cent of the job loss.

This comparison indicates a significant difference between the current upturn and pickups from previous postwar recessions —the growing impact in manufacturing industries of automation and rapid technological change. It indicates too, the seriousness of the employment lag.

When we examine the entire period since the end of the Korean War—from mid-1953 to the end of 1958—we find a record of shocking stagnation. In those 5½ years, real national output of all goods and services rose at an average yearly rate of under 1.6 per cent. As for the basic industrial part of the economy, the output of factories and mines increased at a rate of merely ⁷⁄₁₀ of 1 per cent per year.

The pickup in output since the recession low point is accounted for largely by a rapid rise in productivity, following a decline that occurred during and was caused by the downturn. The great gap between the upturn in production and the slow pickup in jobs can be only partly explained by an improvement in working hours. In manufacturing, for example, the length of the work-week rose from 38.3 hours in April, 1958, to 39.9 hours in September, 1958, followed by a small seasonal increase to 40.2 hours in December. The major part of the gap between the rise in output and the substantial lag in jobs can be explained only by a rapid advance in output per man-hour.

The sharp rise in productivity has meant lower labor costs in many industries and, when combined with the upturn in production, it has meant increased profit margins. Corporate profits, along with productivity, have risen sharply in the past nine months, from the recession low point.

Where is the national economy at present? Output has returned to about the level of mid-1957, leaving a substantial amount of unused capacity. Nonfarm employment has recovered only to where it was more than three years ago and more than 6 per cent of the labor force is jobless. Despite the pickup since last April, economic activity is still no greater than it was two to three years ago.

There is a long road ahead, before employment can reach prerecession levels. It will take a substantial and continuing rise in sales and output to produce 1.7 million new nonfarm wage and salary jobs.

Serious problems will remain, however, even when employment returns to prerecession levels of mid-1957. In the past year and one-half, the labor force has grown and business has expanded its capacity to produce. There are more people able and willing to work and seeking jobs.

There is a much longer road ahead before the national economy can reach full production and full employment. The task of national economic policy should be to speed our advance along that road so as to achieve an expanding, full employment economy as soon as possible.

The sharp decline between the summer of 1957 and April, 1958, was cushioned by effective collective bargaining, the increased percentage of the labor force in service and salary jobs that are less subject to layoffs, and by unemployment insurance. Personal income held up rather strongly, in the face of cutbacks of production, jobs, and hours of work.

While business investment in new plant and equipment, business inventories, and federal government expenditures fell, collective bargaining, shifts within the labor force, and unemployment compensation offset a large part of the drop in personal income that otherwise would have occurred. As Professor Sumner Slichter has stated: ". . . by far the most important cause of the steadiness of personal incomes [during the decline] . . . is the rise in hourly earnings of wage and salary workers."

Other forces worked to bring about an upturn, while the decline was being cushioned. The government belatedly reversed its tight-money policy in the fall of 1957. State and local governments continued to increase expenditures, particularly for roads and schools. Congress adopted measures to make available additional funds for mortgages for moderate-priced homes and to step up roadbuilding. The Administration sharply increased orders for defense goods, after having cut back such orders severely in the first half of 1957.

What factors, however, can be expected to raise output, sales, and employment in the months ahead?

Much less push is expected from the federal government than in the past year. If the Administration has its way, the federal government will be, to an increasing extent, a depressing factor on the level of economic activities in 1959, by curbing and cutting its programs. Even if the Administration does not fully succeed in its effort, there is a danger that the federal government may be a restrictive factor in the second half of 1959, through curbs and eliminations of some current federal programs. Furthermore, the government resumed its tight-money policy last summer. This tight-money policy may restrain economic growth, as 1959 moves on, particularly in the field of residential construction.

State and local government expenditures are expected to continue to increase in 1959, adding moderately to sales, output, and jobs—particularly in highway and school construction and education services. But this continued rise is not assured, by any means. The recession and the persistence of large-scale unemployment have created financial difficulties for many states and critical conditions in several of them. In addition, the federal government's tight-money policy makes it more expensive for state and local governments to borrow money, thus raising costs, which may result in the postponement of expenditure programs.

As for foreign trade, there is nothing to indicate that the recent excess of exports over imports will increase significantly in the months immediately ahead. The economic outlook for 1959, therefore, largely depends on business and consumer activities.

Can we expect a substantial rise in business investment in new plant and equipment in the period immediately ahead? I do not believe that such expectation is realistic. With about 22 per cent of productive capacity still idle, a substantial rise in business investment cannot be expected immediately. Much of any early increases in business investment will probably be for modernization, rather than expansion of capacity—programs that would reduce costs, but would also reduce job opportunities. A significant increase in business spending for new plants and machines depends on a continuing, rapid increase in sales and production that will enable business to operate at maximum levels. The needed continuing rise in sales must come mainly from the consuming public.

In the light of merely a moderate rise in sales and output to be expected from the combined activities of federal, state, and local government expenditures, business investment and foreign trade, the key to the level of economic activities in 1959, therefore, is the consumer. Only a continuing and rapid increase in production and sales—largely dependent on consumer spending—can provide the basis for achieving high levels of production and employment in 1959.

A substantial rise in consumer spending in the months immediately ahead, however, will largely depend, in turn, on consumer buying power.

An improved balance between the economy's ability to produce and its ability to consume is essential in the months immediately ahead. The current lack of economic balance can be seen in recent trends of consumer buying power and productive capacity: Between 1955 and the end of 1958, the buying power of total after-tax personal income rose only 6.4 per cent, compared with a 17 per cent increase in industrial capacity. The rise in productive capacity was more than 2½ times greater than the increase in consumer buying power.

While total consumer buying power has increased at a snail's pace in recent years, the population has continued to grow. The buying power of per capita after-tax personal income, at the end of 1958, was less than it was in 1956. Many families have been compelled to reduce their living standards or to use their meager savings in the past three years.

A boost in consumer buying power is needed in 1959. It is unrealistic to expect a substantial rise in consumer spending— particularly for hard goods and homes—while the buying power of per capita after-tax income is less than it was more than two years ago.

Wage and salary increases and a reasonably stable price level are essential in 1959. With profits rising rapidly from the recession low point in recent months, there can be no rational reason why substantial wage and salary increases cannot be granted without raising living costs.

The economy, obviously, cannot continue, as it has in the past nine months, with almost half of the rise in gross national product going to corporate profits. Corporate profits dropped sharply during the general decline, but they have risen sharply with the upturn in production. Between the first quarter of 1958, the recession low point, and the final quarter of the year, corporate profits rose by a yearly rate of $12.3 billion, almost back to the prerecession level—accounting for 45 per cent of the increase in gross national product. Should anything like this condition continue in 1959, the pickup from the recession will be rapidly undermined.

An improved balance is needed quickly between the economy's ability to produce and its ability to consume. Consumer buying power must be raised sufficiently in the months ahead to provide the basis for a substantial increase of consumer purchases of goods, services, and homes. Government policies must encourage balanced economic growth rather than discourage expansion toward full employment and full production.

Current assumptions of the Administration and business spokesmen are that the nation's total output of goods and services will rise about 6 per cent between the fourth quarter of 1958 and the same period of 1959, as the economy pulls out of the recession. Unless definite steps are taken to encourage this increase, even a 6 per cent rise may be too optimistic. But if we assume such a 6 per cent increase, then, we are likewise assuming a continuation of high unemployment and idle productive capacity. The current assumptions of business and government leaders about economic trends in 1959 bespeak pessimism and defeatism.

In the fourth quarter of 1958, the gross national product was at a yearly rate of $453 billion. Nonfarm employment in those final months of last year was 1.7 million less than when the recession started. The number of jobless was 3.9 million or 6.4 per cent of the labor force.

A 6 per cent rise in total output would bring the gross national product to $480 billion. If this 6 per cent rise represents the real volume of goods and services, without any increase in the price level, it means that unemployment by the end of the year will still be as high as 5 to 5½ per cent of the labor force. It means that about 20 per cent of industrial capacity will remain idle.

A rise in output is produced by some combination of increased employment, and increased output per man-hour, and coming out of a recession, by a pickup in working hours. How would a 6 per cent rise in real national output affect these factors?

Productivity has been rising rapidly since early last year. If output continues to pick up in 1959, productivity can be expected to rise at a rapid pace. Even if the rate of productivity advance slows down during 1959, it is probable that output per man-hour in the fourth quarter of 1959 will be about 4 per cent greater than in the final months of last year—approximately equal to the average yearly advance in output per man-hour during the 1947–1956 decade. This would mean that about two-thirds of the expected increase in real national product would probably be accounted for by the rise in output per man-hour.

The remainder of the 6 per cent rise in real total output would result from a pickup in working hours and employment. A 4 per cent rise in productivity and a modest rise in working hours to prerecession levels would mean less than a 2 per cent rise in jobs. If nonfarm wage and salary employment should increase by 2 per cent, however, that would mean a rise of one million jobs. Should it increase by as much as 3 per cent, it would bring nonfarm wage and salary jobs up by only 1.5 million. It is possible, therefore, that even by the fourth quarter of 1959, nonfarm wage and salary employment may be somewhat less than when the recession started.

In the meantime, however, the labor force is expanding. Commissioner Clague of the Bureau of Labor Statistics told this Committee that the labor force may grow by one million persons this year, following two years of very slow growth, which resulted from economic stagnation. Even if the labor force grows by only 800,000, serious unemployment will persist.

The assumption of merely a 6 per cent increase in real national product, as the economy moves out of the recession between the fourth quarter of 1958 and the final months of 1959, points to approximately 3 to 3½ million unemployed toward the end of this year—5 to 5½ per cent of the labor force, after accounting for seasonal changes.

Since productive capacity is continuing to expand, as the labor force is continuing to grow, a 6 per cent rise in real national output would leave about 20 per cent of productive capacity idle toward the end of 1959, compared with 22 per cent in the fourth quarter of last year.

A 6 per cent rise in real national output from a full-employment level would represent a substantial gain. From the slack level of the end of 1958, however, a 6 per cent increase in the volume of the nation's total output is a very small improvement, indeed.

Furthermore, most observers do not expect a consistent rise in output throughout the year. A higher rate of increase is generally expected in the first half of the year, as business expands its inventories, and a slower pace of increase in the second part of 1959, on the basis of current trends. A slowing down of the upturn in the second half of the year would carry over into 1960. It means a continuation of high unemployment and great amounts of idle capacity in the years ahead.

Joblessness at 5 to 5½ per cent of the labor force is an improvement over 6.4 per cent. Twenty per cent of capacity idle is better than 22 per cent. But these improvements, based on business and government assumptions, are petty, compared to the size of the problem. They indicate the willingness of government and business spokesmen to accept large-scale unemployment and idle capacity as an inescapable price of our free economy.

When the Employment Act of 1946 was adopted it expressed the will and the determination of the American people to reject the negative and defeatist concept that a free society could not deal rationally and effectively with the blind forces of the market place. The Act's passage reflected repudiation by the nation that unemployment is the price of a free economy. The Employment Act of 1946 charged the President with the responsibility of proposing to Congress and the people programs and policies needed to achieve maximum employment, production, and purchasing power.

It was widely accepted by most people at the time the Employment Act was adopted that maximum employment in the

American economy meant a minimum of joblessness at any particular time, representing seasonal layoffs and persons who are temporarily shifting from one job to another in a dynamic economy. This would mean an unemployment rate of 3 per cent or less. Between 1953 and the present, however, the economy has operated at lower levels of manpower utilization—unemployment was over 4 per cent in the period before the recession started. The prospect for the period ahead, based on Administration and business assumptions seems to be a still higher unemployment level—about 5 per cent or more of the labor force jobless.

This picture of economic trends in the period ahead represents defeatism—a continuation of drift and the waste of idle manpower and productive capacity. It is a violation of the intent of the Employment Act. It is not responsive to our national needs in the middle of the twentieth century. It shows a total lack of comprehension of the enormous growth possibilities of the American economy.

The growth potential of any economy is the combined result of increases in its labor force and the rate at which productivity advances. In the past, many economists have conceived of productivity in the United States as increasing at a fixed average rate per year. It was recognized that due to a wide variety of causes there were inevitably changes in the rate of advance from year to year, but it was generally assumed that these changes would average out to a simple annual percentage—figures ranging from 2 to 2½ per cent increase per year have been the most widely used.

Even on this assumption, the rate of growth of our total production for the past five or six years has been less than the "normal" increase in productivity, although to create new jobs for the added number of workers entering the labor force, the rate of economic growth should exceed the rate of productivity advance. Each year, workers not only produce more with an average hour's work, but there are more workers available to help swell the flow of production.

The concept of a fixed average rate of productivity advance, however, does not accord with the facts. It has, in fact, been implicitly rejected for some years by many business executives on the basis of knowledge arising out of their own intimate experience with the facts of industrial life. Thus, for example, Harlow Curtice, then president of General Motors, said at the end of 1954:

. . . Our rate of technological advance is constantly accelerating, which means that every year we can build better cars and build cars better than we could build them before; and second, that the market for automobiles is expanding steadily.

Unfortunately General Motors' price-profit policies were not as forward looking as their production policies, so that the market did not keep on expanding very long; but that was partly due to a failure of judgment in not adopting price policies which took into account this accelerating rate of technological advance.

In the same year, 1954, Henry Ford II, speaking in Cologne, Germany, to a group of industrialists and government officials, said:

Rising American living standards have always been closely tied to our increasing industrial productivity. And productivity does not necessarily depend upon abundant materials, upon large existing markets, or even upon prosperity. Our productivity has improved in bad times as well as good.

In recent years, it has grown at an ever quicker pace. . . .

Recognition of technological acceleration has been expressed outside as well as inside the automobile industry. David Sarnoff, Chairman of the Radio Corporation of America, stated in a pamphlet entitled "The Fabulous Future":

The quantity of new powers and products and processes at man's disposal is important; but even more important is the increasing speed at which these things have come. It is not a case of continued increase but of continued acceleration of increase. We need only project the trend into the future to realize that we are merely on the threshold of the technological age.

The conclusion of industrial executives that the pace of technological advance is accelerating is supported by statistical analysis of long-term over-all rates of productivity advance in the economy. In connection with automobile industry negotiations in 1958, technicians on the staff of the UAW made a careful statistical analysis of the rate of productivity advance in the past half century in the whole private economy. One of the important results of that analysis was the emergence of impressive evidence that productivity has tended to advance at an accelerating rate over time.

What the analysis showed was a definite trend toward speeding up the rate of productivity advance, to the extent of something more than one-tenth of a percentage point every two years. While this rate of acceleration may seem small, what it has meant in practice is that the trend rate of productivity growth has speeded up from 0.9 per cent per year in 1910 to 3.9 per cent per year in 1956.

The latter figure of 3.9 per cent corresponds with the same figure published in the Economic Report of the President, January, 1958, as representing the average annual rate of productivity increase for the years 1947–1956. Although the exact correspondence is coincidental, since one represents the trend at a single point and the other represents the average for a period, it was to be expected that the two figures should not be very far apart.

This is not the first discovery of a trend toward acceleration in the pace of productivity advance. For example, John Kendrick of the National Bureau of Economic Research, who pioneered in the development of measures of productivity change in the national economy, wrote in a paper published by the Bureau in 1956:

. . . One striking fact stands out: there has been a significant acceleration of productivity advance since the end of World War

I as compared with the prior two decades. The acceleration is most pronounced in the output-capital ratio, but it is also unmistakable in the output-labor ratio.

Writing in *Sales Management Magazine* in November, 1955, Professor Sumner H. Slichter of Harvard University said:

Let us sum up briefly the outlook for the next decade.

In the first place, we can look forward with considerable confidence to a more rapid growth in productivity mainly because of the increasing scale of industrial research and the prospective improvement in the art of management.

While the statistical analysis indicates a persistent accelerating tendency over the past half century, the forces which have contributed to it over the past twenty years or so are most readily apparent. For example, as Professor Slichter points out, ever-increasing amounts are being spent by government, industry, and the universities on research and development which directly or indirectly stimulates the growth of productivity. Such expenditures increased from $900 million in 1941 to $8¼ billion in 1957.

Largely in consequence of this increased research, there have been in recent years a number of major breakthroughs in our technologies of production. They include important advances in automation, electronics, the use of plastics and other synthetic materials, new metals, the use of radioactive materials in industry, and important beginnings in the use of atomic and solar energy.

Many of the new technologies are of particular significance, especially in terms of the probable continuing acceleration of productivity advance, because they have wide applicability. These are not inventions whose use is limited to a single process or even a single industry, but whole new technologies which can be applied in a wide variety of fields. In this respect they are comparable to the steam engine that gave birth to the First Industrial Revolution, or to the assembly line principle which opened the door to modern mass production methods.

It is also significant that today's technological revolution is spreading into new fields which in the past were relatively untouched—for example, the substantial penetration of automation into many fields of clerical activity. In a recent article John Kendrick of the National Bureau of Economic Research noted "the speeding up of technological advance applicable to service." He wrote:

Since the service area now employs more than half our labor force, a further acceleration would mean a noticeably faster rate of productivity advance in the economy as a whole, assuming that the commodity-producing industries maintain their past rates of advance.

This new understanding of the accelerating pace of productivity advance compels us to think in wholly new dimensions both as to our economic possibilities and our problems. For example:

1. It is apparent that a substantially faster rate of growth in our economy is possible than has been generally supposed.

2. This faster rate of growth also makes possible more rapid progress in eliminating poverty, increasing leisure through a progressive reduction of the workweek, and raising living standards generally in meeting our public needs and in providing assistance to other lands.

3. Realization of our potential growth rate should minimize the danger of demand inflation, although it will not solve the problem of administered price inflation.

4. Continuation of this higher growth rate will give us new assurance of our ability to win our economic race with the Communist world.

5. Recognition of the magnitude of our potential growth rate gives us a new yardstick against which to measure the cost of our failure to achieve full employment and full production.

6. While a high rate of technological advance permits more rapid growth, we must also recognize that it makes more rapid growth essential, if increasing productivity is not merely to mean spreading unemployment. National economic policies must be framed with this in mind.

As I have already indicated, the rate of growth of our economy must normally exceed the rate of productivity advance, because growth results not only from increasing productivity but from additions to the labor force as well. An annual productivity increase of 3.9 per cent should produce economic growth at a rate of about 5 per cent. Many of us in the past have viewed this goal as one to be achieved only with considerable effort. The recent report issued by the Rockefeller Brothers Fund, *The Challenge to America,* says, for example:

As was pointed out earlier, our growth trend in the long period from 1870 to 1930 worked out to 3 per cent per annum. In the past decade we have been following a 4 per cent per annum upward trend. This record of growth lends confidence to the view that, if we act effectively and purposefully, we may reasonably expect a continuation of a growth rate of 3 to 4 per cent per year over the next decade and beyond. In fact, *a growth rate of 5 per cent is possible if we realize fully our impressive opportunities for economic expansion.* If the problems of growth are formidable, we have also found the impetus of our economy enormous. (Reuther's italics)

What the new productivity figures mean in effect is that a growth rate of 5 per cent can now be considered a normal expectation, with still higher goals possible if we make the fullest use of our potentialities. I do not wish for a moment to suggest that a growth rate of 5 per cent can be achieved automatically, or that it can be expected to develop out of policies of the kind which have produced so many obstructions to growth during the past half decade. It can be achieved only if we exercise both vigor and vision, through programs and policies which look forward to the future, not back to the past. But given those essential qualities of leadership, a 5 per cent growth rate should constitute part of our normal expectation of healthy economic development.

Regular achievement of a 5 per cent growth rate will open wide many doors to social progress which up to now have only with difficulty been kept from slamming shut. The Rockefeller Fund Report put the problem in these terms:

These projections also emphasize the fact that the high and rising level of defense expenditures is a major factor in holding back our progress on other more constructive fronts. We can afford the defense programs essential for survival. In doing so, however, *unless we achieve a 5 per cent growth rate, we shall have to hold back otherwise desirable expenditures in the government field and keep the growth of private expenditures below a level commensurate with our aspirations.* (Reuther's italics)

In other words the rate of growth in our economy, after allowing for the needs of a growing population, represents the margin by which we have more for all purposes each year than we had the years before, the margin available for social progress. If we are faced with the necessity of high defense expenditures, then the rate of growth must be that much greater to allow an adequate margin for progress in meeting other needs. The Rockefeller Fund Report suggests that a 5 per cent growth rate is essential if we are to make the progress to which we aspire.

Even without the element of continuing acceleration, the cumulative effect of a 5 per cent growth rate is most impressive. It means that we can virtually double our production of goods and services every fourteen years. By achieving that goal we can rapidly eliminate poverty from this country, provide a constantly rising living standard with increased leisure for all, catch up rapidly with our unmet needs in such fields as schools, hospitals, homes, highways, and resource development, and at the same time make a contribution worthy of the world's wealthiest country to the economic development of those in economically less advanced countries.

Achievement of a 5 per cent growth rate can be a most effective weapon in minimizing the dangers of a return of demand inflation. Since this is the form of inflation which results from "too much money chasing after too little goods," it becomes apparent that steady, rapid growth of the volume of goods is the best answer to it.

This does not mean, unfortunately, that achievement of a 5 per cent growth rate will solve all our inflationary problems. It should help meet the problem of demand inflation, but there is no assurance that it will be of great assistance in meeting the greater problem of administered price inflation. Since this is a form of inflation unrelated to questions of supply and demand, related rather to the ability of a relatively small number of key corporations to insulate themselves from the forces of the market and set their own level of prices, determined only by considerations of private interest, we must find new and appropriate means of dealing with it. But it must be a solution based on the nature of this new kind of inflationary force, not one which is appropriate only to something entirely different.

Apart from the special problem of administered prices, however, achievement of a high rate of growth should provide much of the answer to our fears of inflation. We have the means at hand today—as our idle productive capacity indicates—to satisfy a far greater effective economic demand than at present exists, and far from producing an increase in prices, such an improvement in demand, by enabling us to use our productive power more efficiently, should make possible some concurrent price reductions.

Achievement and maintenance of a 5 per cent growth rate should make it possible for all groups in society to satisfy their legitimate aspirations for steadily rising standards of living, without the social conflicts that result from efforts to cut up too small a pie, or the hurling of charges that any one group is trying to improve its position at the expense of others.

In passing may I note that in recent months, in addition to the usual false charge that labor is responsible for inflation at home, a number of corporate spokesmen are now claiming that labor is driving American business out of the world markets. I was pleased to note that the Economic Report of the President, this year, while not answering such charges directly, did provide in some detail the reasons why some important American industries are having export difficulties, none of which have any relation at all to the wages paid their employees. As the Report says:

In summary, the relatively sharp decline in United States exports after the middle of 1957 is accounted for by a combination of factors: the disappearance of certain special circumstances which had, for a time, raised shipments of petroleum, cotton, and wheat to exceptionally high levels; and cyclical shifts which had also lifted certain exports, such as steel and other metals, to unusually high levels but which now leave them temporarily depressed.

The Report also points out that the United States was not the only nation to experience inflation, nor the worst sufferer from it.

I hope that the corporation board chairman and other executives who are always eager to make labor the whipping boy for all their difficulties will read and digest the entire section in the President's Economic Report covering our export trade.

Earlier I indicated that if the economies of the United States and the Soviet Union both continue to grow at the respective rates at which they have been growing since 1950, it will be only another seventeen or eighteen years until the gross national product of the Soviet Union will exceed our own. That statement was based on estimates made by Allen Dulles, Director of the Central Intelligence Agency, with respect to the rate of economic growth in the Soviet Union, together with the latest available data as to our own rate of growth.

On April 29, 1958, Mr. Dulles told the 46th annual meeting of the U.S. Chamber of Commerce:

Whereas Soviet gross national product was about 33 per cent that of the U.S. in 1950, by 1956 it had increased to about 40 per cent, and by 1962 it may be about 50 per cent of our own. *This means that the Soviet economy has been growing, and is expected to continue to grow through 1962, at a rate roughly twice that of the economy of the United States.* (Reuther's italics)

Since that time the Soviet Union has claimed to have achieved an even higher rate of growth. The rate implied by Mr. Dulles' figures would come to about 7 per cent per year. On January 27, 1959, Premier Khrushchev told the Communist Party Congress that during the next seven years the Soviet economy would continue to grow at a rate of about 8.6 per cent per year, on which statement, a *New York Times* analyst commented, "Judging from recent performance, he may not be far wrong," and contrasted it with a rate of growth in this country since the end of the Korean War of 1.5 per cent per year.

Taking into account the possibility that Mr. Khrushchev may have raised his figures a bit for purposes of both domestic and international propaganda, it would seem that Mr. Dulles' estimates are worth consideration as a reasonable and realistic forecast.

At the same time, as a result of the recession, even the modest rate of growth which the United States economy averaged between 1950 and 1956 has not been maintained. Between 1956 and 1958 it failed to grow at all. As a result, the average annual rate of growth between 1950 and 1958 comes to only about 2.8 per cent per year.

If the respective rates of growth of the American and Soviet economies are projected forward, it becomes ominously apparent how significant these differences are. In spite of the fact that United States total production is still probably a little more than double that of the Soviet Union, if they had both continued to grow at the same rate as between 1950 and 1956, the Russians would catch up with us by about 1985.

However, if you assume further repetitions of our current recession, and project future growth of the United States economy at the still lower rate which represents the annual average for the period 1950 to 1958, the Soviets will have matched and surpassed us by 1977. It means that unless America provides the dynamic leadership and the effective implementation of bold programs to reverse this trend, the margin of survival between the forces of freedom and of tyranny may soon be reduced to the point of disaster.

Our position would be far less disquieting if we achieve, as we can and should, the 5 per cent annual growth rate that is within our power, even if we make no allowance for continued acceleration of the rate of productivity advance.

With the Soviets expanding their economy at an assumed rate of 7 per cent per year they would still catch up with us eventually—in terms of total although not per capita output.

But the date would be postponed until about 1996, rather than 1977.

Within that period, thirty-seven years, many things can happen, including even the possibility that internal changes in the Soviet Union may help to create a better international climate in which it may be possible for our two nations to live together peaceably in one world.

In any case, the achievement of a 5 per cent growth rate in our economy would give us many precious years of additional time in which to find our answers to the problem of world peace, without having to face the additional problems certain to be thrown at us by a regimented, hostile Soviet economy which had grown greater and more powerful than our own.

Our economy suffered a recession in 1953–1954 and another in 1957–1958, with only a partial recovery in between. If, instead we had maintained full production, full employment, and full utilization of our technological skills, with a steady growth of production at the annual rate of 5 per cent, which we could have achieved under those circumstances, the total value of goods and services we would have produced over that period, expressed in dollars of 1958 buying power, would have been approximately $212 billion greater than it actually was.

That is the measure of the loss we have suffered between 1953 and 1958—$212 billion worth of food, clothing, homes, household goods, schools, hospitals, factories, power dams, economic aid, and all the other goods, services, and facilities that would have helped create abundance.

If we had maintained that rate of growth since 1953, our national production in 1958 alone would have been about $525 billion, or $87 billion more than it actually was—sufficient to have allowed an increase of 20 per cent in every item of expenditures, public and private. This we could have divided among personal and family spending, health, education, and other government services, national defense, help to our friends in other lands, and new plants and equipment to meet our future growing needs.

The high potential for economic growth which is inherent in our economy holds out to us the promise of a fuller, more abundant future, but it also holds the threat of economic disaster if we continue to fail, as we have in recent years, to achieve that potential. A high rate of technological advance, combined with a growing labor force, means that an increasing number of workers each year are able to produce a still more rapidly increasing volume of goods and services. But the other side of that coin is, that unless our increased wealth is fairly shared, and adequate provision made for those common needs which can best be met through public effort, we will find the stream of purchasing power wholly inadequate to sustain a full employment economy. Then, instead of an increasing number of workers, each producing more each year, the number of jobs would begin to shrink so that a smaller number of workers would be producing the same amount or even a smaller volume of goods.

That is exactly the experience we have had in the current recession, and the experience we have had in earlier recessions. It is an experience that we will suffer again in future years, unless we learn the lesson that our economy can be maintained in a state of health and growth only as we learn to expand the purchasing power of the people to match the full potentiality of our economic growth. This is essentially the task of learning to manage abundance by learning to share it. This should be the major objective of national economic policy. Our free economic system has the potentiality for elimination of poverty—but only if we take steps to gear its potential abundance to the needs of all the people. Our system has the potentiality to raise the living standards of us all—but only if we ensure a commensurate rise in consumer purchasing power. Our system has the potentiality to produce all the homes, schools, hospitals, and other public facilities our people need—but only if we carry out programs to build homes, schools, hospitals, etc. Our system has the potentiality to produce additional goods and services which can help build the economies of our friends and neighbors around the world—but only if we initiate programs to provide that assistance.

Potentialities for growth are not enough by themselves. There must be effective programs which will permit those potentialities to become reality. If the programs are not there, what could have been a potentiality for great abundance becomes instead the potentiality of unemployment, hardship, and economic loss.

The problem of a rising price level has been used by antilabor propagandists to attack the American system of collective bargaining, and by conservatives generally as an argument for restrictive economic policies and cuts in federal programs. They are dangerously wrong and the policies they suggest would be disastrous.

The creeping price rises between mid-1955 and mid-1958 were caused by a number of factors, including: the ability of giant corporations in key industries to raise prices despite declining sales, business and government policies that raised industrial costs, crop and weather conditions that affected food prices, and continuing increases in the demand for services that are related to population growth, changing patterns of consumer demand and the spread of suburban living.

The claim has been loudly made that members of large unions have benefited from a rising price level at the expense of other elements in the community, and especially stockholders, who invest their money in the companies. This charge is belied by the facts as they relate to leading corporations in administered price industries. When we look at the General Motors record, for example, we find that stockholders' gains have been several times greater than those of the General Motors worker.

An investor who, at the beginning of 1947, purchased 1,003 shares of General Motors common stock would have received $3,009 in dividends in 1947—exactly the same as the earnings in that year of the average General Motors worker if he were fully employed, fifty-two weeks, without layoff, which is an overestimate of earnings.

Starting with the same annual income in 1947—one as the reward for his work and the other as return on his investment—the stockholder's income from dividends would have risen more than twice as fast as the worker's income from wages. By the end of the third quarter of 1958, after 11¾ years, the worker would have received in pay checks a total of $51,458, and the shareholder would have received in dividends a total of $107,822, or 109.5 per cent more than the worker.

But that is only part of the story. As dividends grew, the corporation's retained earnings increased and the market value of the stockholder's shares also increased, a capital gain he can realize at any time. Based on the average market value of General Motors common stock on the first day of business in 1947, the shareholder's 1,003 shares would have cost him $52,846. By September 30, 1958, as a result of two stock splits, these 1,003 shares would have become 6,018 shares, worth about $48 per share, or $288,864. If the shareholder sold his stock at this price, he would have enjoyed a capital gain of $236,018. Added to his $107,822 in dividends, this would have given him a total benefit from his stock ownership of $343,840—nearly seven times as much as the General Motors worker's earnings from his labor during the same period.

The same facts can be put in another way. If the stockholder in 1947 had invested only $7,909, he would have received, in dividends and eventual capital gain, the same amount as the worker earned. In other words, a worker's sweat and toil and the investment of almost twelve years of his life produced for him the same return as an investment of $7,909 in General Motors' stock.

This illustration points to the utter lack of fact or justice in the barrage of antilabor attacks on American workers as the instigators and beneficiaries of price increases. It also points to one of the nation's important social and economic problems—the ability of key industries, whose prices are administered by huge corporations, to raise prices and cut break-even points to 50 per cent or less of capacity to produce.

The record since mid-1955 clearly indicates the power of industries such as steel, auto, and aluminum to protect their markets from price competition. Prices in such key industries are established by the executives of the dominant corporations to produce high rates of return on investment.

The Senate Antitrust and Monopoly Subcommittee report on automobile industry pricing states the following concerning General Motors, the industry's dominant corporation:

In the past ten years, 1948–1957, the company's average annual return, after taxes, on its stockholders' investment has been an impressive 25 per cent. In the worst of these years, 1957, the rate of return on average stockholders' investment was over 17 per cent, a figure which any public utility would regard with some awe. At the other extreme, the company was able to earn a return of 37.5 per cent in 1950, an exceptionally good year.

The facts brought out by the Subcommittee clearly indicate that it was the quest for these very high profits, rather than wage demands on the part of labor, that were primarily responsible for rising auto prices. In its findings the Subcommittee reported:

. . . it is hard to escape the conclusion that prices and unit profits have risen much more rapidly than unit costs in the past two decades.

The same Senate Subcommittee investigated the pricing policies of the basic steel industry and found that:

the break-even point for both the steel industry as a whole and the U.S. Steel Corporation individually is . . . slightly below an operating rate of 40 per cent. This is to say, the industry and the corporation tend to move out of the "red" into the black when production, as a per cent of capacity, reaches a level of just under 40 per cent.

This means that the dominant U.S. Steel Corporation and the steel industry generally have succeeded in raising prices to the point where they can still make profits with over 50 per cent of their plants and machines idle. In the first half of 1958, for example, U.S. Steel earned $271.65 million before taxes and $135.65 million in after-tax profits, when operating at less than 54 per cent of capacity.

If we are to make any serious effort to achieve a relatively stable price level, we must attempt to find a solution to this problem. Some way must be found to curb the price-raising ability of giant corporations in key industries, in which there is no effective price competition.

Any serious attempt to achieve a reasonably stable price level must also, I believe, be based on a more rapid rate of economic growth than we have had in recent years. Rapidly rising total output makes possible rapid increases in productivity and lower production costs. It also makes possible a large supply of goods and eases the pressures among competing social and economic groups—it is considerably easier to solve the problems of who is to receive what share of the net product if the economic pie is large, than if it is small.

In addition, it would be well for the government to assist in the development of methods to increase productivity and reduce costs, particularly in those parts of the economy, such as the services, where the great possibilities that exist for improvement in productivity can be realized more rapidly through organized effort. In the low-wage service industries, the stimulus that wage increases provide for increasing efficiency can be aided by a rise in the federal minimum wage and extension of that law's coverage to workers in the services.

A reasonably stable price level can be achieved. But it can be achieved only if the propaganda warfare ceases and the realities are squarely faced. A rapidly growing economy is needed to provide the general environment for relative price stability. Special problems, such as the price-raising ability of the giant corporations in key industries, must be solved on the basis of the obvious facts.

What is needed in this area is less heat and propaganda and more light on the economic facts. Congress should make a comprehensive study of the administered price problem in an effort to find an effective and rational way of protecting American consumers and the American economy from the inflationary pressures created by the pricing policies of a few giant corporations in critical sectors of the American economy.

During the recent hearings of the Senate Antitrust and Monopoly Subcommittee, I proposed for my own union, the UAW, that any company which controls, say, more than 20 or 25 per cent of the sales in its industry be required to give advance notice and public justification of price increases it proposes to put into effect, through a public hearing before a government agency which would have access to all the relevant data, and after the hearing would publish the facts as they had been brought out.

In a free society an enlightened public can create the moral pressures essential to make private economic decisions publicly responsible. As I said before the Subcommittee, "In a democratic society, there is always everything to be gained, and never anything to be lost, by giving the people the facts they need in order to make their judgment of the conduct of those whose decisions affect the life and welfare of every man and woman."

There is urgent need for a decisive change in economic policies. Instead of drift and stagnation, we need leadership and a clear statement of goals that are responsive to national requirements in a time of population growth, rapid technological change, cold war, and the economic aspirations of peoples emerging from colonial dependency to national independence.

We have followed a national policy of drift so long, and our economy has stagnated for so many years, that we cannot hope to fulfill unmet national needs in a few months or even years. We can and should, however, make a beginning immediately and start to meet our needs.

There is urgent need for setting forth a program of national priorities in which we begin to put first things first and commit our resources to the achievement of those national priorities.

The requirement at present is to begin to move rapidly and decisively toward and expanding full-employment economy. There is no single pattern for this achievement. A number of steps are essential.

In particular, a decisive change in attitude and direction is needed in regard to federal expenditures and programs. The major test as to whether or not they are worth while should not be cost or budget balancing, but their need. National needs must be met, in the light of the requirements of the middle of the twentieth century.

1. *Distressed Areas.* Federal government assistance for economically distressed communities is essential. The experience of recent years clearly indicates that the changing location of industry and the decline of some industries leave pockets of unemployment, even when most of the nation is fairly prosperous. This problem has grown in size and seriousness, not only because of the recession, but also because of automation and rapid technological change. There is substantial unemployment at present in more than half of the nation's major industrial centers and in 183 smaller labor markets, with the probability that the current economic distress represents a hard-core, chronic condition in many, if not most of them. A concerted program of federal government aid, through loans and grants, is urgently needed to aid these communities to bring in new industries, to retain workers, and to assist workers to move to new communities where jobs are available.

2. *Minimum Federal Standards for Unemployment Insurance.* The unemployment insurance system should be permanently improved by additional federal standards to extend duration and raise benefit payments to unemployed workers. Harsh disqualification provisions should also be removed. As the President's Economic Report recognizes, the unemployment insurance system has proven its great, but limited, effectiveness in offsetting economic declines. The system should be strengthened and improved.

3. *Community Facilities.* Many communities would be happy to relieve local unemployment and at the same time create new or improved facilities for education, health, recreation, police and fire protection, civil defense, parking, or other public needs, if they had the necessary means. Amendments to the Housing Act in 1955 did establish a $100 million revolving fund to provide loans for construction of water, gas, and sewer systems, but the scope of this measure is far too restricted and the funds

entirely inadequate. Congress should pass new community facilities legislation which would provide authority and funds to assist municipalities in the provision of a wide variety of necessary facilities.

4. *Government Contracts for Distressed Communities.* One of the most obvious ways in which the federal government can give immediate aid to communities distressed with serious unemployment is by placing defense and other government contracts in such areas. For some years now, the Administration has given lip service to this principle, but in practice little has been done except to give some priority to such areas when all other procurement considerations are equal. This is not enough. Government procurement policies should be based on the principle that reasonable additional costs involved in placing contracts in distressed areas will be offset by resulting avoidance of the heavy financial costs and other tragic consequences of unemployment, both to such communities and to the nation.

5. *Minimum Wage.* Congress should extend the coverage of the Fair Labor Standards Act to millions of workers in retail and wholesale trade and in services, and should raise the minimum wage under the Act from the present $1.00 to $1.25 an hour. Such action would not only aid in increasing consumer buying power, it would also be a step toward eliminating poverty from the American scene.

6. *Social Security.* The Social Security Act should be improved through increased benefits, liberalized eligibility, and medical care provisions for those receiving Social Security benefits.

7. *Committee on Technological Change.* We must devise social and economic programs to cushion the dislocations that result from automation and rapid technological change. For several years now we have been living through a silent revolution in the United States—a revolutionary change in production and distribution processes, manpower requirements, composition of the work force, and location of industry. This silent revolution is continuing and, in the not too distant future, there will be the widespread introduction of nuclear energy for peacetime uses,

with the possibility of a vast impact on the location of industry, on opportunities for employment and on the skills of the labor force.

It is irrational to move blindly, without direction or information, through a period of radical technological change. Information is needed to help guide government and private groups in devising policies to minimize social and economic dislocations.

This Committee of the Congress has made a start in this direction. Much more information and examination of varying policy proposals are needed. A permanent National Commission on Technological Change should be established to investigate and keep abreast of these important issues. Such a National Commission should be composed of representatives of labor, farmers, management, consumers, and government. It should keep under continuing review developments in automation, atomic and solar energy, and other technological innovations, and make recommendations to Congress and the President to assure that the fruits of technological advance are fairly shared and full employment sustained.

8. *Progressive Reduction of the Workweek.* The Fair Labor Standards Act should be amended to provide for a progressive reduction of the standard workweek, with provision for periodic review by the proposed National Commission on Technological Change, so that, as our technology continues to advance, workers can enjoy, through a shorter workweek, an increasing measure of creative and purposeful leisure instead of suffering the tragic and wasteful idleness of unemployment.

Historically, we in America have always taken part of the fruits of advancing technology in the form of reductions of working hours, while at the same time increasing our supply of goods and services. The accelerating rate of productivity advance makes it possible to progress faster in both respects.

The rate of reduction of the standard workweek should take into account both the rate of technological advance and the extent to which our growing power to produce is actually being used to raise living standards, to meet our national needs for more and improved homes, schools, hospitals, highways and re-source development, and to provide for generous international economic aid and an adequate defense. When workers are un-employed, or suffering short workweeks, or faced with the threat of unemployment, they can scarcely be asked to accept the argu-ment that a forty-hour week is needed to attain our national ob-jectives while their government takes no steps to assure that their available working hours are fully utilized.

9. *Aid to Education.* There is a growing need for federal aid for education to strengthen the basic human resources of our country. This should mean, not only aid for school construction, but also a federal scholarship program.

10. *Housing.* A national housing program is needed to provide good homes in decent neighborhoods for all American families. The program should provide adequately for public housing for low-income families, slum clearance, and urban redevelopment, and low-interest, long-term mortgages for privately constructed moderate-priced homes and apartment developments. In this connection, too, a federal loan program for the improvement of community facilities is needed.

11. *Hospitals, Highways, Resource Development.* Other essen-tial federal programs include hospitals and other medical facili-ties, highways and natural resource conservation and develop-ment. These, and similar programs to strengthen our human resources and to promote more efficient use of our material re-sources, contribute to full employment, facilitate economic growth, and add to national security in a troubled world.

12. *Adequate Defense.* The national defense effort is in need of careful examination in terms of the military requirements for the defense of freedom. The U.S. lag behind the Russians in some areas is obvious even to a layman. Informed experts have chal-lenged the adequacy of the President's defense budget proposals. Defense expenditures should be stepped up wherever necessary, to meet our national security needs.

13. *Economic Aid.* Economic and technical aid for the peo-ples that are emerging from colonialism should be considered as

a major aspect of national policy. Such programs of loans and grants—both directly and through international agencies—should be greatly expanded as part of a long-term effort by the United States to assist the economically underdeveloped nations.

14. *Consumer Buying Power.* Consumer buying power must be raised substantially in order to lift sales and output in the months ahead. Wage and salary increases, and a reasonably stable price level, therefore, are essential. The President and the Congress should declare their essentiality, as part of a concerted effort to eliminate the waste of idle manpower and machines.

15. *Tight Money.* The government should indicate its support for a policy of rapid economic growth to full employment and full production by halting the tight-money policy which is generally restrictive. Instead of attempting to restrain the entire economy while over 6 per cent of the labor force is unemployed because prices in one economic sector, the stock market, have risen, the government should use specific measures to curb excessive stock market speculation. A step in this direction would be the effective enforcement of the elimination of margins on all stock purchases.

16. *International Trade.* International economic and trade policies of the United States likewise require bold and realistic measures to meet the needs of the times. Vice President Nixon's experience last year in South America dramatized, for example, the need to move in the direction of stabilizing raw material prices on an international basis.

17. *International Fair Labor Standards.* The United States must build its trade relations with other countries, particularly since we need a wide variety of imports as well as foreign markets. But we cannot avoid the problem of unfair competition with some American products from low-wage, highly efficient foreign producers. In this connection, the United States should propose, through the International Labor Organization, the creation of international fair labor standards provisions on wages and other labor conditions in export industries directed at raising wages in such industries, step by step, to levels justified by productivity. This would bring to an end unfair international competition

based entirely on depriving workers of their fair share of the fruits of their labor.

18. *Fair Employment Practices.* Opportunities should be opened for members of minority groups to contribute fully to and share fairly in social and economic growth through enactment of federal fair employment practices legislation.

19. *Meeting the Cost.* Admittedly, not all of these programs can be gotten under way in time to affect the level of economic activities in 1959. But their initiation now would change the direction and tone from defeatism to optimistic faith in the ability of the national economy to move forward in response to the needs of our times.

We have been told often—and it will be repeated in the future —that this nation cannot afford to meet both the defense and public service needs of the middle of the twentieth century. The truth is, first, that under dynamic leadership the means at hand are ample not only to meet our needs in both areas but also sufficient to make up rapidly for time already lost in meeting them and, second, that what we can afford least of all is to fail to meet them.

A more rapid rate of economic growth—higher employment and increased utilization of productive capacity—will, in itself, generate personal and business incomes and federal revenues. A large part of the increased expenditures for expanded government programs can arise from an increased rate of economic growth.

Still more additional federal revenues are available, without raising tax rates, by closing current loopholes in the tax structure. As much as $9 billion in additional revenue can be raised if these numerous loopholes were closed. Certain immediate steps in this direction would raise about one-third of that amount of additional revenue by closing the following loopholes of special privilege for wealthy families and corporations. To gain this much revenue we need merely:

(a) Repeal the favored tax treatment granted to dividend income from stocks by the Revenue Act of 1954.

(b) Require witholding taxes on the payment of dividends and interest, similar to the present system of withholding taxes on wages and salaries.

(c) Repeal excessive depletion allowances such as those for oil and gas and remove such tax privileges from many of the metals and minerals now covered.

(d) Tighten the capital gains structure by lengthening the holding period for long-range gains and increasing the current 25 per cent tax rate.

(e) Remove from capital gains treatment the many types of income not originally included.

Full employment, a more rapid rate of economic growth, and steps toward closing the numerous tax loopholes can raise more than enough revenue to cover the increased federal expenditures to meet our national needs.

Above all, this nation needs leadership and direction to move out of stagnating, rudderless drift into a firm faith in the future of our free society. We have the human resources, skills, and ingenuity. We have the productive equipment. What we need is a decisive change in national policies that are firmly rooted in an optimistic conviction about our nation's ability to grow and to solve its many problems.

History has thrust world responsibility upon America and we have become the custodians of human freedom. No nation is better equipped to meet these new and challenging responsibilities, for we are blessed with tremendous economic and human resources and a great democratic heritage.

The American economy is the most productive in the world. It is freedom's greatest material asset and if its potential abundance is fully mobilized and intelligently and responsibly distributed, it is equal to the challenge we face.

We must reject the counsel of the men of little faith who would sell America short by preventing the realization of the full growth and the maximum potential of the American economy. As a people and as a nation we must act in the knowledge that we are engaged in a struggle for peace and our survival, and that the challenge of peace is equally compelling and costly but more complex than the challenge of war.

The American people and the American economy responded to affirmative leadership following Pearl Harbor. The challenge today is no less imperative and the American people and the American economy will once again respond to bold and imaginative leadership.

We cannot hope to overcome our fiscal deficit until we first overcome our leadership deficit. We need bold leadership and direction to move out of economic stagnation and drift. We need leadership with a firm faith in the future of our free society that can call into play our great human resources and skill and our ingenuity and our productive capacity.

We need decisive changes in our national policies that are firmly rooted in the conviction that our nation has the ability and the capacity to grow and expand and find answers to these challenging problems.

We need first of all to overcome the crippling and corrupting influence of complacency.

We need to comprehend more fully the dimensions of the Soviet challenge and the totality of the threat with which we are confronted.

I share the concern expressed by General Omar Bradley when he said: "I am sometimes discouraged not by the magnitude of the problem but our colossal indifference to it."

As a people and as a nation we need to get our values in sharper focus. We need to think through together the values that we are defending and trying to extend in the world.

We need a list of national priorities for peace and survival, and we need the will to commit our resources, both human and material, in total effort to achieve these national priorities. We have to put first things first so that we do not dissipate our time, our energies, and our resources.

We need to recognize that new problems and new challenges

will require new concepts and new approaches, and we need to dare to try such new concepts and new approaches, for we cannot solve tomorrow's problems with yesterday's tools.

We need above all a sense of national urgency out of which we can achieve the same measure of national unity and singleness of purpose to win the peace that we demonstrated in winning the war.

We must recognize that business-as-usual, whether in government, industry, or labor, will not make us equal to the challenge before us.

I have unlimited faith in the capacity of free men to win over those who slave under systems of tyranny. In the words of Abraham Lincoln, "If we could first know where we are, and whither we are tending, we could then better judge what to do and how to do it."

Address before the Berlin Freedom Rally

West Berlin, Germany
May 1, 1959

It is a great joy for me to be in Berlin once again. I greet you and extend to you the hand of friendship and solidarity in behalf of the 16 million members of the American trade union movement.

Berlin is once again the testing ground for freedom. It is not your freedom alone that is being challenged by Soviet tyranny. It is our freedom as well as your freedom, for freedom is an indivisible value and when the freedom of one is threatened the freedom of all is in jeopardy. No man and no people live as an island unto themselves. We all live in one world—a world which grows smaller and smaller every day as science and technology move forward. You do not stand alone. Your American trade union colleagues stand firmly with you. The people of America and the people of the free world stand firmly with you in defense of our common freedom.

As you know, I am no newcomer to your city. I first came here during the dark days of 1933 when the shadow of Hitlerism fell across your city. I was with you again at the war's end as you struggled to reestablish the basis of normal economic life and when blind prejudice tried to prevent the restoration of essential industry. I was with you speaking out against the evil policy of dismantlement. But the new despotism of the East was not content to dismantle factories. It was soon obvious they were determined to dismantle freedom and life itself. Their effort to starve you into submission through the blockade failed because of your courage and determination. The blockade failed because the entire free world stood firmly with you. In the days of the blockade the cause of freedom had as its champion our late good friend—the courageous and dedicated leader of free Berlin,

Ernst Reuter. Today the whole free world is again thankful that Willy Brandt carries on freedom's fight in the best tradition of Ernst Reuter. I am confident that your courage and solidarity in the face of the new threat will remain unshaken, and I assure you that we are determined to continue to stand firmly with you in this crisis as we did during the blockade. The real test of friendship and solidarity is not where one stands when the weather is fair and the sun is shining but rather where one stands at a time of storm and stress. We shall stand with you in Berlin no matter how strong and cold the Soviet winds blow from the East.

Today, as I stand facing the Brandenberg Gate, I think not only of the threats to our mutual freedom but also of the millions who live on the other side of this gate and on the other side of the Iron Curtain which locks out freedom and human dignity. I hope that our voices from this great rally of free men might carry through and beyond the Brandenberg Gate, penetrating the Iron Curtain, not only to East Berliners but likewise to the heroes of Poznan and Budapest and, yes, to the latest victims of Communist aggression in remote Tibet.

They must all know they are not forgotten. We must reassert with new determination and faith that freedom, like peace, can be made secure only as it is made universal. There is no ultimate basis for peace in Germany except as all its people, East and West, are united in freedom and democracy. No one outside Germany, and this includes the men in the Kremlin, has a right to dictate the terms for such unification. This choice, to be valid and workable, must be made by the democratic will of the German people attested to by appropriate representatives of the community of nations, and within the framework that will strengthen European stability and ensure world peace. The free world must continue to strive for peaceful answers to achieving a free and united Berlin in a free and united Germany. We must negotiate from unity and strength and stay firm on matters of principle and flexible on matters of procedure. I am told there is ever present danger that totalitarian leaders, unaccustomed to soliciting or heeding the views of others, may underestimate the mood and determination of free people to resist encroachment on their rights. For this reason I thought it wise to tell Deputy Premier Mikoyan to his face during his visit in America that on the question of safeguarding the rights of Free Berlin and securing a Germany united in freedom and democracy, the American people are more united than on any other issue.

I talked to Mikoyan with first-hand knowledge about the Soviet Union, for I worked in an automobile factory in the Soviet Union for eighteen months and learned about the Soviet Union as a worker. The Soviet Union has made great industrial progress and the Soviet workers have won more bread but they have not won more freedom. We in the free world want both bread and freedom. Soviet workers, people everywhere on both sides of the Iron Curtain, share the same hopes and dream the same dreams of a world in which people can live in peace, in freedom, in friendship, in which no one would be denied either bread or brotherhood.

One cannot come to your bustling city, teeming with new construction and industrial activity, and speak only of tensions, threats to freedom, and other reminders of hot or cold wars. Berlin, like other great industrial centers, serves as dramatic evidence that the world has crossed the threshold of the Second Industrial Revolution. For centuries man has struggled to divide up economic scarcity. There was too little food for the hungry —too little clothing for the naked. Now for the first time in the history of mankind, we have within our grasp the economic tools of unprecedented abundance which can end man's ageless struggle against want and misery. The same scientific and technical know-how which brought forth the H-bomb and guided missiles gives to the world automation and the tools of economic abundance. Will mankind have the vision and common sense to use the new tools of abundance to usher in an era of human progress and human fulfillment?

The free labor movement is in the vanguard of the struggle for peace and freedom because we have understood that the struggle for peace and freedom is inseparably tied together with the struggle for social justice. Peace and freedom cannot be made secure in a vacuum. They must be made secure in a world in which pressing human problems cry for solution.

I can say in truthfulness that the only war in which the American people wish to engage is this war against poverty, hunger, against ignorance and disease. In such a war all mankind will be victors. The promise of such a world at peace, dedicating its combined resources to the fulfillment of human needs everywhere, will kindle the same hopes and warm response in the hearts of Russian people as among the people in the free world.

The German trade union movement (DGB) and the American trade union movement are united in the great family of the free world labor movement, the ICFTU (International Confederation of Free Trade Unions).

This is our goal. A world of peace, freedom, and social justice for all people everywhere.

In this hour of tension and uncertainty keep strong your faith in freedom's cause—keep strong your faith in yourselves. Your freedom and the freedom of the whole world is being put to the test in Berlin. Stand fast, for you do not stand alone. The people of America—the people of the free world—stand firmly with you in friendship and solidarity. Together we shall keep the door to freedom open in Berlin. Together we shall build a world of peace, freedom, security, social justice, and brotherhood.

Medical Care for the Aged

Statement to the House Committee on Ways and Means

Washington, D.C.
July 16, 1959

The promise of a long and healthy life has been held out to the aged. Dr. Edward Bortz, a former president of the AMA and a prominent member of its committee on the health of aging, last year made this dramatic statement:

Already we have enough information at our command that if we would utilize it we could control about 50 per cent of the sickness being caused by four diseases that are now the major causes of death in old age. . . .

Dr. Bortz predicted that the average span of human life will approach the hundred-year mark.

As stated in the HEW report, three-fifths of all Americans sixty-five and over are receiving cash income from all possible sources of a thousand dollars a year or less and four-fifths are receiving less than two thousand dollars. When three out of five older Americans have no greater income than one thousand dollars a year, it does not take a mass of statistics and it does not take a means test to demonstrate that we are dealing with a group in great need.

The basic problem is that this period of life is one in which people face a tremendous increase in their need for health care and at the same time a radical drop in income. This glaring discrepancy between needs and resources has become so great that we commonly accept the notion that a large group of our older people, accustomed to supporting themselves, become indigents immediately upon facing any substantial medical expense.

The report does not hold out much hope for great improvement in the income of the overwhelming number of aged people. It warns that—

Any assessment of the probable situation of beneficiaries in the future must take account of the fact that persons on the beneficiary rolls are getting progressively older. . . . The aging of the beneficiary rolls can be expected to be accompanied not only by higher medical costs but by the using up of savings and less opportunity to supplement benefits with earnings. . . .

Let us take teeth for example: In a study of people over the age of fifty, it was found that more than half of those in the low economic group had no teeth, compared with only 4 per cent in the high economic group. Similarly, only one out of four in the low economic group had ten or more teeth, compared with 71 per cent in the high economic group. . . .*

Let us look at nutrition: A vitamin C shortage was found in 87 per cent of industrial patients, 42 per cent of those in the low economic group, and none in the high economic group.†

Even so crucial a form of health care as admission to hospitals is also related to the means possessed by patients. The access of older people to the hospital is strongly influenced by whether or not they have hospitalization insurance. Those with insurance go to the hospital more often, are cared for earlier, and stay for shorter periods than the uninsured. The OASI study for 1957 shows, for example, that for every one hundred with insurance fourteen were hospitalized; among the uninsured fewer than nine were hospitalized.

The uninsured, who are by far in the majority among older people, often wait until the need to be hospitalized can no longer be put off. When finally admitted, they stay longer and are more severely ill.

Because of the limited means of older people, the whole range

* "Nutritional Status of the Aging," by Drs. Harold D. Chope and Lester Breslow, appearing in the *American Journal of Public Health* for January, 1956.

† Drs. Chope and Dray in *California Medicine* for February, 1951.

of health facilities available to them is often inadequate. The Minnesota Commission on Aging found that only with respect to hospitals do the majority—80 per cent—of the counties in that state consider the present facilities adequate for older persons. The results showed that in 55 per cent of the counties, the licensed nursing homes were inadequate for the care of older persons; in 76 per cent of the counties, low-rent housing was rated as inadequate.

. . . A prominent state official has recently reported that 90 per cent of the nursing and convalescent homes in his state are dangerous with regard to possibility of fire. . . .

The use of readily combustible materials in construction is a common hazard, causing rapid spread of fire. In two of the worst fire disasters in homes caring for older people, the fire was out of control from the very beginning largely because of the use of fiberboard and plywood construction. Of some 451 nursing homes in one state, only 29 are built of fire-resistant materials. . . .

Many homes lack even the simplest measures of fire and smoke control. . . .

. . . When telephone lines were destroyed in a recent nursing home fire, someone had to drive the several miles to the nearest fire department, and by the time help arrived, nothing could be done to save trapped patients. . . .

. . . A great many patients were trapped when a fire broke out in a one-story nursing home where no one was assigned to be on duty at night. . . .

Overcrowding, restraints, and oversedation are not only injurious to residents but are highly dangerous in emergencies. . . . It is known in some instances that overcrowding made it impossible to remove patients in time. Sometimes patients have been trapped because they were locked in their rooms and could not be removed. . . .*

The same report comments on the status of health and medical care as follows:

Poor health and medical care practices exist in many homes under any type of auspices. Many homes provide no medical super-

* "Standards of Care for Older People in Institutions," National Committee on Aging, sec. II, pp. 11, 12.

vision and no assurance of hospital care when needed. Some accept patients for whom they are not licensed to care, such as persons with severe mental conditions or tuberculosis. Often the sick and well are kept together in long wards. Infirmary arrangements are frequently makeshift and inadequate. . . . Abusive treatment has been reported in some homes where patients are left on bedpans for hours at a time, or where calls for assistance and personal care are ignored. Irresponsibility in relation to needed medical attention and medication has been found in many places. . . .

A 1950 study by the Kentucky State Health Department of the private nursing homes in Jefferson County comments:

Medical care is quite inadequate quantitatively and many patients have had little or none. Insofar as could be determined, few patients had had complete medical workups and diagnoses were frequently several years old. Treatment consisted largely of drug therapy and it was impossible to determine how closely this followed physicians' orders. Much of the medical followup was episodic and only in relation to acute episodes or illnesses.

More than one-eighth of the private medical care received by people 65 years or older was provided through public assistance in 1956.

Moreover, to most older Americans the test of need for old-age assistance as applied by public welfare agencies is most onerous, and many go without care rather than apply for relief. In most instances, laws and regulations require that practically all liquid assets be exhausted. The amount of assistance received may constitute a lien against property. Various relatives (sons, daughters, parents, and in some jurisdictions grandchildren and even certain in-laws) are required to contribute before either medical aid or a grant can be authorized. Older people are often understandably reluctant to push off on relatives in modest circumstances the obligation of support implicit in an application for public assistance.

Expressing his support of the union's efforts in behalf of the Forand bill, one rank-and-file member wrote, on May 6, 1959:

This is written in regards to the Forand bill. Our elderly citizens do need some consideration after years of spending their lives bringing up their children and doing without to give them the education and training to become good citizens themselves. At a time when the elder ones could sit back and enjoy each other and the few years they have left together, they have new worries to upset them. If one got sick how in the name of all that's holy could they pay their bills? Should they get the children who, after all they have done to help them become independent, to help? No parent wants to feel that he or she is imposing on their children. It's true no child in their right mind would let their parents down, but a lot of them can't afford to help two homes and pay two sets of bills.

We people in the United States take it for granted that the families will provide for their elders, but has anyone asked the elders what they want? Just because they get to the age where they can't work any more and have to retire, doesn't mean they want to be charity cases. The elderly folks desire and deserve the good care and respect that they gave to their own when they were able.

In addition to the means test, there are further bars to receiving help. Residence requirements, local and state, are quite common and constitute all too effective a bar in a period of increased population mobility. Even where states and localities have provision for granting aid to the so-called medically indigent who are not receiving public assistance, it is often done grudgingly and under conditions which make it extremely difficult for a self-respecting person, with a lifetime record of independence, to accept help.

Further, in many jurisdictions, the medical care available to those occupying the long lines of cots in county hospitals is inadequate medically. While some advances have been made in the provision of charity medicine in a way that does not offend the patient, the unrelenting struggles of harassed personnel with heavy caseloads, insufficient staffs, and inadequate budgets too often lead to an inescapable erosion of medical standards and a common disregard of the sensibilities of the sick in hospital charity wards and outpatient charity clinics. Is it not high time that we turn away from the indignities of assistance and charity for our older citizens in favor of an insurance system as we have done with retirement income?

There are no accurate figures available on the number of aged people covered by health insurance and the degree of protection that they have. There are strong grounds for skepticism about the reliability of the figures that have been advanced. The Health Information Foundation in its 1957 survey estimated that 38.6 per cent of people sixty-five and over were covered by some form of voluntary health insurance. The survey, however, acknowledged that: "relatively little is known about the details of this coverage."

In many household surveys, people who believe that they have hospitalization insurance are classified as insured. Efforts to verify coverage are often not feasible and people are sometimes counted as insured who have negligible protection or none at all.

The survey of OASI beneficiaries in the same year of 1957, reported that among those with hospitalization insurance as many as 16 per cent of the aged couples and 13 per cent of the non-married beneficiaries did not receive any benefits when hospitalized. It is possible to explain some of this away by people who received free care. However, much of the discrepancy is undoubtedly the result of counting as insured people who failed to receive benefits because they were actually not insured and because of cancellations, limitations, and exclusions in their coverage. I seriously question both the correctness and the true meaning of the current estimates that 41 or 42 per cent are now insured.

The fact that the number of older people still uncovered is substantially higher than those covered is hardly surprising. The enthusiasm of insurance companies for covering the aged is of very recent origin. Not before legislation of this type began to be seriously considered was there any significant effort on the part of insurance companies to make available to people of advanced years their individual accident and health policies. As late as 1957, a tally of insurance companies, showing the highest age at which they could issue individual policies, revealed that 90 per cent ordinarily do not sell insurance to persons past a stated age. A few have set the maximums at very high ages, but almost half still will not write such policies for applicants over sixty-five and some of them adhere to limits of fifty-five and sixty. While I know there has been some progress I question whether very many major carriers have unfrozen those age limits for most of their policies.

Within the age-limit provisions, moreover, coverage was effectively denied for people who were in need of protection by the requirement of insurability whereby the individual had to undergo a medical examination to establish his good health and testify to his previous good health by giving a medical history. If, perchance, he successfully ran this gantlet, he became insured. And if he subsequently became ill and needed his insurance, he could be weeded out as a bad risk by refusal of the company to renew, or by outright cancellation.

As for group insurance, before acquiring their new-found zeal for covering the aged, the insurance companies were discouraging employers from providing health insurance for older people and often, in many situations, refusing outright to provide such coverage. The rate manual of one of the most prominent insurance companies stated: "In general, hospital, surgical, medical, diagnostic, and other special features may not be continued for retired or pensioned employees or their dependents."

The company discouraged the employer from covering the retired people.

The claim rate for this class of employee is several times higher than that for active employees and their dependents and the continuation of coverage for this class of employee may have an adverse effect upon the experience under the policy.

Under certain circumstances and subject to certain conditions where the employer, after being fully acquainted with the probable cost, feels that for employee relations it is necessary, coverage may be continued . . . subject to prior home office approval.

Approval, however, was considered only if the case numbered at least one thousand active employees in size and was subject to other qualifying conditions. Even so, coverage was limited to hospital and surgical insurance and there were benefit limitations. And the premium rate was three times that for the corresponding active employees or dependents. These conditions were typical and they made it extremely difficult to get any significant coverage of retired workers before 1953.

In that year, our union began a concerted drive to get carriers and employers to agree to voluntary insurance for our retirees. The automobile companies agreed to open enrollment for retirees, but refused to bear any part of the cost, thus making it necessary for the retired workers, themselves, to pay the full cost of protection out of their pensions. A checkoff for this purpose was agreed to.

Blue Cross and Blue Shield plans, after some initial resistance, generally agreed to provide this coverage, although the rules were made very strict. The retired workers were offered a single lifetime opportunity to become enrolled. An employee who was not covered by Blue Cross and Blue Shield at the time of his retirement was unable to obtain group coverage. A retired worker who, for any reason, missed a month's or quarter's premium was permanently removed from coverage. If for any reason the employed group ceased to be enrolled by Blue Cross and Blue Shield, the retirees were stranded. Several groups have lost coverage when plants closed. Others have been continued under precarious arrangements at the sufferance of Blue Cross with the chance that they may be discontinued. And if this sounds restrictive, the Blue Cross and Blue Shield have been the more cooperative among carriers. The experience with commercial insurance has been far worse.

About four out of five UAW retirees have tried to hang on to their hospital-medical coverage. To do so, however, the average retiree has to spend about $6 a month if he is single, and about $15.50 a month if he is married. On the average, this means that elderly couples have to spend about one-fourth of their negotiated pensions for health insurance. For some, the amount spent for health insurance is more than half of the pension.

When retirees, living under limited income, have to allocate this kind of money for health insurance, it hurts. Hardly a day goes by that we don't get letters at Solidarity House such as these:

You will please find enclosed receipts of records pertaining to my Blue Cross and Blue Shield insurance. By comparison of receipts herein, they will just about rob me of my entire Ford pension. This last raise given them is just about highway robbery. We have no help from Ford Motor Company as do those that are working and, too, we have no cost-of-living escalator clause. Personally, I almost feel disposed in canceling this highway outfit, but I hate to be without some protection.

This retired worker enclosed receipts showing that out of a negotiated pension of $25.31 a month, his deduction for health insurance had increased from $9.45 to $16.13, leaving a monthly pension of only $9.18. Although part of the increased deduction covers an improvement in benefits, the majority of it represents increases in prepayment cost.

Another letter from a Ford retiree:

They have took $4.32 more out of my Blue Cross and Blue Shield. They are taking out $16.13 out of my Ford pension which is $33.75. That don't leave enough to pay my gas bill. Is there anything you can do about it?

From still another letter from a General Motors worker:

When I was in the shop and making good wages, the company paid part of the cost, as you know, and thanks to you fellows at the table. But now, out of my $61 Chevrolet pension, the Blue Cross takes $11 for me and my wife and from what I read in the papers this week, I expect it to be raised again.

And he was right.

"Being sick," says this worker, "is the most dreaded of all the problems of growing old." . . . "Do you think there will ever be anything done to relieve the pressure of mounting cost?"

We are drifting further and further away from a solution to this problem because of unrelenting increases in health care costs.

The cost of hospitalization leads all items on the Consumer Price Index. The cost of drugs and medicines has been going up and often reaches unmanageable levels for older people. The phenomenal inflation which has taken place in the cost of hospital and medical care over the past few years has hit the retired worker especially hard. A dramatic example of how inflation has eaten into retired worker income occurred just these past few months. In September of last year our union, after hard-fought negotiations, was able to secure an increase in pension benefits for UAW retirees. On January 1, 1959, there was a rate increase in Michigan Blue Cross-Blue Shield which at one stroke completely wiped out the entire average pension increase.

As you have seen from the parade of witnesses from organized medicine, a great many of the medical societies are fighting this bill.

It is a regrettable truth that the American Medical Association resisted the early development of the voluntary health insurance system which they now claim they are defending. Organized medicine has spent millions of dollars to confuse the American people with such slogans as "socialized medicine." Over a 3½-year period, through Whittaker & Baxter, a highly paid public relations firm, they spent $4,678,000, pumping to the public millions of pieces of spurious propaganda about "socialized medicine," a term which, according to the current issue of *Harper's* magazine, Whittaker & Baxter have themselves, "conversationally abandoned."

Only recently the AMA opposed disability benefits under Social Security, a feature that was earlier incorporated into the social security system of practically every civilized country in the world.

We did not adopt disability benefits until 1956, and then only after the program had been delayed and resisted for years, and after the insurance companies and doctors had so long threatened the Congress with almost every kind of danger, that the late Senator George rose in indignation and made an impassioned plea to the Congress to support the measure.

What is the AMA now proposing? The AMA is exhorting

state and county medical societies to extend Blue Shield coverage to older people and to establish cut-rate fees for their care. The March 14, 1959, *Journal of the American Medical Association*, describing this program, claimed that: "Such arrangements would make it possible to provide the coverage at low rates and constitute a program that persons living on retirement income could easily afford."

If the doctors of America really were living up to their principle of charging according to ability to pay, the present campaign for reduced fees would be entirely unnecessary. This is literally a plan to force upon physicians the responsibility for a systematic subsidy of the medical care of older persons. It is questionable whether it will be generally accepted by the profession. In *Medical Economies* of April 27, Dr. Harold J. Peggs asserts: "Doctors can't beat the Forand bill." He says in part: "All over the country doctors are being asked to accept reduced fees to help beat the Forand bill. This gesture is not only futile, but downright dangerous."

Dr. Peggs concludes:

. . . Some version of the Forand bill will go sailing through Congress in 1960. It's inevitable, as everyone knows—everyone, apparently, except us doctors.

The hospitals and Blue Cross won't seriously fight it. Both labor and management will be relieved to have the burden of health care for the aged shifted to Government. . . .

So why must we stand alone? In the name of common sense, why don't we put aside this quixotic gesture? Nothing doctors can do will solve the problem of the aged. But it isn't too late for us to work toward preserving the rest of private practice. Let's get on with that job.

The AMA proposal to cut fees for the aged is indeed quixotic. Even if its members should accept this proposal, which apparently is not entirely certain, and agree to provide service benefits at reasonable cost for the aged people, it would do nothing to assure them hospitalization—a cost that will not be reduced by any medical fiat, or by some sleight of hand. How will the aged meet the cost of hospital care and nursing home care, and how will they meet the substantial cost of programs even after fee reduction without employer contributions to help pay for the cost?

The political doctors of the AMA have come up with an unworkable scheme. I would seriously urge the doctors of America to consider on its merits the Forand proposal, which would relieve the older patients of financial stress in obtaining hospital care, nursing home care, and surgical care. No fee cutting will replace the necessity for a decent insurance program—it just won't work.

In their testimony on the Social Security Amendments of 1955, the National Association of Life Underwriters asserted that all this is socialistic. They said:

It would seem that many of our lawmakers in Washington have dedicated themselves to the implementation of this socialistic philosophy and are determined to forge the OASI program into a compulsory system of cradle-to-grave benefits, so comprehensive and costly that the citizens of this country will find it both unnecessary and financially impossible to fend for themselves. If it happened in France, let us in the life insurance business not delude ourselves into believing that it cannot happen here.

It is high time that the organized medical profession and the insurance companies and a few of the businessmen's organizations of this country stop ganging up on the country's vulnerable older citizens.

Apart from an entirely unfounded optimism that they will somehow catch up with this problem, what have the insurance companies offered as solutions of their own? To meet the threat of federal legislation, some insurance companies have agreed to recommend the discontinuance of such practices as cancellations and failures to renew insurance for older people.

This outburst of social responsibility, even under pressure, to stop shabby practices that should have been illegal years ago is welcome but what does the industry offer by way of constructive solution? A few companies have been spending a small fortune to advertise prominently a type of individual accident and health insurance designed for the older people of the country—the so-called sixty-five-plus contracts.

The few liberalizations in these policies expose the indefensibility of previous practices of these same insurance companies. At that, they were unable to part with some of their customary tricks and even under these new policies, the status of people with preexisting conditions is compromised by a six-month period of denial for any illness or condition for which the policyholder received treatment or had been advised to receive treatment before the policy began.

Accordingly, the benefits are appallingly inadequate. Hospitalization benefits in one such policy for example, are limited to ten dollars a day when room rates often run about twice as much. This policy provides a maximum of thirty-one days, although one-third the bed-days occur for people over sixty-five after the thirty-first day of hospitalization. The one hundred dollar maximum for other hospital expenses is obviously insufficient at a time when the therapeutic charges, which would be covered without cash limits under the Forand bill, are almost as expensive as room and board. The surgical benefits are mere indemnities and offer no assurance of their acceptance as full payment by physicians.

Moreover, the monthly premium of $6.50 per person—$13 for an elderly couple—are attractive only in comparison with the previous offerings of insurance companies. I question whether, without employer contributions to help defray the cost, many of the aged people of our country will be able to enroll for these expensive but still inadequate benefits.

The time may come to challenge basically the long-accustomed practices of individual accident and health insurance. Consider the results of last year's total underwriting experience with this class of insurance. For calendar year 1958, 420 insurance companies with combined assets of $101 billion, played this kind of game with their individual health insurance business.

On hospital and medical insurance, they took in over $550 million in net premiums (after dividends to policyholders). They repaid in benefits a total of $305 million. On noncancellable accident and health insurance, they took in $219 million in net premiums. Here they paid back only $96 million in losses. On their accident and health insurance they took in $443 million and paid back $219.

With all the health needs of people, it takes a lot of doing to keep from paying back more on premiums than 1 out of every 2 dollars. This is accomplished by the restrictive language, the "fishhooks," the gimmicks in these policies and by years of tradition of insuring the profit of the carriers rather than the health of the policyholder.

Proposals to prefund health care for older people—that is, to set aside money for it before retirement—are being advanced. These proposals may sound reasonable, but they come far too late and are impractical.

The HEW report refers to a "recently issued policy" which would provide for a $10-a-day benefit, with $150 maximum for miscellaneous services. There would be a substantial advantage in having such a policy issued early, say at age twenty-one when it would cost only $22.80 a year, compared with over $100 at age fifty-nine. However, a $10-a-day benefit is even now palpably inadequate when a hospital bed in Detroit costs about $20 a day. In less than twenty years hospital room rates have about tripled. Today's twenty-one-year-old has no way of knowing what protection he will need in the year 2008 when he reaches age seventy.

We cannot abandon the present generation of the aged for such an unreliable solution to this immediate problem. Prefunding is not a practical way to meet the basic problem of health care for the aged.

While the insurance companies have made a few gestures toward older people, their practice of experience rating has done more harm than any other single factor in keeping satisfactory health insurance out of their reach. Instead of trying to spread the cost of high risk groups over as large a portion of the population as possible, insurance companies have stressed a sales approach of paying dividends to so-called more favorable groups. Thus groups are discouraged from meeting their responsibilities toward older people and induced to cut their protection or to exclude them.

Broad risk sharing is an essential part of any serious proposal to deal with the aged. Experience rating is directly opposed to this necessary risk sharing. The direction of voluntary health insurance has been toward, rather than away from, experience rating. Under the pressure of competition from commercial insurance companies, even Blue Cross and Blue Shield plans, which earlier embraced community rating and broad risk sharing, have been increasingly moving toward experience rating.

The Forand bill does not even attempt to meet all of the health needs of those Social Security beneficiaries it proposes to cover—the aged, widows, fatherless children, and dependent parents of the insured population. A strong case should be made that this bill should go much further into the range of care provided and the duration of its benefits.

But in spite of these limitations, I wholeheartedly endorse Representative Forand's bill and I strongly urge its passage. It would put a stop to the neglect of a segment of our population too long ignored. The provision of fully paid hospital care for up to sixty days is probably the most important segment of all health care and it would be extended to people now largely without such protection. The nursing home benefits provided in conjunction with hospital care would greatly raise the standard of treatment. Surgical services would provide a valuable form of protection against some of the more serious medical hazards. Obviously, the Forand bill will not solve all of the problems that I have enumerated which now face its potential beneficiaries. No initial piece of legislation of this type was ever perfect at its inception. The Forand bill will establish an advisory council that could study the operation of the measure and its ultimate effects on health care.

We recognize that the new benefits will cost money, and we stand ready to meet the cost. Under the Forand bill, Social Security taxes would be increased by a quarter of 1 per cent of taxable payrolls, both for employees and employers.

The estimates made of the cost of the Forand bill appeared to be competently derived on the basis of the best available evidence —I accept these estimates and believe that they serve as a valid basis for legislation. The Social Security system as it now stands is sound. The chronic accusations against its solvency are phony. The additional benefits which would be provided under the Forand bill would be fully supported by increased contributions.

The Forand bill is a well considered, carefully thought out, practical proposal. It is essentially sound and we stand ready to join with other constructive forces in America to support this legislation. The time is now long past when there was any real doubt as to what has to be done. We have to act now.

Free Labor Meets Khrushchev

Text of interview with Premier Nikita S. Khrushchev

San Francisco, California
September 20, 1959

Besides Walter P. Reuther, American participants included James B. Carey, President of the International Union of Electrical Workers, and George L. P. Weaver of the IUE; Joseph Curran, President of the National Maritime Union; Karl Feller, President of the International Union of Brewery Workers; O. A. Knight, President of the Oil, Chemical and Atomic Workers International Union; Paul Phillips, President of the United Paperworkers of America; Victor Reuther of the UAW; and Emil Rieve, President Emeritus of the Textile Workers Union of America. Premier Khrushchev was accompanied by Foreign Minister Andrei Gromyko; Mikhail A. Menshikov, Soviet Ambassador to the United States; and other Soviet officials.

Chairman Khrushchev and his party appeared in the Golden Empire Room exactly at 8 P.M., as previously arranged.

As the group went to the dining table, President Reuther pointed out to Mr. Khrushchev that it had been discovered that the table legs fell precisely at the center of the oval, therefore he had shifted Mr. Khrushchev slightly to the right.

MR. REUTHER: Even though I have shifted you to the right, Mr. Chairman, I assure you there is no political significance in it.

MR. KHRUSHCHEV (laughing): No matter how much you move me, I will still hold to a basic Communist position. Everything is fluid and everything progresses toward Communism.

MR. CURRAN: Has this part of your journey been fairly restful?

MR. KHRUSHCHEV: What do you think?

299

MR. CAREY: We are impressed by the statements you are said to have made at the Lincoln Memorial in Washington. We are afraid, however, that you may have seen too many bankers and businessmen.

MR. KHRUSHCHEV: That is because you didn't want to meet me. (Laughter.)

MR. REUTHER: Tell the Chairman we are happy he is going to the Garst farm. He must understand that here we eat corn as well as feed it to cattle. When my brother and I were in the Soviet Union in 1934 we went down the Volga to the Dongas and to Yalta and Batum and to Baku.

I'd like to tell this little story. We know you have made great progress in terms of food since we were there in the early thirties. In the stores there was always one kind of canned goods we could readily buy—Amerikanski corn, because the Russians did not eat corn. When we got to Baku we bought four cans of corn, took it home and found it was pork and beans. The cans were so old the labels had worn off. We went back and asked for eight more cans, specifying we preferred ones without labels. The man at the store said it was the same with the paper or without the paper, so we got eight without labels. We again found they were all pork and beans and as a result we lived like capitalists for a while. I bet they still don't eat corn to any extent in Russia.

MR. KHRUSHCHEV: Not much. Some of our northerners can't conceive of eating corn. Some tried to eat it raw and found it impossible.

MR. REUTHER: In Iowa you'll see big corn and we hope you will be able to use our techniques to raise more food and therefore raise living standards.

MR. KHRUSHCHEV: That is so, and we thank you. But we want you to know we are at no lower level than the U.S. on corn growing.

MR. REUTHER: Your major problem is with meat?

MR. KHRUSHCHEV: Our hybrid corn is no worse than yours. Garst knows that. What we need is to extend the growing of corn. Now we are extending limits up to the farthest north. We now want to devote one-third of the land of those northern areas to corn.

Mr. Carey (laughing): By the way, this chicken is corn-fed.

Mr. Khrushchev: I once said that to take away corn from Americans would be to starve them to death.

Mr. Carey: No, not that, but certainly it's one of our most important grains. President Curran, here, of the Maritime Union, knows that. He raises cattle and knows the importance of corn.

Mr. Reuther: I worked in the technical division of the Gorky auto plant. I trained Russians to do what I did in Detroit. I worked eighteen months and then made an 18,000-mile tour from one end of Russia to another. So I saw Soviet Russia during that period quite clearly. (Khrushchev inquired about an engineer at Gorky who had worked at Ford, now a U.S.S.R. minister.)

Mr. Reuther: What is the production in the Gorky auto plant these days?

Mr. Khrushchev: I don't think I could even suggest any figure.

Mr. Curran: In 1945, when I went through the Gorky plant, they were making chiefly trucks then. I sailed to your country in the early thirties, bringing Ford motor equipment and other materials to Russia.

Mr. Khrushchev: I remember in 1922 a group of United States workers came to the mines where they worked with their own tools. Fine men. A lot left when they saw the conditions.

Mr. Reuther: I grew up in West Virginia, in a coal mine country and came to know mines, and I have been into mines all over the world. I paid special attention to the mines in the Donbas.

Mr. Khrushchev: The Donbas mines are the most difficult for workers.

Mr. Reuther: Like the most difficult mines for the British workers that extend out under the seas. One thing we must do, most of all, in the future, is to harness the atom for peace and get all of the miners out of the earth.

Mr. Khrushchev: Our scientists tell me we are approaching that. They want to produce coal by utilizing the hydrogen atom.

Mr. Reuther: This is a venture in which we would favor

a mutual effort to pool the abilities and scientific knowledge of all nations.

MR. KHRUSHCHEV: A very noble goal.

MR. CAREY: We are familiar with the speech that the Chairman made at the United Nations and your splendid comments at the Lincoln Memorial. We are familiar with the eloquent speech you delivered to the U. N. General Assembly on disarmament. We are also familiar with the history of the past efforts to get agreement on effective control measures, which we of labor consider to be at the heart of the disarmament problem. Will you tell us what specific implementation you have in mind with respect to enforcement of any disarmament agreement?

MR. KHRUSHCHEV: What is it you have difficulty understanding?

MR. CAREY: It appears now that 25 per cent of Soviet production goes for military purposes, and 8 per cent to 10 per cent of U.S. production goes to military services. All nations of the world are spending now about $100 billion a year for military purposes. Of this, the U.S. spends about $40 billion a year, and the Soviet Union spends about $40 billion. The rest of the world spends about $20 billion. Certainly with disarmament a large percentage of this could be devoted to development of underprivileged nations and areas.

MR. REUTHER: I think we can all agree that the most pressing problem is how we can preserve the peace. We all understand that the United States and the Soviet Union have produced the kind of weapons that make war inconceivable, that make war now a question simply of human survival. The question today becomes, what will we do in a practical sense. The only war America wants to fight is war against poverty, hunger, ignorance, and disease. It's the only war mankind can win.

The Chairman has said repeatedly that he believes in no interference in the internal affairs of the United States and the kind of government we prefer to live under, and we share that feeling about the kind of government the Russians may prefer to live under. We think the people of Russia have a right to choose their own government and all other people should have the same right.

Therefore, as we see it, the "cold war" is not an attempt to change each other's systems of government, but to influence those that are uncommitted. Therefore, I want to ask the Chairman, is the Soviet Union prepared to contribute to the ending of the "cold war" by joining the United States and other countries through the United Nations in a cooperative effort to aid the underprivileged nations to abolish poverty and ignorance?

MR. KHRUSHCHEV (talking very quietly and into his napkin): In our proposal, which I submitted on behalf of the U.S.S.R., it is made clear that the outlays on armaments would be greatly reduced and a certain percentage of the reduction switched from the amount saved to the underprivileged countries.

MR. REUTHER (reminds Khrushchev of a proposal Reuther submitted to the President of the United States in 1950 and passes a copy to him): It seems to me that if we wait for disarmament to start we lose great opportunities. Our proposal would create the better climate in which disarmament could be carried forward faster and more effectively.

MR. KHRUSHCHEV: I am not familiar with your program so at this moment I cannot comment on it. But we are not waiting for disarmament to render this economic aid to needy nations.

MR. ADZHUBEI (editor of *Izvestia*): We already render such aid through the United Nations and through the various funds, medical and food funds, and we have bilateral agreements to aid underprivileged countries. For example, we have contributed our designs and our equipment to chemical and pharmaceutical plants in India. (He continued to cite the Arab countries, Indonesia, Ethiopia and others who received Soviet aid. He placed emphasis especially on the thousands of students who are brought to Russia as part of the aid program.)

MR. CAREY: Let us go back for a moment. When there is such a tremendously high percentage of the national incomes of both countries spent on military preparations, doesn't it become more and more demanding that we find a formula of control and inspection? Your country is spending $40 billion a year on the military, our country is spending $40 billion a year. If there were a completely safe inspection and control system how much more aid could we provide to the underprivileged countries of the world?

MR. KHRUSHCHEV: We agree. And that's why we submitted our proposals.

MR. REUTHER: There's no value in this, just going around the barn, as we seem to be now. I am familiar with the steel plant in India and other enterprises. When you do it, it's part of the "cold war." When we do it, you charge it's capitalist imperialism. Why can't we do it together? Through the U.N.? Do it together for their benefit, not for our separate advantage.

MR. KHRUSHCHEV: We don't agree.

MR. REUTHER: Why not?

MR. KHRUSHCHEV: America has now surrounded us with military bases, alliances such as NATO and SEATO, and by these means the United States wants to obtain world domination. In the United Nations we are always outvoted. Thus it would be up to the United States to decide how the money would be used.

MR. REUTHER: How about a U.N. commission with equal representation? Equal representation of Russia and the United States and U.S. friends and Soviet friends.

MR. KHRUSHCHEV: That would already be progress, but it won't be accepted.

MR. REUTHER: Why not expose the two positions to public air? That's what we do with unreasonable employers.

MR. KHRUSHCHEV: So long as we are surrounded by U.S. bases, we can have no agreement on this.

MR. REUTHER: Why can't we work together to fight poverty and hunger with the U.S. entitled to no advantage, and the U.S.S.R. entitled to no advantage?

MR. KHRUSHCHEV: But we do take part in these programs.

MR. REUTHER: You do it unilaterally, and that's the basis for the charge that you are penetrating economically and subverting politically.

Mr. Khrushchev: When the U.S. sends arms and creates bases, what kind of penetration is that?

Mr. Reuther: But what we are proposing here is an equal commission with equal control. After all, most of the people who are hungry are workers and peasants.

Mr. Khrushchev: Unilateral bread has no smell. If it has a Socialist smell, it is a pleasant smell.

Mr. Reuther: If it's politically motivated, it's not a pleasant smell.

Mr. Khrushchev: We've sent to Yemen thousands of pounds of wheat. That's not a Socialist country.

A few words more on the preceding subject, one more motive in my United Nations speech. The United States exploits the wealth of other countries, underdeveloped countries, for profits. England and France do the same. They exploit the wealth of countries that need aid. We do not exploit any country—we only engage in trade.

Mr. Reuther: You exploit the workers of East Germany.

Mr. Khrushchev: Where did you dream that up?

Mr. Reuther: If you don't exploit them, why should 3 million of them cross the border into West Germany?

Mr. Khrushchev: You are feverish. (Several voices interchanging across the table.)

Mr. Reuther: The workers in West Germany are free.

Mr. Khrushchev: We are free, too.

Mr. Reuther: Do you have credentials to speak for the workers of the world?

Mr. Khrushchev: Do you have credentials to poke your nose into East Germany?

Mr. Carey: This is part of our difficulty: the fear of the Chairman that the United States actually wants to dominate the world.

Mr. Khrushchev: Not just wants—striving!

Mr. Carey: And the other way around, there is the fear in the United States, based on much evidence, that the Soviet Union wants to dominate the world.

Mr. Khrushchev: The Soviet ruble does not kow-tow to the

American dollar. [At this point, Khrushchev raised his voice loudly and vehemently.] You have been spoiled by everyone bowing down, by everyone cringing and crawling.

MR. CAREY: It is a privilege having this sort of discussion. We have been given reason to wonder whether the Chairman's U.N. speech was chiefly for propaganda purposes. I want to reemphasize that unless we can find some way to implement the Chairman's disarmament proposals then we might have to start hunting all over again. A reduction in the $40 billion military budget of the Soviet Union and our $40 billion budget, that reduction could be devoted to helping underprivileged nations as the Chairman cited as the most desirable objective.

MR. KHRUSHCHEV: It is not $40 billion, but $25 billion, and that's no small sum either. I, as a former miner, have to say that I pity you as representing the working class, but your thinking is not of the working class. When Hearst says it, I am not offended. But when a representative of the workers says it, it is different.

MR. REUTHER: The key is universal inspection and control, and to stop hydrogen bomb testing. We expect the same conditions as you expect. We believe that neither nation should be treated as a second-class power. Why can't you agree?

MR. KHRUSHCHEV: Why are you so familiar with the Dulles arguments and not with the Khrushchev proposals?

MR. CAREY: Dulles is dead.

MR. KHRUSHCHEV: We say what we are saying because we have already clarified these issues.

MR. REUTHER: You will not agree to universal inspection and control?

MR. KHRUSHCHEV: Have you been asleep all the time? That is what we are for. I am sure you haven't read my speech.

MR. CAREY: Yes, we have read your speech, and other propaganda. But we failed to find the basis for implementing the proposals.

(Knight again raised the self-determination question.)

MR. KHRUSHCHEV (interrupting): I've never liked fleas when they jumped all over.

MR. REUTHER: We would prefer not to jump all over. We

would prefer to exhaust one question at a time, but it's all a matter of time. Tell the Chairman we will go slower if he has the time.

MR. VICTOR REUTHER: The Chairman has said he wants to talk to workers, and these are workers' representatives.

MR. REUTHER: How much time will the Chairman be willing to give?

MR. CAREY: We want to be considerate of our guest but . . .

MR. KHRUSHCHEV: 10:30, another hour. Disarmament is the question of questions, and if you misunderstand this there is almost no way out. What the Americans propose is control first, and then disarmament. What does this mean? Nothing! Let us station our bases in Mexico and Canada, then maybe you will have an understanding.

(There was a fast two-or-three-minute interchange across the table. At one point Khrushchev, talking at Curran, exclaimed: "How can you open your mouth like that and represent the workers? Do you want a discussion, or is this a bazaar?" At this point Khrushchev became quite excited and pounded the table.)

MR. CAREY: Here is the question on disarmament (passing it across the table) as I have phrased it. We fear there is lack of attention being given by you and your colleagues to the whole question of inspection and control.

MR. KHRUSHCHEV: I would like to tell you, gentlemen, so long as America continues to manifest a high-handed attitude toward other people there can be no agreement.

MR. CURRAN: We ought to talk sense here, and we're not talking sense yet. I don't want to be confused with statesmen. I am a worker speaking for workers and I'm pretty sure the rest of the guys here do.

(Rieve raised the question of Socialism versus Communism, and particularly public ownership under capitalism, pointing out that social ownership is compatible with the highest forms of political democracy as practiced in Scandinavia.)

MR. KHRUSHCHEV: There is a different understanding between us. Capitalist countries can own production and it doesn't make them Socialists.

MR. REUTHER: It is more than a matter of degree. We think

that the country in the free world nearest to democratic socialism is Israel. Yet the Russian attitude toward Israel has been most unfriendly.

MR. KHRUSHCHEV: We don't have an instrument that could measure the Socialism there. (He tossed his head almost disdainfully here.)

MR. REUTHER: You haven't been there, I have been there, and I have seen how Histadrut, the magnificent Israel labor movement, which owns 60 per cent of the production, supports the nation and aids its progress.

MR. CURRAN: I appreciate the Chairman's fatigue. (Here came a heated interchange with Khrushchev, for the most part, apparently, over the interpretation of fatigue.)

MR. REUTHER: Mr. Chairman, you are agitated again. You don't even understand a friendly question. Curran was inquiring about your weariness after a tough schedule.

MR. CURRAN: Please accept my apologies. I was asking about your tiredness from your journey.

(Curran, returning to issues under consideration, mentioned his sailings to Russia in 1945. Curran's question was "Specifically, will workers be permitted to exercise freedom to secure redress of their grievances by the only test of industrial democracy, the right to strike, the right collectively to withhold their labor power? When will workers be able to negotiate agreements in Russia, including the right to strike?")

MR. KHRUSHCHEV: I quite understand you, but you do not understand anything of the workings of the Socialist system. I do not want to offend you—You just do not know, you have not been there. You measure everything by U.S. standards. What I like about you is that you do have a class sense, that feeling, yes, they do have those rights. [Presumably this refers to the right to negotiate agreements and strike.] I understand your question. The working class does have the juridical right to strike. Does the worker have the right to exercise the right to strike? Yes. Have there been strikes since the October Revolution? Yes, I spoke at some of the strike meetings. Are there strikes now? No. Because

workers and unions and the government have one thought, because in what other country would the government announce
that wages would be raised and the working day reduced without
pressure? In capitalist countries they would need to fight for this.

I would think that if our disarmament proposals were accepted—we are now planning a six-hour day in 1964—we could
immediately reduce it to a six-hour day and raise wages. Our
workers are all organized in unions and they are learned and they
know the economic conditions and the economic possibilities in
our country.

MR. CURRAN: But in spite of that, knowing economic conditions and possibilities, do they have the right to strike?

MR. KHRUSHCHEV: Juridically, yes.

MR. REUTHER: I grew up in a working-class home in West
Virginia.

(Interruption by Khrushchev, with hand waving.)

MR. REUTHER: Is he afraid of my questions?

MR. KHRUSHCHEV: I am not afraid of the devil and you're a
man.

MR. REUTHER: I worked with the anti-Hitler underground
in Germany before going to Russia. What bothers me about your
social system is not that you're not making economic progress
for the workers and peasants. You're making tremendous technical progress. And I know all about your rationale of workers
not striking against themselves. But the Chairman himself exposed—in his exposure of Stalin's crimes—the cult and power
of an individual. How could the worker in that period get justice
if he would not strike or publicly protest?

MR. KHRUSHCHEV: His trade union.

MR. REUTHER: The union is an extension of government, the
Soviet government. Does a union ever disagree with the government? Can you give us one single example in which one of your
unions ever disagreed with government policy?

MR. KHRUSHCHEV: Why poke your nose into our business?

MR. REUTHER: Freedom is everybody's business. You are
always expressing a concern for the workers of Asia. There is a

thing called international labor solidarity. When I was in Russia I was a member of a union, and it was what we would call a company union.

(Fast and frequently indignant interchanges between the Chairman and the labor side of the table, too fast to be recorded.)

MR. REUTHER: Every time we push a sharp question, the Chairman gets angry.

MR. KHRUSHCHEV (Getting red in face, and just slightly loud): And what we call what you represent—capitalist lackeys.

MR. REUTHER: Every time I ask a question he has no answer for he gets angry.

MR. KNIGHT: Mr. Chairman, since it took me so long to get the floor, I want to exercise my democratic rights and ask two questions. Mr. Chairman, you have made repeated statements regarding self-determination and the freedom of people from outside interference.

We agree with you on both of these principles. However, we cannot understand, since you say you favor the right of the German people both East and West to decide for themselves on unification, how do you visualize the German people making this decision since you continue to oppose a free and democratic vote by the German people on this issue?

My second question is, in view of your statements favoring self-determination and noninterference in the internal affairs of other nations and your statements supporting peaceful coexistence, how do you reconcile these statements with the harsh military suppression of the Hungarian Freedom Fighters by the Soviet military powers?

MR. KHRUSHCHEV: The capitalists have certainly trained some very good cadres. May I just voice my thoughts aloud! Do you know anything about Germany? Have you ever been there? The German Democratic Republic is based on the most democratic foundations. There is no private ownership of the means of production.

MR. KNIGHT: If it is on the most democratic foundations, then they should not be afraid of a democratic election.

MR. REUTHER: In Eastern Germany there is only a one-party system.

(Interchange of ten voices.)

Mr. Knight: Why do you oppose a democratic vote for reunification of Germany?

Mr. Khrushchev: It depends not on me but on the two Germanies.

Mr. Knight: But you take a position against democratic reunification in your propaganda throughout the world.

Mr. Khrushchev: Tell me where I said that. Hungary has its own constitution and laws, and is freely developing.

Mr. Knight: Why did the Russians interfere in Hungary?

Mr. Khrushchev: There was no interference. There was a counterrevolution, thugs and hooligans who received arms from outside and took power in Budapest. And the government asked us for aid and we gave it, and we're proud of it. We are proud of it as a feat. There would be Fascism there if we had not.

Mr. Reuther: Was Nagy a Fascist, I thought he was a Communist?

Mr. Khrushchev: Don't mix things with dirt. (Exchanges around the table.) Have we exhausted the Hungarian question?

Mr. Carey: We have touched on it; we have certainly not exhausted it.

(Phillips brought up the question of radio jamming of Radio Free Europe and Voice of America.)

Mr. Khrushchev: What do you prefer to have for dinner? [Looking at Phillips] What is your favorite dish?

Mr. Phillips: Probably roast beef.

Mr. Khrushchev: I, borscht . . . You continue to enjoy roast beef, and I, borscht.

Mr. Reuther: But you prescribe and insist on borscht for all.

Mr. Khrushchev (rising to his feet at 10:22 p.m.): If you don't read what I have stated, what can I expect?

Mr. Reuther: You advocate more trade. How come you oppose a free flow of ideas?

Mr. Khrushchev: As head of the working class I will protect workers from capitalist propaganda.

(At this point, unexpectedly, Khrushchev, still on his feet, gave a burlesque demonstration of his idea of the can-can he witnessed during the Hollywood rehearsal of the forthcoming film *Can-Can*. He turned his back to the table, bent downward, flipped his coat up and gave an imitation of the can-can.)

MR. KHRUSHCHEV: This is a dance in which girls pull up their skirts. You're going to see that, we are not. This is what you call freedom—freedom for the girls to show their backsides. To us is pornography. The culture of people who want pornography. It's capitalism that makes the girls that way.

(Khrushchev still on his feet while saying this.)

MR. PHILLIPS: Does the Chairman think that the girls should be prohibited by law from showing their backsides?

MR. KHRUSHCHEV: There should be a law prohibiting the girls from showing their backsides, a moral law.

MR. CAREY: I may not see it, I may not want to see it . . .

MR. KHRUSHCHEV: Your children will go to see it.

MR. REUTHER: Perhaps it was a stupid movie—it was stupid of them to show it to you. But that has nothing to do with our question of why not a free flow of ideas between our countries.

MR. KHRUSHCHEV: Why don't you want to trade with us? The sausage tastes the same in all countries.

(Khrushchev referred to the press conference statement by Georgi A. Zhukov on cultural exchange.)

MR. CAREY: I will read this press statement and I'm sure that all of our colleagues will follow it up.

MR. SATYUKOV (editor of *Pravda*): We printed in *Pravda* in full Reuther's statement at the unemployment conference in Washington. We didn't change a word, but at the same time the New York papers said that it was a Red scheme. We wrote back in *Pravda* there was no collusion between us and Reuther. The Voice of America didn't broadcast it. If it did, we wouldn't jam it.

MR. REUTHER: No, you wouldn't because that report on unemployment would reflect upon us. But why didn't you and why don't you publish my May Day speech of this year in West Berlin? I invite you to publish and broadcast that speech.

MR. KHRUSHCHEV: We only publish speeches that contribute to friendly relations between countries.

MR. REUTHER: There were at least 600,000 workers who

heard my speech in West Berlin, and I am certain that my speech was far less provocative than the May Day speakers in the Eastern Sector of Berlin.

MR. CAREY: I think the Chairman answered the question, in part, in his reply to Spyros Skourus. Actually Skourus knows little about the problems of unemployment in the United States.

MR. REUTHER: The record of struggle of U.S. unionism stands for itself. Personally, I have been shot and beaten. I have been criticized by the reactionary press as a Moscow agent and by you as a lackey of Wall Street.

MR. KHRUSHCHEV: Without sharp edges, I would like to ask whether we cannot find a common approach. But we think differently. We pity you.

MR. REUTHER: We don't want your pity.

MR. CURRAN: Maybe the word he wanted was sympathize. Pity is a bad word. We don't want his pity.

MR. KHRUSHCHEV: We are progressing toward Communism. You want to strengthen capitalism.

MR. REUTHER: We are interested in how best to advance the interest of the workers under freedom. We disagree on how best to advance the interests of the workers.

MR. KHRUSHCHEV: You have your point of view; we have ours. They are irreconcilable.

MR. REUTHER: Why can't we believe in our system of individual freedom without your feeling it is a necessity to say we are betraying the workers?

MR. KHRUSHCHEV: We did not come to this meeting to aggravate our relations. They are bad enough as they are. Let's not raise questions that disunite us. Let us join our efforts for peace. Let us not be hotheaded. Questions like Hungary are pinpricks. What good do they do? Suppose we raised the question of Guatamala?

MR. REUTHER: We criticized the situation in Guatamala but the most important fact is that no one in Russia could or did criticize your intervention in Hungary.

MR. CAREY: We are making some progress, however, when

we can have meetings like this. This is more pointed than any discussion we have had in recent years. If this kind of discussion is continued it holds some hope for the future.

MR. FELLER: Mr. Chairman, I cannot understand since the Communist party proclaims itself to be the liberator of the working class, yet we see mass exodus of workers in other countries following the Communist seizure of power. You have the example of 3 million workers fleeing from East Germany to West Berlin, and about 3 million fleeing from North Korea to South Korea, and, as mentioned a moment ago, 300 or so thousands of Hungarians braved arrest and death in escaping to freedom.

Mr. Khrushchev, can you tell us of a single instance where, following Communist seizure of power, there has been a mass influx of workers from surrounding non-Communist countries into the Communist country? If the Communist party is the liberator of the working class, why don't we see this phenomena?

MR. KHRUSHCEV: Is that all? Think it over. Drink your beer. Perhaps that will help you to find the answer to your question.

MR. FELLER: That certainly is no answer and apparently nothing will make you understand why millions want to escape from Communism.

MR. KHRUSHCHEV: I've told you, I'm not afraid of the devil.

MR. CAREY: Wall Street says Reuther is a representative of the devil.

MR. REUTHER: Wall Street says I am an agent of Moscow, and Moscow says I am an agent of Wall Street.

MR. WEAVER: I would like to pose this question, Mr. Chairman. In fact, one of the problems as I see it and which you just referred to—for example, Hungary as a "pinprick"—is how do we establish a basis of trust which must precede understanding? Recently I served as a labor representative at a conference of the World Association of United Nations, in Geneva. At this conference, the U.S.S.R. and the United States delegations agreed on a resolution attempting to diminish the tensions of the "cold war." However, at the same time the friends of the Soviet Union from the Eastern European countries were raising the kind of provocative questions you just referred to, that do not lead to understanding. How do we arrive at a basis of understanding with this kind of attitude? For our people the questions that have been raised here with you this evening must be answered.

Mr. Khrushchev: It is true that there are many issues on which we differ. Let us have more contacts. We may not solve all the issues at once but through contacts we can begin to settle the little issues which will lead to more progress. Let us not aggrevate our relations. It is only our opponents who will benefit. Do you want to see a change in the social order of our country? No! We don't want to see a change in the social order of your country. I confess I myself have never been a trade union functionary. But why shouldn't you gentlemen visit us? You won't become Communists.

Mr. Carey: We've been there; we've seen your country, time and again. I've been there three times; our other colleagues have been there.

Mr. Reuther: It is important that the Chairman understand that changes are occurring here in the United States and that we have people as dedicated to advancing the working class as there could be anywhere else (throwing across the table to Khrushchev U.S. wage rates). How can we say these people are wage slaves exploited by capitalism, making these kinds of wages in America? How can he say that they have nothing to lose but their chains!

Mr. Khrushchev: We say what we do in retaliation for what you say about us. Take, for example, Meany's speeches. I read most of them. They sound like Dulles—they sound like Dulles.

Mr. Reuther: We have our disagreements and we recall you had some disagreement with Molotov. However, when we have disagreements, no one is exiled.

Mr. Carey: We thank the Chairman. I suggest our guest of honor has been quite generous with his time. We thank you for joining us, and may our two great countries work together for peace and the good of all mankind.

The Mike Wallace Interview

Text of television interview

New York, New York
October 17 and 18, 1960

MR. WALLACE: This is Mike Wallace with another television portrait in our gallery of colorful people. A Detroit businessman once called our guest the most dangerous man in Detroit because no one, he said, is more skillful in bringing about revolution, without seeming to disturb the existing forms of society. Our guest is Walter Reuther. As President of the United Auto Workers and second in command of the AFL-CIO, he is one of the most powerful men in America today. What are Walter Reuther's views on the future of America and the American working man? How much of a welfare state is Walter Reuther after?

Walter, first of all, let me ask you this: You have been a kind of a prophet, because a good many of the things that you have stood for from the beginning of your career have seemed to come about in the United States: Social Security, pension plans, minimum wage, unemployment benefits, union power. So, as a prophet, I'd like for you to project for us now, the next ten years. What are your specific social goals for the next ten years?

MR. REUTHER: Well, to begin with, I think we've got to first raise the question of whether or not America is going to have the kind of affirmative leadership that we need in order to mobilize the great potential of the American economy. If we can achieve full employment and full production, and then gear the abundance of automation to the basic needs of the American people, then I believe the American economy is equal to meeting our needs at home, and also to meeting our responsibilities in the world. On the basis of our ability to achieve full employment

316

and full production, I think we need to work out a list of national priorities in which we put first things first. I would put first on my list of goals the achievement of the best and most adequate educational systems, so that every American child can have the benefit of educational opportunities that will enable him to grow to his maximum stature. Second, we've got a tremendous job to be done on the medical front, and certainly what we have been working for in the last session of Congress, which Senator Kennedy sponsored, of building into our Social Security system medical and hospital care for our aged, is one of the top priority items, because millions of older American citizens cannot afford the prohibitive cost of medical care.

MR. WALLACE: Do you want me to interrupt you as you go?

MR. REUTHER: Any time at all.

MR. WALLACE: All right, as far as education is concerned, do you mean college education for every American?

MR. REUTHER: I think that every American should have the kind of education that will facilitate his maximum growth. If a child has the capability . . .

MR. WALLACE: Government supported?

MR. REUTHER: When necessary; I think that one of the things we need to do is to avoid the tragic waste of human potential, and—

MR. WALLACE: And if necessary—

MR. REUTHER: Do you realize that more than 250,000 of the most capable high school students are washed out without any opportunity to go to college because of economic reasons? Now if we had the kind of federal scholarship program so that these students on a competitive academic basis could qualify for a scholarship, they would be given the opportunity of developing their capabilities so that they could be more useful citizens, and society would get the benefit of their greater contribution.

MR. WALLACE: Understood. Now as far as medical aid is concerned, are you keeping it at medical aid for the aged, or do you think that ten to fifteen years from now the issue might be medical care for everybody?

MR. REUTHER: Well I think that the immediate urgency is

the question of providing medical care for our aged, because they have the most compelling need. Their economic resources obviously are limited and they can't afford to pay the cost of the medical bills. So that's the first step. I think that the whole medical care program in America will develop quite differently than in any other country, because we come out of a different background. I am for encouraging the development of nongovernmental voluntary group medical approaches, but where there are areas that cannot be filled by the nongovernmental approach, I am for the government filling those areas of the total problem.

MR. WALLACE: Socialized medicine only if private medicine fails?

MR. REUTHER: That's right. I only want the government to do what we are unable to do on a nongovernmental basis, but I do not want the vacuum to continue just because we are waging ideological warfare.

MR. WALLACE: What about minimum wage?

MR. REUTHER: Well now, here's the problem: In the last session of Congress Senator Kennedy again took the lead in trying to raise minimum wage from a dollar to $1.25. In other words, to raise the income of millions of American families from $40 a week to $50; I don't know how you can raise a family even on $50, yet Mr. Nixon and Mr. Eisenhower, the Republican Administration, fought against that.

MR. WALLACE: Let's not be too political, let's just talk about what Walter Reuther wants.

MR. REUTHER: I'm merely stating what happened.

MR. WALLACE: Yes.

MR. REUTHER: Now I hope that stating the facts is not political; I hope that this is a matter of making the record straight. Now those people are opposed to the government helping the lowest income families.

MR. WALLACE: How high a minimum wage would you like to see in 1970?

MR. REUTHER: Now this depends upon the level of our technology. Obviously, our basic economic problem in America is not that we don't know how to make things; we know how to make things. We're making tremendous technological progress in automation and the new tools of science and technology. Our problem is to learn to manage abundance by learning to share it, and the only way that you can have full employment and full production in our kind of free economy is by the achievement of a dynamic expanding balance between greater productive power matched by greater purchasing power. When you give a low-income family $10 more a week to spend they don't put that in salt brine and keep it. That's high-velocity purchasing power that gets into the stream of the economy. I say that if we have full employment and full production, we ought to be able to look forward to 1970 for a $2-an-hour minimum wage. In terms of the economic realities, this is more than a matter of economic justice to the wage earner. This is a matter of economic necessity, because unless you expand the purchasing power at the base of the economy by giving people who have the greatest needs the purchasing power to translate need into demand, the economy gets in trouble.

MR. WALLACE: A few years ago, Walter, you wanted a profit-sharing plan for your union, the automobile industry, and you were defeated on the issue. Are you going to go after profit-sharing again?

MR. REUTHER: Well, we have made no decision; we will have a conference in our union in the early part of 1961, where the rank-and-file members of our union will make that decision. But what I tried to point out in 1958 on profit-sharing was that we've got to find a more rational and a more intelligent way of sharing the fruits of our developing technology among workers and stockholders and consumers. I happen to believe that this is the crux of where we're going in terms of the future of the American economy. I think that the basic problem is to find a way to work out the competing equities among the three groups: the worker, the stockholder, and the consumer, so that we share the abundance in a way that would create the dynamics of growth and expansion.

MR. WALLACE: But according to our system the creativeness,

the thinking, and the risk that goes into capital—all of that—is rewarded by profits. The working man is not responsible for any of that creative thinking, or for the risk. You want them not to be involved in the creative thinking and the risk, but you want them to be involved in the profits.

MR. REUTHER: You'd have a hard time convincing an unemployed automobile worker or unemployed steel worker, that he doesn't take any risk; they throw him on the street when they don't need him—that's about as great a risk as you can take. The point is, that this transcends the question of equity, and we will not meet the problem of tomorrow by talking about yesterday's concepts. The problems of tomorrow require whole new concepts of how a free economy can work. As the tools of production become more productive, it means that we've got to find the markets by which people can absorb this greater productivity. Unless the fruits of technology are shared among workers and stockholders and consumers more equitably, the economy gets in trouble because you develop a lag between the ability to create wealth on the one hand, and the inability of people to consume the wealth that we know how to create.

MR. WALLACE: This summer, I traveled around the country for about six weeks after the conventions, and I went to the Chevrolet plant in Cleveland where I talked to one of your United Auto Workers there. I think he said that he was making $115 a week and I asked him if he wanted more. He said yes. And I asked him, "Do you think that you deserve more for the work you do?" And he said, "No, the job isn't worth more, but I'm an American, and I feel entitled to improvement in my wage." I want to know if you share his views.

MR. REUTHER: Well, obviously, I don't share his views. The question here again, you see, is how do you share abundance so that the economy of America can maintain the dynamic qualities of growth and expansion. This transcends the narrow concept of economic equity between worker and investor, and it's a question of how do you gear the abundance so that in creating abundance you can maintain the dynamics of growth. The real key, I think, Mike, is the question of what are we going to do with abundance. Now, after we've met our basic economic needs of housing and medical care and adequate clothing and education and so forth, we will soon get to that point in American history, because of the onrush of technological progress, when we've got to make a very basic decision: Do we want more gadgets, or do we want more leisure? I think we need now to begin to prepare for a reduction in the workweek, so that when we do get a shorter workweek, because the tools of production are so productive we can create all the material wealth we need with fewer hours of work, we've got to be certain that when we get this increased measure of leisure we can use it constructively and creatively.

MR. WALLACE: Do you look forward to a 30-hour week?

MR. REUTHER: Oh, in time—there's no question about it, because—

MR. WALLACE: And what, a 48-week year?

MR. REUTHER: Well, this is a matter of how we decide to work out the distribution of our leisure. This is, I think, the great—

MR. WALLACE: But, is that sensible—48 weeks, instead, out of 52 and 30-hour work week minimum wage of $2 an hour?

MR. REUTHER: Well, I think this will take many forms; I think that the real problem will be that to provide leisure in meaningful packages so that you can do something. The reason I personally have felt that going, say from a 40-hour week on an 8-hour day basis to a 7-hour a day, 5 days a week—I think that's meaningless. Give a fellow one hour more leisure a day; it's not in a large enough package so that he can do something with it. I think that maybe we'll work out a kind of industrial sabbatical leave every once in a while, so a fellow can really go out. Maybe he wants to study music—maybe he wants to study literature, maybe he wants to try to paint.

MR. WALLACE: Take a year off.

MR. REUTHER: Take the whole year off. The point is that—

MR. WALLACE: At full pay.

MR. REUTHER: That's right. When we get to the place in the development of our society where the tools of abundance can take care of the material needs of the outer man with less and less human effort—the real emphasis then has to be shifted to enabling the inner man to grow. In other words, we've got to develop new appetites, new interest in the nonmaterial things. And this really, I think, means the first opportunity for the great mass of human beings to participate in culture.

MR. WALLACE: Won't the state have to get more and more into it, though, to effect that kind of thing—the kind of life that you're talking about?

MR. REUTHER: I personally believe very much in trying to encourage voluntary groups to do as much as they can in these areas, and I am for the state only doing what people are unable to do in the absence of the government's action.

MR. WALLACE: And if the people are either unable or unwilling to do it, then—

MR. REUTHER: Well then you have the choice between the vacuum of nothing being done, or the state doing it.

MR. WALLACE: Nothing being done the way you want it done.

MR. REUTHER: Nothing being done to meet the basic problem.

MR. WALLACE: Will you state the problem?

MR. REUTHER: Well, the point is, that if we're going to have the choice between mass unemployment, or more creative leisure, then obviously, I am for more creative leisure, because there's nothing so tragic as an able-bodied man or woman who is willing and able to work but who can't find a job; there is nothing more tragic than the waste of human—

MR. WALLACE: Agreed. These able-bodied men and women —do you think that they like—do they take pride in their work?

MR. REUTHER: There's no question about it. The average American wants a job where he can earn a livelihood for himself and those for whom he's responsible, and he would like a job that gives him a sense of achievement—the sense of participation. Now this becomes more difficult as automation takes over. Here's a fellow that may spend his whole life pressing buttons. Now that isn't very creative, and this is why in his leisure hours, we have got to satisfy his creative urge.

MR. WALLACE: Two years ago a full-page spread was given in your own union's newspaper, *Solidarity,* it was back in January of 1958, to an article which said this, and I quote the article: "The factory worker's attitude toward his work is generally compounded of hatred, shame, and resignation. The plain truth is that factory work is degrading." Now how do you reconcile that with your talk about pride, and—

MR. REUTHER: Now I say that a worker would like a job where he earns a good living and a job that gives him a sense of participating—a sense of creation, but this becomes more difficult all the time. If you were just tightening five nuts on a wheel, eight hours a day, five days every week, you would find that very degrading. I think any human being would—even though they paid you quite well for doing it. I think that in addition to earning your bread and butter, that work ought to give you a sense of participation in the creative process.

MR. WALLACE: Is it possible to do that, though, Walter?

MR. REUTHER: It gets more difficult and this is why we've got to satisfy this inner need in terms of our leisure time.

MR. WALLACE: Outside of the job.

MR. REUTHER: That's right, and this is why we've got to plan because if we don't plan for the constructive and creative use of the growing measure of human leisure that we're going to have based upon our technological progress, we can wind up as a well fed nation of morons.

MR. WALLACE: Walter, Jack Kennedy, your candidate, has said this; he said that "The goals of the labor movement are the goals for all Americans, and their enemies are the enemies of progress." Now that sounds as though it might just as well have come out of the mouth of Walter Reuther. Who are the enemies of labor—is Richard Nixon an enemy of your group?

MR. REUTHER: Well, I think the important thing is not who are the enemies of labor, but who stand in opposition to the things that the labor movement is trying to get America to do. I mean, who are the forces that are opposed to adequate aid to education, or who have opposed medical care for our retired workers, who have tried to block the kind of adequate housing programs essential to clearing out the slums and the social cesspools?

MR. WALLACE: Certainly Nixon cannot be indicted for any of these—

MR. REUTHER: Except that you can't separate Mr. Nixon from the Republican party. Every time there has been a tie vote in the United States Senate since Richard Nixon has been serving as the Vice President, he has cast his vote along the lines of the Republican party and in harmony and agreement with Senator Barry Goldwater. You cannot deny the fact, that in this election the contest is not just between Jack Kennedy as a person, and Richard Nixon as a person—this is a contest between two basically different concepts of the role of government in a free society.

MR. WALLACE: You believe, then, that Nixon is an ally, a real political and intellectual ally of Barry Goldwater?

MR. REUTHER: I think that the Republican party is more nearly in the image of Barry Goldwater and that Richard Nixon has, in his public life, cast deciding votes in harmony with that basic concept of the Republican party.

MR. WALLACE: Well, how do you account for the moonlight meeting last summer then, between Nelson Rockefeller and Richard Nixon?

MR. REUTHER: Oh, that was just—

MR. WALLACE: And the move forward that the Republican platform took after that meeting?

MR. REUTHER: That was just a clever piece of, I think, political manipulation to try to create a more liberal image so that the Republican candidate could run in the election in the framework of that more liberal image.

MR. WALLACE: Well, he's running on the platform—

MR. REUTHER: Sure, but he's—

MR. WALLACE: It wasn't manipulation—he did it out in front of everybody—told everybody about the meeting—

MR. REUTHER: But look, there were really no basic concessions made. On the question of economic growth where Rockefeller agrees with Kennedy, 5 per cent is essential to full employment and full production. Nixon didn't yield on that. The platform didn't reflect that. It didn't reflect increased military expenditures, it didn't meet the needs on medical care. Rockefeller agrees with the social security approach on medical care. Nixon and the Republican party are opposed to it. I think you've got to get it down to this: There are two basic concepts of the role of government. Franklin Roosevelt put it quite well in 1932; he said that you've got to judge the worth of the government not by what it does to help the few who have too much to get more, but what government does to help the many to get enough. Now this essentially is the difference between the Republican party and the Democratic party. Philosophically, the Republican party believes that if you help big business to earn higher profits they will then invest more money in plants. That will create more job opportunities. That will create full employment. They've got this trickle-down theory that you can build prosperity from the top down. The Democrats basically believe that you've got to build prosperity from the bottom up by expanding purchasing power, by doing the things that will make it possible for all the American people to participate in prosperity.

MR. WALLACE: By confiscating property in the form of taxes, too.

MR. REUTHER: Well, call it what you will—the fact is that we can't get our kids in school because there are inadequate schools. We've got a brand-new school in Dearborn, Michigan, a wonderful new school, and it's not open. It's standing idle right now, and children are going to school on double shifts in other schools because we can't get enough teachers. Now why can't we get enough teachers? Because we aren't willing to pay the kind of salaries to attract more young Americans into the teaching profession.

MR. WALLACE: Well, as Dick Nixon points out, now wait just a second—

MR. REUTHER: Mr. Nixon cast his vote on that very issue when the vote was 44 to 44 in the United States Senate last spring, Mr. Nixon cast the deciding vote against aid to teacher's salaries. Now he covers up his position by saying he's opposed this because of federal control. Nobody wants federal control of education, and nobody thinks that if the federal government helps to provide funds, as the bill that Mr. Nixon voted against proposed doing, that would mean federal control. Under that bill, a state would have been offered "X" dollars per student, and whether they use part of it to help pay teachers' salaries, or all of it to help build classrooms was a decision the state would make. There was no federal control, but Mr. Nixon voted with Senator Barry Goldwater against aid to education. That's why we're against Mr. Nixon, because he's against the things we think are good for America.

MR. WALLACE: Mr. Nixon, I believe—correct me if I'm wrong—has suggested that he feels that the federal government should give money for the construction of school buildings, thereby freeing money on the local level which would go into the building of schools in order to raise teachers' salaries, so it's —he wants the same thing—it's just a question of method.

MR. REUTHER: The bill provided that the state would make that determination. In other words, if the State of New York said we'll spend all the federal grant for classrooms, that would be their decision—this would be a local state decision. Now if Mr. Nixon believes in all this local autonomy and local authority, and local responsibility, why didn't he vote for the bill, so that each state could have made the decision itself on how it would allocate the expenditures of the funds?

MR. WALLACE: Doesn't it really come down to this in the argument between Kennedy and Nixon, the argument momentarily between Reuther and Wallace, although you can see that I'm just playing the role of devil's advocate here. Doesn't it come down to this, though, the Democrats want the government to get more and more into the fabric—more and more into our social fabric. You want government to have more and more to do with us as individual human beings, it's as simple as that.

MR. REUTHER: No, it is not.

MR. WALLACE: Fulton Lewis has written this—perhaps we should put it this way—and have you answer Mr. Lewis rather than Mr. Wallace. He has written that you are bent on winning control of the Democratic party, and then conceivably, control of the federal government. Lewis has this to say about Reuther: He says the government that you will produce would make the Nazi dictatorship of Adolf Hitler look namby-pamby.

MR. REUTHER: It sounds like some of the things that Barry Goldwater would be saying. The point is, that if America followed the political and economic philosophy of the ultraright, the Fulton Lewises and the Barry Goldwaters, America would default in doing those things which essentially are the responsibilities of the whole community. Now I share the basic philosophy of Abraham Lincoln when he said that the purpose of government is to enable the people to do together through the instruments of government what they are unable to do without the aid of government.

MR. WALLACE: Dwight Eisenhower feels the same way.

MR. REUTHER: Yes, except that he hasn't been implementing that philosophy very effectively.

MR. WALLACE: Not the way you would implement that philosophy.

MR. REUTHER: Just take education. That's the test. Here we are, the richest country in the world, and yet, no one can deny the fact that millions of American children and American youth are being denied the kind of education that will facilitate their maximum growth. We want the government to do what must be done to fill the deficit on the educational front. We want the government to take affirmative action on the medical front so that our aged citizens will have medical care in the autumn of their lives. We want the federal government to do what it must do to help the local communities to wipe out our slums, because the tax structure of the local community is not adequate to take care of the decay in the cores of our big metropolitan cities; the federal government must help do this job. And doing these things is not a matter of extending the power of government as an arbitrary thing over the lives of people. Helping a child to get more adequate education, helping an old person to get adequate medical care, helping a family to escape the—

MR. WALLACE: Everybody's for that, Walter. Everybody's for that, it's the means.

MR. REUTHER: The test is not whether you give lip service to it, but whether you're willing to agree to affirmative action to deal with the problem. Now you take the Social Security approach to medical care—

MR. WALLACE: Under those circumstances why bother with free private enterprise at all, why not simply socialize the government, and have a good government that will do all of these things and achieve these ends and forget about the whole thing.

MR. REUTHER: There are many, many, many things that free enterprise can do better than government.

MR. WALLACE: What?

MR. REUTHER: Well, I'm in favor of General Motors making automobiles. I'm opposed to government doing it, but I know that General Motors is not going to meet the medical needs of the old-timers.

MR. WALLACE: Why do you want General Motors rather than the federal government to make automobiles?

MR. REUTHER: Well, because I only want the government to do the things that you can't do without the government, and General Motors seems to do quite well building automobiles.

MR. WALLACE: Well, you can give power to people—the government felt it was necessary to step in to give federal power— the federal government could do all kinds of things, probably do it just as well.

MR. REUTHER: Well, I'm in favor of the government building a power dam—take the Tennessee Valley Authority—the private utility industry had a hundred years of opportunity, they could have gone down there, they could have invested the capital, but they opposed the development of the hydroelectric power potential of the Tennessee Valley Authority. Why? Because they wanted to have a limited supply of power so that they could exact the highest possible price for the power that they were selling in a market where the supply was inadequate to meet the demand.

MR. WALLACE: But your opponents will tell you that you will destroy individual fiber, you will destroy individual initiative,

you will destroy the very freedom on which this country was
built if you continue to let the government infiltrate more and
more and more as it has infiltrated in the quarter of a century in
which you've been working.

MR. REUTHER: The question of the degree the government
gets involved in the activities of a society is not an absolute
thing, but a relative value. It depends upon the complexities of
the problem that a society is dealing with. Obviously, government intervention in the lives of the people was less necessary
in certain economic areas in a very simple agrarian economy
than it will be in the economy based upon automation and
electronics. In other words, as the problems of society become
more complex, then government is the only instrument that could
help solve certain of the problems—now—

MR. WALLACE: Wait a minute, wait a minute, who opened
up this country?—

MR. REUTHER: Barry Goldwater is for abolishing Social Security, Barry Goldwater is for abolishing federal aid to education and all—

MR. WALLACE: Let's talk about Walter Reuther. Who opened
up?—

MR. REUTHER: Now that you're talking about Fulton Lewis,
Jr., and he and Barry Goldwater are political bedfellows.

MR. WALLACE: Who opened up this country, industrially, the
government or free private enterprise? Are you not grateful to
the capitalists, the businessmen of the United States for anything, Walter?

MR. REUTHER: I'm grateful for the contribution they made,
but even in the early days of capitalism the government helped
a great deal: The railroads got tremendous land grants, the
steamship companies got subsidies—they still get subsidies—the
airlines got subsidies; none of these great industries developed
without some assistance from the government. The whole question here, Mike, the whole question is not are you opposed, or
are you in favor of government intervention into certain areas
of our free society? The question is, whenever people are either
unable or unwilling to do what must be done to maintain the
health and advance the well-being of the whole of society, then

government is the only instrument that the whole people have to look to do that job. Now, I'm for limiting that; I'm for encouraging voluntary nongovernmental approaches. This is why I try to do everything I can at the collective bargaining table; this is why we fought on the Social Security front, on the pension front—but when you've got a problem like education or medical care for the aged that you can't solve on a nongovernmental basis, then the government must do the job.

MR. WALLACE: Perhaps I'd better get Barry Goldwater here instead of me to effect it.

MR. REUTHER: Well, it would be interesting.

MR. WALLACE: How do you get along with—ah—don't you talk at all, you two?

MR. REUTHER: Well, you see, I have nothing against Goldwater. I think he has the finest eighteenth century mind in the U.S. Senate.

MR. WALLACE: But you don't talk, either socially or professionally, do you?

MR. REUTHER: I have no basis for it. I mean that this is not a personal thing. I just think Barry Goldwater just doesn't understand the forces at work in the world. If you took his book, this little book that he's put out called *The Conscience of a Conservative,* and translated that into governmental action, the Communists would take over the world in the next five years, because we would make the free world impotent to meet the basic economic and social forces that are changing the world in revolution.

MR. WALLACE: Walter, we have just about a minute left, and I want to put one question to you, maybe two. Is Jimmy Hoffa an enemy of labor?

MR. REUTHER: I think Jimmy Hoffa is bad for the American labor movement, because I believe that he is surrounded by forces who are interested in a fast buck, and I think that anybody in the leadership of the American labor movement has got to be dedicated to the advancement of the well-being of the rank-and-file and their families, and whenever they're interested in a fast buck, they ought to be on the other side of the table.

MR. WALLACE: Thank you very much, Walter Reuther.